Learning to Teach Religious Education in the Secondary School

D0531356

Learning to Teach Religious Education in the Secondary School provides insights from current educational theory and the best contemporary classroom teaching and learning, and suggests tasks, activities and further reading that are designed to enhance the quality of initial school experience for the student teacher.

Key themes addressed include:

- the place of Religious Education in the curriculum
- state and faith community schooling
- developing schemes of work
- language and religious literacy
- teaching religion at 16 plus
- religion and moral education
- collective worship

This revised edition has been thoroughly updated throughout to take account of changes to policy and the curriculum. It includes two additional chapters on 'Religious Education and Citizenship' and 'Teaching Religious Education at A Level', as well as new versions of three original chapters 'Teaching Children with Special Educational Needs', 'Religious Education and Moral Education' and 'Resources for Religious Education'.

Supporting teachers in developing levels of religious and theological literacy, both of individual pupils and the society as a whole, this comprehensive and accessible text will give practising teachers and students an introduction to the craft of teaching Religious Education in the secondary school.

L. Philip Barnes is Senior Lecturer in Religious Education at King's College London. He has been a Head of Department in both secondary and grammar schools in Northern Ireland, and director of the PGCE Course in Religious Education at the University of Ulster.

Andrew Wright is Professor of Religious and Theological Education at King's College London. He has also been director of a number of PGCE courses as well as Head of Religious Education at three contrasting secondary schools.

Ann-Marie Brandom is Lecturer in Religious Education at King's College London where she co-ordinates the PGCE Religious Education course. She was also a teacher of Religious Education and Head of Department in a London comprehensive school.

Related titles

Learning to Teach Subjects in the Secondary School Series

Series Editors
Susan Capel, Marilyn Leask and Tony Turner

Designed for all students learning to teach in secondary schools, and particularly those on school-based initial teacher training courses, the books in this series complement *Learning to Teach in the Secondary School* and its companion, *Starting to Teach in the Secondary School*. Each book in the series applies underpinning theory and addresses practical issues to support students in school and in the training institution in learning how to teach a particular subject.

Learning to Teach in the Secondary School, 4th Edition
Edited by Susan Capel, Marilyn Leask and Tony Turner

Learning to Teach English in the Secondary School, 2nd Edition
Edited by Jon Davison and Jane Dowson

Learning to Teach Modern Foreign Languages in the Secondary School, 3rd Edition
Edited by Norbert Pachler, Ann Barnes and Kit Field

Learning to Teach Physical Education in the Secondary School, 2nd Edition
Edited by Susan Capel

Learning to Teach Science in the Secondary School, 2nd Edition
Edited by Jenny Frost and Tony Turner

Learning to Teach Mathematics in the Secondary School, 2nd Edition
Edited by Sue Johnston-Wilder, Peter Johnston-Wilder, David Pimm and John Westwell

Learning to Teach Religious Education in the Secondary School, 2nd Edition
Edited by L. Philip Barnes, Andrew Wright and Ann-Marie Brandom

Learning to Teach Art and Design in the Secondary School
Edited by Nicholas Addison and Lesley Burgess

Learning to Teach Geography in the Secondary School, 2nd Edition
David Lambert and David Balderstone

Learning to Teach Design and Technology in the Secondary School, 2nd Edition
Edited by Gwyneth Owen-Jackson

Learning to Teach Music in the Secondary School, 2nd Edition
Edited by Chris Philpott

Learning to Teach ICT in the Secondary School
Edited by Steve Kennewell, John Parkinson and Howard Tanner

Learning to Teach Citizenship in the Secondary School
Edited by Liam Gearon

Learning to Teach Using ICT in the Secondary School, 2nd Edition
Edited by Marilyn Leask and Norbert Pachler

Starting to Teach in the Secondary School, 2nd Edition
Edited by Susan Capel, Ruth Heilbronn, Marilyn Leask and Tony Turner

Learning to Teach Religious Education in the Secondary School

Second edition

A companion to school experience

Edited by L. Philip Barnes, Andrew Wright and Ann-Marie Brandom

Routledge
Taylor & Francis Group

LONDON AND NEW YORK

First published 2008
by Routledge
2 Park Square, Milton Park, Abingdon, Oxon, OX14 4RN

Simultaneously published in the USA and Canada
by Routledge
270 Madison Avenue, New York NY 10016

Routledge is an imprint of the Taylor and Francis Group, an informa business

Typeset in Bembo by RefineCatch Limited, Bungay, Suffolk
Printed and bound in Great Britain by
TJ International, Padstow, Cornwall

British Library Cataloguing in Publication Data
A catalogue record for this book is available from the British Library

Library of Congress Cataloging in Publication Data
Learning to teach religious education in the secondary school: a companion to school
experience / [edited by] L. Philip Barnes, Andrew Wright and Ann-Marie Brandom.
    p. cm.
    1. Religious education–Great Britain. 2. Religion–Study and teaching (Secondary)–
Great Britain. I. Barnes, Philip (L. Philip). II. Wright, Andrew, 1958–
III. Brandom, Ann-Marie.
  LC410.G7W75 2008
  200.711'241–dc22

                                        2007052721

ISBN 10: 0–415–42046–6 (pbk)
ISBN 13: 978–0–415–42046–4 (pbk)

Contents

Illustrations

FIGURES

TABLES

TASKS

Contributors

Jo Backus is Senior Lecturer in the Study of Religion and Religious Education at Bath Spa University College. She holds degrees in Philosophy and Theology and in Religious Studies. Before moving into higher education she taught RE in secondary schools and ran a Department of Religious and Social Studies. She has considerable experience in initial teacher education, both as school tutor and as PGCE RE Programme Director.

L. Philip Barnes is Senior Lecturer in Religious Education at King's College London. He has published widely in the philosophy of RE and on the role of RE in liberal democratic societies, contributing to such journals as the *British Journal of Educational Studies, British Journal of Religious Education, Journal of Philosophy of Education*, and *Studies in Philosophy and Education*. He is currently in the process of completing a major study of British religious education entitled *Multiculturalism, Religion and Education: Developing a New Model of Religious Education*, to be published by the University of Wales Press.

Ann-Marie Brandom is Lecturer in Religious Education at King's College London, where she co-ordinates the PGCE RE course. She was a visiting lecturer at Goldsmiths College, University of London, providing RE input on the Primary BEd course. Previously, she was a teacher of RE and a Head of Department in an Inner London comprehensive for ten years. She is undertaking research into the cognitive abilities of students in relation to religious and theological understanding.

Andrew Clutterbuck is Head of the School of Humanities at the University of Hertfordshire. A former teacher of RE and Head of Department in a comprehensive school, he now contributes to BA and BEd Study of Religion and Religious Studies courses. His previous publications include *Growing up in Sikhism, The Reader's Guide to Women's Studies* and articles in journals such as the *International Journal of Human*

Computer Interaction. His PhD concerned structural knowledge representations and Muslim children's understandings of Islam.

Sue Cooke is an experienced teacher who is Assistant Head and Head of Department of Religious Education at Wallington County Grammar School for Boys, Wallington, Surrey.

Trevor Cooling is Director of Transforming Lives, a project promoting teaching as a Christian vocation based at the Stapleford Centre in Nottingham. Previously, he had many roles in RE, including head of department, university lecturer, curriculum developer and diocesan adviser. He is an Honorary Research Fellow at the University of Gloucestershire.

Clive Erricker is Hampshire County Inspector for Religious Education. Previously, he was Reader in the Study of Religions at University College Chichester. He is the author of, contributor to and editor of a number of publications in the area of RE and spiritual education. He is co-director of the Children and World-views Project and joint editor, with Jane Erricker and Cathy Ota, of the *International Journal of Children's Spirituality.*

Jane Erricker is Associate Dean of the Faculty of Education at the University of Winchester, where she lectures on Education Studies and Science Education. She has authored and contributed to a number of publications in the fields of spiritual and moral education. She is co-director of the Children and World-views Project and joint editor, with Clive Erricker and Cathy Ota, of the *International Journal of Children's Spirituality.*

Liam Gearon is Professor of Education in the School of Education and Senior Fellow in the Crucible Centre in the School of Business and Social Sciences at Roehampton University. At Roehampton University he was founder and former Director of the Centre for Research in Human Rights. He has published widely in the fields of religion and literature as well as education; and has taught in schools in the North-West and South-West of England, being former Head of Religious Education at St Dunstan's School, Glastonbury.

Fred Hughes has recently retired from the University of Gloucestershire, where he was Head of Theology and Religious Studies until 2003. He has a MEd and PhD from Nottingham University. Before entering academic life, he taught RE in Essex, Gloucestershire, Leicester and Uganda. He is the author of *What Do You Mean – Christian Education?* (Paternoster Press, 1992).

Vanessa Ogden qualified as an RE specialist and is currently Head Teacher at Mulberry School for Girls in the London Borough of Tower Hamlets. As Sir Halley Stewart Teacher Fellow, she undertook full-time research into post-16 RE. She has taught on the Masters programme in RE at the Institute of Education, London, and been part of working parties for QCA on RE.

John Rudge worked for 18 years at the Westhill RE Centre in Birmingham, and contributed to the development of the Westhill Project RE 5-16. After teaching PGCE RE at Westhill and Birmingham University, he moved to East Anglia where he now works as a freelance consultant. He is involved in the inspection of teacher training and of RE subject teaching in schools, and is Chair of Examiners with Edexcel.

Linda Rudge is the Director of the Keswick Hall Centre for Research and Development in Religious Education at the University of East Anglia in Norwich. She was a secondary RE teacher and Head of Department between 1980 and 1990, and an Essex LEA curriculum adviser on RE between 1990 and 1993. Her research interests are the history and politics of RE, the professional lives of RE teachers and the relevance of RE to the 'silent majority'.

Joy Schmack was formerly Religious Education Adviser in the London Borough of Croydon. She is an experienced secondary school teacher and Head of RE. With Ann Lovelace, she is co-author of *Beliefs, Values and Traditions* (Heinemann, 1996). Joy has contributed regularly to a number of secondary PGCE courses, both as external examiner and as visiting lecturer. She was a director of a series of St Gabriel's Trust-sponsored Action Research Initiatives developed jointly by Croydon LA and King's College London.

Alison Seaman is an adviser, researcher, writer and consultant in religious education. She is an experienced facilitator for groups wishing to reflect on their own educational and working practice at conferences, workshops and in-service training. She is the author of a wide range of books and support materials for pupils and teachers on RE and spiritual development.

Derek Webster is an Anglican priest working in the Diocese of Lincoln, who until recently was Reader in Education in the School of Education, University of Hull. A former teacher, he taught in colleges of education in London, Leeds and West Yorkshire before being appointed to his university post in 1972.

Andrew Wright is Professor of Religious and Theological Education at King's College London, and co-ordinator of the Centre for Theology, Religion and Culture. He has been in charge of PGCE RE programmes at King's College, the Roehampton Institute and the London Institute of Education. Prior to his move into higher education, he was Head of the RE departments in three contrasting secondary schools. Among his publications are *Religious Education in the Secondary School* (David Fulton, 1993), *Spirituality and Education* (RoutledgeFalmer, 2000) and *Religion, Education and Post-modernity* (RoutledgeFalmer, 2004). His current research is concerned with critical realism and religious literacy.

Angela Wright is an RE PGCE Tutor at King's College London. Previously, she taught RE in two London schools. In 1995, she was awarded the Sir Halley Stewart Fellowship for Religious Education and spent the year investigating the issue of teaching RE at Key Stage 4. This coincided with the development of the new GCSE short courses, in which she was involved. She is part of the team of authors of *Religion in Focus*, the textbook series devoted to the teaching of the short courses published by John Murray.

Abbreviations

ACCT	Association of Church College Trusts
ACT	Association of Christian Teachers
AfL	assessment for learning
AREIAC	Association of Religious Education Inspectors, Advisers and Consultants
AS	Agreed Syllabus
ASC	Agreed Syllabus Conference
ASDAN	Award Scheme Development and Accreditation Network
AT	attainment target
AULRE	Association of University Lecturers in Religion and Education
BECTA	British Educational Communications and Technology Agency
BFBS	British and Foreign Bible Society
BHA	British Humanist Association
BJRE	*British Journal of Religious Education*
BTEC	Business and Technology Education Council
CEDP	Career Entry and Development Profile (formerly CEP)
CEM	Christian Education Movement
CEP	Career Entry Profile
CKSA	Common knowledge, skills and attributes
CTC	City Technology College
DCFS	Department for Children, Families and Schools
DES	Department of Education and Science
DfE	Department for Education
DfEE	Department for Education and Employment
EA	Education Act
EAZ	Education Action Zone
EBD	Emotional and Behavioural Difficulties
EFTRE	European Forum of Teachers in Religious Education

ERA	Education Reform Act
FE	Further Education
GCE	General Certificate of Education
GCSE	General Certificate of Secondary Education
GM	Grant-maintained (of schools; designation no longer used)
GNVQ	General National Vocational Qualification
HEI	higher education institution
ICT	information and communications technology
IEP	Individual Education Plan
IHE	Institution of Higher Education
INSET	In-service Education for Teachers
IT	information technology
ITE	initial teacher education
KS	Key Stage
LA	Local Authority
ME	Moral Education
MLD	moderate learning difficulties
NASACRE	National Association of SACREs
NASEN	National Association of Special Educational Needs
NCC	National Curriculum Council
NCET	National Council for Educational Technology
NGfL	National Grid for Learning
NQT	Newly Qualified Teacher
NS	National Society (Church of England) for Promoting Religious Education
NVF	National Values Forum
NVQ	National Vocational Qualification
Ofsted	Office for Standards in Education
OHP	overhead projector
PCfRE	Professional Council for Religious Education
PDP	professional development portfolio
PGCE	Postgraduate Certificate of Education
PRU	Pupil Referral Unit
PSE	Personal and Social Education
QCA	Qualifications and Curriculum Authority
QTS	Qualified Teacher Status
RE	Religious Education
REC	Religious Education Council of England and Wales
RI	Religious Instruction
SACRE	Standing Advisory Council on Religious Education
SCAA	Schools Curriculum and Assessment Authority
SEN	special educational needs
SENCO	special educational needs co-ordinator
SLD	severe learning difficulties
SMSC	spiritual, moral, social and cultural
TDA	Teacher Development Agency

TES	*Times Educational Supplement*
TTA	Teacher Training Agency (now TDA)
UMS	Uniform Mark Scale
WRERU	Warwick Religions and Education Research Unit
WWW	World Wide Web

Introduction: Becoming a Religious Education teacher

L. Philip Barnes, Andrew Wright and Ann-Marie Brandom

We introduced the first edition of this book with the claim that Religious Education (RE) is flourishing: 'brash, bold and self-confident'. The old assumption that the subject is no more than a missionary wing of the Christian churches is now long dead, and those still subscribing to such a dogma must rely increasingly on memory rather than an appeal to current reality in sustaining their argument. Similarly, the misplaced reaction against RE as Christian nurture, which led to the reduction of the subject to forms of personal and social education, is itself quickly becoming a thing of the past. Admittedly not without effort, RE has learnt to resist the temptation to replace religion with 'mere morality', though under the guise of citizenship mere morality has made a comeback. The last quarter of a century has seen the emergence of a third way, in the form of a modern RE committed to the integrity of its subject matter and to the professionalism of the task of teaching religion. In the light of recent international events, the responsibility of RE to develop deep understandings of the ultimate beliefs, commitments and transcendent truth claims of adherents of different religious traditions – rather than merely paper over the cracks of society through a vacuous blanket appeal to tolerance when so much around us is unambiguously and profoundly unworthy of acceptance – is all the more urgent. The establishment of a (non-statutory) National Framework for RE, the rapidly increasing uptake of the subject at GCSE and A Level, and the recognition by Ofsted that standards of teaching and learning in some areas show signs of significant improvement, suggest that our initial claims were not too far off the mark.

This book is designed to support student teachers at secondary level who, recognising the sea change that has swept the subject, have chosen to embark on a professional career as teachers of RE. It is also hoped that this book contains much of value for established professionals. Student teachers using this book are strongly urged to read it in conjunction with the lead book in the series, *Learning to Teach in the Secondary School*, 4th edition (Capel *et al.* 2005) which has established itself as standard text for many PGCE courses.

THE ART, CRAFT AND CHARISMA OF TEACHING

One popular, though misplaced, view of the teaching profession subscribes to the theory of 'personal charisma'. Good teaching is dependent on the possession of an effervescent personality, able to enthuse and motivate otherwise reluctant pupils. If you embark on your teaching career committed to this particular myth you may find yourself looking enviously at fellow students who are simply more charismatic than you are, and rather smugly down at those grey colleagues whom you know instinctively are not going to make the grade. It is important to ditch this myth at an early stage in your initial teacher education (ITE). Though it possibly contains a fragment of truth, it remains ultimately flawed.

Most good teachers base their professional credentials not on force of personality but on hard graft. As a student teacher you must learn the craft of the classroom by becoming an apprentice to experienced tutors. The way to establish yourself as a teacher is by the observation and discerning imitation of those who, with years of experience behind them, know how to operate effectively in the classroom. The model of learning to teach as a craft, however, is only part of the story. Teaching is a profession, and becoming a professional teacher is all about becoming a 'reflective practitioner'. The profession of teaching goes beyond mere imitation and transcends the mere passing on of traditional wisdom. As a teacher you must become critically aware and responsible in your role, capable of using your insights into the nature and purpose of education to take initiatives to develop and transform your practice.

Responsibility for ITE is shared between schools and higher education institutions (HEIs). This partnership reflects an understanding of the teaching profession rooted in the dual models of teaching as a 'craft' and the teacher as 'reflective practitioner'. You may learn much of the craft of teaching from your school-based tutors and more of the art of critical reflection from your IHE tutors but both sets of tutors contribute to your professional development. Perhaps the key issue is the recognition that craft without reflection, and reflection without craft both lead to the diminishing of your competence as an effective RE teacher.

ABOUT THE BOOK

The contributors to this book were selected to reflect the ITE partnership between school and HEI, and the crucial balance between craft and reflection. The authors are either established and effective classroom teachers of RE with experience of tutoring students, or experienced HEI tutors on initial teacher education courses. Some contributors have experience of both roles.

The brief given to each contributor was to support and enhance the teaching and tutoring that takes place on Postgraduate Certificate of Education (PGCE) RE courses by:

- providing a clear and balanced introductory survey of the designated topic of their chapter;

- highlighting those areas of dispute and contention that form the cutting edges of contemporary developments in the subject;
- offering their own specific opinion or slant on their topic so as to encourage critical reading on the part of student teachers.

In setting out these ground rules for contributors we hoped to ensure two things: (1) that you are provided with clear and balanced introductions to key themes and issues facing the contemporary RE teacher; and (2) that at the same time you are confronted with the need to read the book critically, acknowledging that the particular standpoint of an author does not necessarily reflect any general consensus in the RE world, thereby enhancing the development of your reflective practice.

We have tried to ensure that each chapter is self-contained, so that it can be read independently without reference to any other chapter. This decision has led to a limited amount of overlap and repetition and reflects the pedagogical concept of the spiral curriculum: the notion that we learn not in a linear fashion, but by constantly addressing the same themes at different levels and on different occasions.

THE STRUCTURE OF THE BOOK

Though each chapter in this book is self-contained we have, nevertheless, attempted to provide a coherent structure and flow to the text as a whole.

Part I: The context of Religious Education

Part I sets out to locate the task of teaching RE at the beginning of the third millennium within its broad educational setting. In Chapter 1, 'The Place of Religious Education in the Curriculum', Linda Rudge maps the contours of the subject's increasingly successful struggle to secure its proper place within the school timetable and generate a sense of its own identity and integrity. In Chapter 2, Fred Hughes and Philip Barnes consider the place of 'Religious Education in state and faith schools', underlining the importance of recognising that the increasingly diverse range of types of school available in the UK both demand and create a plurality of approaches to the teaching of RE.

Part II: Teaching and learning

Part II takes us to the heart of the pedagogical process: teaching and learning itself. In Chapter 3, Jo Backus offers guidance on the process of preparation and planning for teaching through 'Developing programmes of study'. In Chapter 4, Trevor Cooling addresses the process of 'Pupil learning', paying particular attention to his pioneering model of 'concept cracking' as a means of enabling pupils to effectively tackle religious questions.

Part III: Classroom issues

In Part III a range of classroom issues are addressed that inevitably arise once you have become familiar with the context of curriculum and schooling, and begun to learn the craft of teaching and learning. Ann-Marie Brandom explores the importance of teaching for religious literacy in Chapter 5, 'The role of language in Religious Education'. John Rudge guides us through the minefield of pupil and programme 'Assessment in Religious Education' in Chapter 6. In Chapter 7, Angela Wright explores 'Learning to teach Religious Education at Key Stage 4', paying particular attention to GCSE teaching, and Sue Cooke does the same for 'GCE A Level Religious Studies' in Chapter 8. Finally, Chapter 9 finds Vanessa Ogden unpacking 'Establishing and enriching Religious Education at 16-plus', and reminding us that there is much more going on here than just A Level examinations.

Part IV: Religious Education and the whole school

In Part IV we recognise the fact that RE exists only alongside, and in intimate relationship with, the broader curriculum of the school. Here three areas of overlap with the educational task facing the whole school are explored. In Chapter 10, Clive Erricker and Jane Erricker guide us through an issue that has been more significant than most in recent years: 'Spirituality in the classroom'. Derek Webster cautions against dismissing the educational value of 'Collective worship' too lightly in Chapter 11. Philip Barnes invites us to take a fresh look at the relationship between 'Religious Education and Moral Education' in Chapter 12. Finally, Liam Gearon addresses issues of 'Religious Education and Citizenship: a human rights approach' in Chapter 13.

Part V: Supporting professional development

The PGCE and similar courses can provide no more than an initial teacher education. Learning to teach is an ongoing, indeed lifelong, task. Consequently, in this final part, we look at ways of supporting and resourcing your professional development, both during your ITE course and beyond. In Chapter 14, Andrew Clutterbuck unpacks one of the most significant growth areas in recent years, 'Information and communications technology', and in Chapter 15, Joy Schmack offers pearls of wisdom concerning your 'Professional development' enabling you to become a reflective practitioner of the craft of teaching religion in future years when your present PGCE course is a distant memory! The book concludes with an Appendix listing some useful addresses and websites, compiled by Alison Seaman and L. Philip Barnes.

FURTHER READING

Barnes, L.P. and Kay, W.K. (2002) *Religious Education in England and Wales: Innovations and Reflections*, Leicester: Religious and Theological Studies Fellowship. Short, critical and provocative review of developments in RE.

Baumann, A.S., Bloomfield, A. and Roughton, L. (1997) *Becoming a Secondary School Teacher*, London: Hodder & Stoughton. Designed to help support PGCE students achieve Qualified Teacher Status, this balanced and practical text is intended to help you 'on that journey from novice to expert'.

Capel, S., Leask, M. and Turner, T. (2005) *Learning to Teach in the Secondary School: A Companion to School Experience,* 4th edn, London: Routledge. The indispensable foundation stone of the *Learning to Teach* series, of which the present book is part.

Watson, B. and Thompson, P. (2007) *The Effective Teaching of Religious Education*, London: Pearson Longman. A balanced and insightful book, and as good a place as any to begin your own exploration of the contours of RE.

Wright, A. (1993) *Religious Education in the Secondary School: Prospects for Religious Literacy*, London: David Fulton. A basic introduction to some of the key issues facing RE teachers.

Part I

The context of Religious Education

1 The place of Religious Education in the curriculum

Linda Rudge

INTRODUCTION

This chapter begins with an overview of a range of factors influencing the place of Religious Education (RE) in the curriculum. It then explores some controversial aspects of RE's development, exemplified by the fact that the subject is both compulsory but optional and local but national. School collective worship is mentioned, but only as part of RE's history. The ownership of RE, the subject's aims and its relationship with religion(s) are also discussed. The concluding section considers present and future possibilities for RE with the introduction of the new *Non-Statutory National Framework for RE* (QCA 2004).

Any review of RE's place in the curriculum has to take account of wider debates about the whole curriculum in state schooling, from the early years of education to (and through) adulthood. The perceived purposes of education affect RE's position. This chapter explores the maze of structures, institutions and communities that influence and support the subject in a variety of different educational contexts. An appreciation of the diverse forms religious education can take and the factors that influence its nature will prepare the student to develop a critical but constructive perspective on the challenge of preparing to teach religious education in schools.

OBJECTIVES

By the end of this chapter you should be able to:

- understand some of the debates surrounding the purpose of RE and its position in the curriculum;

> ● be familiar with aspects of Agreed Syllabus construction, and the aims of RE;
> ● be able to formulate a justification of RE's place in the school curriculum.

RELIGIOUS EDUCATION: REALITIES AND RUMOURS

The place of RE in the curriculum presents you with many possibilities and, inevitably, some problems. Here are five possible aims for the subject, though there are many more possibilities. RE can:

● be an important contributor to personal development, enabling pupils to develop their own beliefs and values, and to consider thoughtfully those of others;
● provide an academic and rigorous way of understanding the world in which we live, introducing pupils to the fascinating realm of rituals, ceremonies, symbols and lifestyles;
● help develop critical thinking and skills of communication and expression, providing a literacy for dealing with religious questions and experiences;
● offer pupils a chance to reflect on the ultimate questions in life;
● stimulate interfaith dialogue and understanding, and offer an interface between the secular and the spiritual.

This is a tall order. Some, or all, of the above claims for RE may have been why you decided to become an RE teacher. This chapter is not only about RE's place in the curriculum, it is also about aims for RE and for RE teachers. As you develop a rationale for the subject, which in turn may have implications for the teaching methods you employ, you need to consider where that rationale has come from, and what alternatives exist. You also need to be hard-headed about the realities. How is it possible to fulfil any of these aims given the complexity of the task and, if government guidelines are actually met, a mere 5 per cent of curriculum time is available?

Task 1.1 Developing a professional rationale for RE teaching

Before you read any further, think about the question 'What is RE?' During the course of your career you may encounter many definitions and models of RE, and you may find yourself identifying with one or more of them. Despite this diversity, most good RE teachers work with a clear understanding of, and commitment to, their own personal rationale for the subject.

● Look at the five suggested aims of RE outlined above, and try to place them in descending order of importance according to your own developing approach to the subject.

- Are there any possible aims you would like to add to the list?
- Write down a summary of your professional aims as an RE teacher and share your perspectives with those of other student teachers of RE.
- Seal your summary in an envelope and put it in your Professional Development Portfolio (Capel *et al.* 2005: 3). In a year's time go back to it and consider how your views have changed.

RE is a comparatively new subject, although it has many ancient and contemporary relatives, such as Theology and Religious Studies. RE was effectively created by teachers and other educators during the period between 1944 and 1988, and it was legally recognised and given its current name by the 1988 Education Reform Act (HMSO 1988). During those forty-four years it also officially (if inadvertently) become divorced from its partner, collective worship. RE, like all school subjects, continues to evolve and develop, reflecting the changing nature of society and of schooling. In thirty years, between 1945 and 1975, the subject changed (at different speeds in individual schools and regions) from semi-confessional religious instruction, usually based on Christian Bible study, through thematic approaches to social and ethical issues, usually addressed from a Christian viewpoint, to a multi-faith experience in which pupils became engaged in the phenomenological study of religion(s). After 1975, the year of publication of the ground-breaking Birmingham Agreed Syllabus and its accompanying teacher's handbook *Living Together* (City of Birmingham Education Committee 1975), the stage was set for the developments and debates about RE's place in the curriculum described in the rest of this chapter. By 1988, RE had to be reviewed alongside controversial proposals for a state National Curriculum and broader aims for schooling as a whole.

A curriculum is a programme for learning within and across subjects, and outside them. There is a curriculum in each school, and there is a basic formal curriculum that educators, politicians and others refer to in discussions about schools, their purpose and their effects. Part of this basic curriculum is the National Curriculum, another part is RE.

> RE is required to be included, alongside the National Curriculum, in the basic curriculum which all maintained schools must provide for their registered pupils . . . The special status of RE as part of the basic but not National Curriculum is important. It ensures that RE has equal standing in relation to National Curriculum subjects within a school's curriculum.
>
> (DfE 1994a, para. 20)

The current realities affecting RE's place in this curriculum are presented below in some detail. The detail is provided so that you can become professionally informed about RE, and be able to deal accurately with queries about the place of RE in the curriculum. These realities are not unchanging, but they are the givens that impact upon the place of the subject, its aims, and its rationale at present.

The teacher of RE

Teachers of any subject influence its perception by others. Professional standards, combined with personality, values and attitudes send messages about the subject, its aims and content. These in turn affect the religious education of pupils. The formal standard you have to reach to become a teacher, published by the Training and Development Agency for Schools (TDA), emphasises this central role of the teacher (TDA 2007). RE teachers face specific challenges in their training, because the subject is not organised through one set of national Statutory Orders (DfEE 1998a, and QCA 2004). In certain circumstances teachers can decline to teach RE (DfE 1994a, paras 141, 144) but as a specialist teacher of the subject your future employers will assume that you will not use that right (DfE 1994a, para. 145).

The pupils, their families and their communities

Attitudes to religion in society inevitably influence attitudes to RE. At a time when secularism, individualism and religious diversity have increased, public and professional perceptions of the subject are often confused and contradictory. Consider the following broad range of opinions that can be found within society: RE should

- teach children to be religious;
- mould them into good Christians;
- teach pupils about religions;
- encourage them to learn from religion(s);
- educate them in religion, or spirituality.

RE can be inspiring, interesting and relevant, but given this broad spectrum of opinion it is not surprising that some of the expectations for RE of different people in society are not met. Most pupils and teachers can be loosely affiliated to the 'religion of the silent majority'; that is, those in society whose religious beliefs and attitudes are often implicit and even invisible, being related primarily to forms of civic and common religion rather than formal religious institutions (Wolffe, in Parsons 1993). There are also, however, pupils who come from families and communities where formalised religious belief and activity are still a central part of life.

  Just as teachers have a right not to teach RE, parents and guardians have the right to withdraw their family members from all or part of RE (DfE 1994a, para. 44). The withdrawal clauses continue to be controversial, particularly among those who support and practise non-confessional religious education: if there is no element of nurture in RE, why should it not be compulsory like other National Curriculum subjects? In practice, the number of secondary school withdrawals is very small compared with the total school population. Nevertheless you may become aware of a parental request for a child to be withdrawn from your lessons, in which case your school tutor will deal with the request.

Task 1.2 Investigating changing attitudes to RE

Identify a group of adults, including other student teachers from any subject in your PGCE year, teachers in schools, family, friends and acquaintances. Try to ensure that the group embraces a broad age range capable of reflecting changing attitudes towards the subject.
Ask each member of your selected sample to:

● recall their own primary or secondary religious education;
● express their attitudes and feelings towards their experiences;
● outline their perceptions of the nature and purpose of contemporary religious education.

Consider the responses as a whole. What patterns emerge? Which issues constantly push themselves centre stage?
Do the members of your sample have a fair and balanced understanding of your chosen professional role or are you misunderstood? Is, in your judgement, your sample typical of public understanding of RE? How should you and your colleagues respond to public perceptions of RE?
Use your findings to write a short summary of your inquiry and share it with your RE group.

Pupils contribute to RE's place in the curriculum by their attitudes and responses to it, and by their use of their religious education in their wider communities. They help mould the identity of RE together with their teachers and their peers. Their lives, and the lives of teachers, are part of the substance of the RE curriculum itself.

The RE department

The department with the delegated responsibility for RE usually has a head of department and other delegated staff working alongside him or her. Sometimes RE is organised through a Humanities faculty or Personal and Social Education (PSE) team. The staff teaching RE will have a range of qualifications and experience, and you must expect to find yourself working alongside non-specialists, some of whom may be unwilling conscripts to the team. The department's schemes of work, the resources it deploys, and the school's internal syllabus for RE, with its interpretation of the local Agreed Syllabus (i.e, the aims and content prescribed for RE by the Local Education Authority), all affect RE's place in the curriculum of individual schools. Standards in departments across the country will also affect national policy and so help determine RE's future.

The school

RE takes place in a variety of types of schools, including special schools. The focus here is on maintained schools (of which there are three categories: community, foundation and voluntary), though some of the discussion is relevant to teachers in denominational schools, e.g. Faith Academies. The place of RE in the secondary school curriculum has to take account of developments in primary education, and standards for Qualified Teacher Status require you to consider issues of continuity and progression in RE. The variety and types of schools have had a complicating effect on these matters. However, reports from the Office of Standards in Education (Ofsted 2007: 5, for example) indicate that there is an overall improvement in the standard of RE. The type of school, its relationship with feeder primary schools, its management and ethos have an effect on RE's place and its achievements in its curriculum.

The RE syllabus

> The 1988 Education Reform Act requires all syllabuses to reflect the fact that the religious traditions in Great Britain are in the main Christian while taking account of the teaching and practices of the other principal religions represented in Great Britain.
>
> (Education Reform Act 1988, Section 8.3)

> RE aims to help pupils to: acquire and develop knowledge and understanding of Christianity and other principal religions represented in Great Britain; develop an understanding of the influence of beliefs, values and traditions on individuals, communities, society and cultures; develop the ability to make reasoned and informed judgements about religious and moral issues with reference to principal religions represented in Great Britain; enhance their spiritual, moral, social and cultural development; develop positive attitudes towards other people, respecting their right to hold different beliefs from their own, and towards living in a society of diverse religions.
>
> (SCAA 1994a: 3)

> Religious Education actively promotes the values of truth, justice, respect for all and care of the environment.
>
> (QCA 2004: 8)

It is important to be aware that, apart from the requirement to address Christianity and other principal religions represented in Britain, there is no stated aim for RE in national law and no prescribed curriculum content, although *The Non-Statutory Framework for RE* (QCA 2004) gives much more detailed advice to LEAs and Agreed Syllabus Conferences (who have the task of producing syllabuses for their local areas) than previous central documents. Unlike subjects in the National Curriculum, the aims and material content of RE are determined locally. Most pupils in England and Wales in state education encounter their RE through school schemes of work which are most frequently based on locally Agreed Syllabuses, issued by each Local Education Authority (LEA), though there are separate arrangements regarding the scope and content of RE in community, foundation and voluntary schools. GCSE and A Level examination courses also have their own prescribed content for Religious Studies (RS is the term designating RE as a formal examination subject), and most Agreed Syllabuses are written to take account of these courses. These issues are dealt with in detail in Chapters 7 and 8. Historically the legal requirement that RE should be provided for all pupils, from nursery to tertiary stages of education, has tended to flounder in the face of the demands of public examinations at Key Stage 4, though recent developments are encouraging with large numbers of pupils pursuing Short Course GCSE Religious Studies. These new short courses offered by the Examinations and Awarding Boards often mean that pupil effort and achievement at Key Stage 4 in Agreed Syllabus RE can now be recognised nationally.

A syllabus is a tool for planning teaching and learning; its reception by teachers affects the RE of the pupils in individual schools and the place of RE in the curriculum as a whole. Although there are no national Statutory Orders for RE, the relevant clauses in the Education Reform Act, and subsequent legislation and advice, have provided a national basis for syllabus development in LEAs. The publication of national Model Syllabuses in RE as advice to LEAs and Standing Advisory Councils on Religious Education (SACREs) (SCAA 1994a, 1994b) was intended to homogenise RE syllabuses in England and Wales, but diversity and variety still dominate, as more LEAs have created their own syllabus rather than adopt those of other LEAs. The recently published *Non-Statutory Framework for RE* (QCA 2004) represents a further attempt to bring uniformity to syllabus construction and content. It also, of course, represents a further attempt to centralise control over RE.

Some Agreed Syllabuses emphasise the importance of spiritual development in their aims and approach, others the exploration and/or systematic study of beliefs and values, and others the opportunities RE provides for pupils to explore, and respond to, religion. Each syllabus either prescribes or offers schools choice concerning which religions are to form the basis of study for the achievement of these aims. Some include detailed schemes of work, programmes of study, attainment targets and assessment procedures, while others are less detailed.

Although there could be 126 locally Agreed Syllabuses in England and Wales, it has never happened, as local government reviews, SACRE recommendations and local elections mean that syllabuses are always at different stages of development. It was not until 1993 that LEAs were required by law to review their syllabuses to check that they were in line with 1988 legislation and national government advice. Since the 1993 legislation, syllabuses have to be reviewed every five years following their adoption, if not requested to do so sooner by the relevant SACRE (DfE 1994a, para. 29).

An LEA adopts a syllabus after taking the advice of an Agreed Syllabus Conference (ASC). An ASC may recommend adopting an existing syllabus from another LEA, choose to revise the syllabus currently in use, or opt to write a new one. The ASC is made up of committees representing various sectors (including religious ones) of the local community, education and local government. The ASC meets only at the direction of an LEA, after a recommendation by its SACRE, and can have an active life ranging from days through months to years. However, its only official function is to recommend a syllabus (ibid., para. 24). ASC membership is supposed to represent the 'proportionate strength' of religions and denominations (other than the Church of England) in a local area (ibid., para. 103).

The quality of LEA syllabuses is directly affected by the procedures and expertise of the conferences that produce them. Agreed Syllabuses have an impact on RE in the curriculum both at a national level, via debates about aims and standards, and in each school as teachers use them in their day-to-day planning. The focus in the last decade on the syllabus content of RE, on what pupils are to study and learn about, has provided most of the ammunition for a clash of interests and cultures between teachers, educators, faith communities and politicians which is still being resolved. The QCA *National Framework for RE* (2004), even though it is non-statutory, is another development intended to alleviate these potential problems and to improve pupils' experiences of RE.

Task 1.3 Exploring the aims of RE

Collect a sample of current locally Agreed Syllabuses, the internal syllabuses used in your experience schools, together with the QCA Non-Statutory Framework for RE.

- Identify and record in outline the various aims and objectives set out by these documents.
- Note how the form, structure and language through which the purpose of each syllabus is expressed either differ from, or are similar to, other syllabuses.
- Is there any particular set of aims you have encountered that you particularly dislike? Explain your selection.
- Is there any particular set of aims you have encountered that you particularly like? Explain your selection.
- Does any consensus emerge across the various documents? Are we in a position to identify a common national perception of the nature of RE that transcends local differences? Or are you dealing with incompatible diversity?

Local government and SACREs

As RE's place in the curriculum is subject to local democratic procedures, and local involvement (including in aided schools), the role of LEAs, and their ability to provide support, are central to RE's position. Local government reviews and elections, and initiatives such as the creation of a diversity of school types since 1997 (see Introduction to this chapter) and of Education Action Zones in 1998 (EAZs are groups of schools which are determined to raise educational standards in some of the most challenging urban areas) have also affected RE's position.

> Detailed arrangements for the provision of religious education and collective worship are properly a matter of local responsibility . . . Nevertheless the Government seeks to encourage improved standards and secure comparable opportunities for all pupils in non-denominational schools.
>
> (DfE 1994, para. 6)

The origins of SACREs go back to the 1944 Education Act and since 1988 every

LEA has been required to have a SACRE to advise it on aspects of RE and collective worship, and to recommend a review of the LEA syllabus when necessary (ibid., paras 90–2). The SACRE also receives inspection reports on schools in the LEA area. A SACRE comprises representatives of four (or five) groups representing similar interests to members of the ASC, but not necessarily through the same people. Details of the make-up of both SACREs and ASCs are set out in Figure 1.1. SACREs have kept RE on the agendas of Local Education Committees, and some have been forums for interfaith dialogue, and on occasions, for confrontation. There is now a National Association of SACREs that has also had some influence (NASACRE has a dedicated website, www.nasacre.org.uk/). The effects of the existence of SACREs on RE's place in the curriculum have been far-reaching, double-edged and controversial. The quality of their activities can support and improve RE, and the position and training of RE teachers. The quality of the relationship between a SACRE, schools and teachers is vital, and as a student teacher of RE you would be well advised to find out more about the SACRE in your local area from staff in your school experience school.

Central government and RE

The government also attaches great importance to the role of religious education and collective worship in helping to promote a clear set of personal values and beliefs among pupils and in promoting respect for and an understanding of the beliefs and religious practices of others. These aims are pursued through legislation in RE such as the 1988 Education Reform Act. Wider government policy also affects RE: local government review and reorganisation, educational emphases on school effectiveness,

---

The following summary of the constitution of SACREs and ASCs post-1993 is taken from the DfE Circular 1/94, Religious Education and Collective Worship (DfE 1994a, paras 103, 105). A SACRE may also include co-opted members who are not members of any of the other groups. There is no provision for an ASC to include co-opted members. A SACRE and an ASC each comprise four (or five) groups or committees representing, respectively:

- Christian denominations and other religions and religious denominations, the number of whose representatives shall, 'so far as consistent with the efficient discharge of the committee's functions, reflect broadly the proportionate strength of that denomination or religion in the area' (DfE 1994a, paras 111, 112);
- the Church of England;
- such associations representing teachers as, in the opinion of the authority, ought to be represented, having regard for the circumstances of the area;
- the Local Education Authority;
- other relevant maintained schools, such as Foundation Schools.

Figure 1.1 Composition of Standing Advisory Councils and Agreed Syllabus Conferences

the National Curriculum, management, quality assurance, standards, literacy, numeracy, citizenship and values, etc. National bodies such as the QCA, Ofsted and the TDA also influence RE, its standards, its nature and aims.

RE associations and professional groups

Although RE in maintained (and aided) schools is designed and implemented locally, the national view of RE is influenced by suggestions (and objections) from teacher associations, teacher educators, higher education groups, RE associations and charitable trusts. Research projects and curriculum development materials are used by teachers as they experiment with different methods of teaching and learning in RE. In some LEAs, where support for RE has been slow to emerge, commercially produced materials have often been a vehicle for change. Some charitable trusts (for example, the Saltley Trust) have entered into informal partnership with SACREs through school RE competitions, or through support for RE training and research (e.g. All Saints Trust, St Gabriel's Trust, the Farmington Institute and the Keswick Hall Trust). The actions of RE associations and professional groups have kept the debate open on RE's place in the curriculum; sometimes they have appeared to be in direct conflict with central (and local) government and advice, but more often they have acted as mediators, filtering the advice to support the teacher in the classroom, and other RE educators.

Religions and religious denominations

The opinions, beliefs and values of members of religious groups and denominations also have a direct influence on RE (and indirectly on other subjects) and on RE's position in both local and national legislation and policy. Members of all six major religions (and others) represented in Great Britain have been involved in national working groups, local SACREs and ASCs. One challenge facing teachers of the future is how to keep RE relevant to those participants (teachers and pupils) who are not members of the vocal minorities who influence national policy and local syllabuses.

These are some of the current realities facing RE and its teachers. Where they came from is the topic of discussion in the next section of the chapter.

RE: AGENDAS AND OWNERSHIP

The previous section dealt with the givens of the place of RE in the curriculum. The current realities of RE's status will continue unless there is a change in the law. They are the factors that most immediately affect you as a teacher as you plan your RE lessons, and some of their implications are covered in later chapters of this book. These factors are necessarily bound up with religious and social history, and the actions, beliefs and opinions of key personnel and groups. You need to consider the following related issues as you develop your rationale for teaching and learning, since RE continues to develop, and you are now part of this development.

The 1988 legislation on RE and collective worship arguably showed that RE had been 'there and back again' (Parsons 1994: 164). Though the subject in the classroom had changed beyond recognition from the Religious Instruction of 1944, the legislators and their advisers seemed determined to recreate the past. Several reasons for the continuation of RE's local position were given:

- lack of central government interest;
- fear of change and controversial legislative procedures;
- appreciation of good practice in local curriculum development;
- the idea that RE really does affect religious belief and commitment, and that pupils in any local area should not be affected too much by the religious beliefs and values of others.

The national government in the early 1990s made attempts to influence decisions on RE's content and pedagogy, both through legislation and through advice. Alterations to the composition of SACREs and ASCs (Figure 1.1) were intended to bring local pressure to bear on syllabus development and implementation. Local ASCs, while recognising the national picture, were expected to recommend a local form of RE which kept local communities happy, and which would ensure the protection of the majority religion(s). The debates on the role and intentions of the Model Syllabuses published by SCAA in 1994 illustrated further central pressures on the local nature of RE, and highlighted the concerns of some about the relative benefits of thematic or systematic teaching in RE. These debates continue.

The speed and the complexity of change in RE over fifty years, highlighted earlier in this chapter, have given rise to a range of controversial issues. Here we can deal in detail with only three: the nature of the educational enterprise and its aims; the place of Christianity and other religions in RE, and the question of the ownership of the RE curriculum.

RE: nature and aims

Views of the nature and aims of education affect approaches to RE, just as interpretations of religion affect educational models of the subject. This results in different approaches to RE, three of which we will consider.

RE as induction into community and culture

First, there is a view of education (and therefore of RE) as nurture in communities of culture, beliefs and values. The main aim of RE in this setting is to nurture both the pupil and the wider society into a particular faith, and even into a particular denomination. The 1944 Act sought, implicitly, to nurture children into Christianity, though not into any specific Christian denomination. Contemporary debate now focuses on whether any form of proselytism, regardless of its being illegal in maintained schools, can ever be genuinely effective. A counter-argument views all education as a type of nurture or indoctrination, and claims that RE teachers are inevitably engaged in nurturing the faiths of pupils in the class. Teachers can also be seen as bolstering interest in religious perspectives on life in an increasingly secular world. Of all the approaches to RE, teachers (of all subject backgrounds, primary and secondary) feel most nervous about nurture. It has problems of relevance and credibility in the classroom, and can appear to fly in the face of equal opportunities and anti-racist policies. However, many RE teachers with a strong commitment to a religion recognise the need for objectivity and distance in the way they handle material and implement lessons in the classroom.

RE as the liberal study of religion

The second model of education may be described as liberal. In this model, the teacher tries to become the mediator of controversial material and opinions by adopting a distanced neutral stance and by developing in pupils the skill and ability to use knowledge and understanding to make well-informed judgements. This model's commitment to religion itself and to an attitude of openness makes it the approach which is favoured by most RE teachers. It is essentially focused on 'out there' and not 'in here', and on 'them', not 'me'. One of its main aims is to promote respect for religion, and for the human right to belong to a particular religion. The problem, of course, lies in the practical classroom reality. There is no such thing as the neutral teacher, although we all aim for neutrality at times. The selection of material and methods of teaching immediately betray interests and preferences. Dialogue and body language in the classroom reveal prejudices and likes and dislikes. Pupils can become experts in the minutiae of religious practice, and yet ignorant of the wider value of encountering beliefs. 'What is religion?' and 'What or who constitutes religions?' are basic questions that are rarely addressed and which often get overlooked by concentration on the minutiae of learning about religion.

RE as an agent of humanisation

The third model primarily views education as humanising concern. It addresses the 'whole' person, and is focused on issues of justice as well as respect, and with empowerment as well as community. The aims of RE in such an education are concerned with how we educate pupils to grow and develop spiritually through reference to, and the expression of, religion in general rather than any one religion in particular. Knowledge of religion is the instrument, not the goal, and an RE of this kind has to take full account of secular world-views. It also has to consider the uncomfortable fact that theologies and religious philosophies may be constraining as well as emancipating, illiberal as well as liberal. It is essentially a reflective approach to RE based on rigorous study, but it also implies a critique of religion and religions. Once again, the pitfalls lie in the translation of theory into practice. With only 5 per cent of curriculum time, perceived pressures of assessment and recording and a large number of classes and pupils to deal with each week, many secondary RE teachers find themselves appreciating the theory, and avoiding it in practice. Others find the notion of a critical stance in RE inherently unsettling.

In reality, pupils in both primary and secondary schools receive their RE from a range of professionals who combine aspects of all three approaches and their related rationales. You may find yourself using all three in your classroom at different times.

The place of Christianity, and of other religions, in the curriculum

The second issue highlighted at the beginning of this section concerned the place of different religions in RE. Christianity is defined by the 1988 Education Reform Act as the 'predominant' religion in Great Britain. This usage gave rise to debate at the time, as some proponents of a multi-faith approach interpreted the reference as intended to undermine current practices and methodologies in RE. Critics of multi-faith RE who presented it in public debate as an 'incoherent mishmash', creating contamination between faiths, and a 'mess of secular pottage' were challenged by John Hull, Professor of Religious Education at Birmingham University (1991: 9). He argued that those who opposed multi-faith RE chose to present themselves and their beliefs as requiring separateness and space in order to avoid contamination and maintain their individual holiness. Hull proposed an alternative way of considering the holiness and integrity of faiths:

> In myself, I am not particularly holy, and perhaps in yourself you are not wonderfully holy, but the ground between us is holy. The boundary which separates shall become the holy ground, the common ground, the mutuality of response and responsibility which makes us truly human

> (ibid.: 38)

Transferring this radical approach into the classroom means that the RE teacher chooses material and methods which present religious beliefs and traditions with integrity. Pupils are encouraged to respond to them with similar integrity. A great deal has been written and said about the integrity of faiths in the RE classroom, little about the integrity of RE teachers and, more importantly, their pupils.

Ownership of RE's purpose and agenda

The final issue is about ownership of RE's purpose and agenda. It is linked to the question of the position of religions in RE, and it is contentious and complicated. Is RE 'owned' by professional educators, by the religious communities or by politicians and their advisers? Is shared ownership feasible in the future? It has certainly been difficult in the past. Religious groups play an important role in defending and developing RE, but there are times when some teachers feel that religion is trying to own RE, and to control their professional freedoms. Religion can be defined in various ways, and sometimes religions do not appreciate being defined by education. However, religion in its different forms affects all of us, it is part of the common heritage of humanity, and if the nature of education is to be concerned with human development, religion is a matter both for educational concern and for educational enhancement. Presumably, the interests of religious communities have to be balanced with the interests of education and professional educators. Religious communities expect that their commitments will be properly represented, while educators will insist that what religious communities regard as true should be the subject of debate and discussion in the classroom.

RE: CULTIVATING HUMANITY

This section of the chapter looks to the future, yet the wider purposes of current legislation cannot be ignored when considering RE's future place in the curriculum: schools are expected to contribute to the spiritual, moral, social and cultural (SMSC) development of pupils. For example, if spiritual development has to do with the acquisition and application of spiritual wisdom, regardless of age and intellect, then RE certainly has a wealth of material and experiences to contribute. The present interest in citizenship and values is a direct result of the SMSC debates, and RE's contribution to these cross-curricular issues is valued and recognised by some, though denigrated by others (Watson 2003). Analysing and measuring that contribution are not easy, though schools and RE departments have been pressed to address them fully through inspection and advice. How does RE make a difference to the development of personal identity?

Internationally, RE in the UK is regarded with a mixture of curiosity, incredulity, sometimes admiration and sometimes criticism. Its positive achievements, especially as a major contributor to the field of multicultural education and interfaith dialogue are well known, if disputed. To those looking in from the outside, the fact that RE is still here is astonishing. Historical precedent, tangled legislation, pressure groups and professional commitment certainly protect its position, but that does not necessarily explain why religious components of state schooling persist in Britain. Elsewhere it is either handled at a distance through denominational schooling, by visitors to schools providing voluntary supplementary education to pupils from specific communities, or by complete banishment from state classrooms. Perhaps RE is there in the curriculum to inoculate the population against the worst excesses of religion! What would the British curriculum, and British society, look like without RE? Where, and how, would religion be encountered? Can you learn from religion without a structured form of learning about it?

Establishing a rationale for RE is important, and, as we have seen, there is more than one rationale. To do so for any subject requires making some idealistic claims, and those listed at the beginning of this chapter may appear to be daunting, or even impossible, in the light of what you have subsequently read. Ideals, however, are important, and though reality only rarely lives up to them, what has been described as the 'dumbing down' of RE is not the answer. Religious literacy, religious knowledge, religious spirituality, religious understanding, religious dialogue, religious reflection – all are part of the RE curriculum. RE's place in the curriculum is to provide an opportunity for an education in the emotions as well as the intellect, and a focus on critical reasoning; it may be an education that is concerned with social justice, seeking to empower teachers, and emancipate learners. Teachers of RE, including student teachers, have an important contribution to make to education.

Task 1.4 RE and values

The extract below is from a *Guidance for Schools: The Promotion of Pupils' Spiritual, Moral, Social and Cultural Development* (QCA 1997: 35). The values that underpin the document were compiled by the National Forum for Values in Education and the Community between 1996 and 1997.

> We value truth, freedom, justice, human rights, the rule of law and collective effort for the common good. In particular we value families as sources of love and support for all their members, and as a basis of a society in which people care for others.

> *On the basis of these values we should:*

- understand and carry out our responsibilities as citizens;
- refuse to support values or actions that may be harmful to individuals and communities;
- support families in raising children and caring for dependants;
- support the institution of marriage;
- recognise that the love and commitment required for a secure and happy childhood can also be found in families of different kinds;
- help people to know about the law and legal processes;
- respect the rule of law and encourage others to do so;
- respect religious and cultural diversity;
- promote opportunities for all;
- support those who cannot, by themselves, sustain a dignified lifestyle;
- promote participation in the democratic process by all sectors of the community;
- contribute to, as well as benefit fairly from, economic and cultural resources;
- make truth, integrity, honesty and goodwill priorities in public and private life.

Write a short commentary on the values above by answering these questions:

1   Which values would you select to promote RE? Explain why you reject any values listed.
2   Identify any problems or contradictions in your choice of values and ways you might ameliorate them.
3   Write three statements supporting a rationale for teaching RE for your chosen set of values.

Compare your selection of values with those of other student teachers of RE.

SUMMARY AND KEY POINTS

The place of RE in the curriculum is dependent upon legislation, official organisations, communities and people. RE is simultaneously compulsory yet optional and local yet national. The realities facing RE in the first decades of the twenty-first century can appear complicated and daunting: they have arisen through the relationship between religion(s) and education, and through the speed of social, economic and cultural change in post-war Europe. The issues for RE which have emerged since 1988 are concerned with the position and appropriate aims of RE in a changing educational system, the place of Christianity and other principal religions in RE, and questions about the ownership and agendas of the RE curriculum. As a teacher you should be aware of the need to consider and reconsider your own rationale for RE, and your professional contribution to its place in the curriculum. RE is concerned with learning about religion, learning from religion and learning through religion. The encounter between teachers, pupils and world-views is the key to effective and affective RE in a broader curriculum which seems to be moving again towards an education for being and becoming human.

FURTHER READING

Barnes, L.P. (2008) *Religious Education: Taking Respect for Difference Seriously*, Oxford: Philosophy of Education Society of Great Britain. Important, recent critique of British religious education.

Copley, T. (2008) *Teaching Religion: Religious Education in England and Wales 1944 to 2007*, Exeter: University of Exeter Press. A useful, very readable and informative review of RE over the past sixty years, using a range of historical evidence, including otherwise inaccessible source material from politicians.

Hull, J. (1998) *Utopian Whispers*, Derby: CEM. A collection of editorials from the *British Journal of Religious Education* focusing particularly on government legislation and the politics of religious education.

Parsons, G. (ed.) (1993) *The Growth of Religious Diversity: Britain from 1945, vol. I, Traditions*, London: Open University/Routledge.

Parsons, G. (ed.) (1994) *The Growth of Religious Diversity: Britain from 1945, vol. II, Issues*, London: Open University/Routledge. Both volumes provide essential background information about the increasing secularisation and religious pluralism of modern British society. These two volumes contain accounts and analyses of the social, religious and cultural changes in Britain up to the 1990s. Excellent background reading to the development of RE, and detailed information about religions in Britain today.

2 Religious Education in state and faith schools

Fred Hughes and L. Philip Barnes

INTRODUCTION

This chapter aims to introduce the broad context in which Religious Education (RE) takes place, in particular, the system of schooling in England and Wales. It first describes the dual system of partnership between the state and a variety of faith communities in terms of the provision of schooling, focusing especially on the various types of school and their historical background. It then goes on to outline the current legal requirements for RE and collective worship, as well as the current school inspection arrangements in these two areas of the curriculum. The final part of the chapter explores and explains the nature of the basic distinction between 'confessional' and 'non-confessional' RE.

OBJECTIVES

By the end of this chapter you should be able to:

* understand some of the differences between RE in different types of schools;
* clarify your understanding of the distinction between confessional and non-confessional RE;
* form a professional opinion regarding the confessional and non-confessional RE debate.

THE DUAL SYSTEM: STATE SCHOOLS AND SCHOOLS WITH A RELIGIOUS CHARACTER

In England and Wales, the context of RE is dominated by the dual system of partnership between the state and various faith communities, which work together to provide primary and secondary education for all children. We begin by looking at the various types of school you are likely to encounter in your career. We must take a little time with this, since recently the situation has undergone considerable change. We then unpack some of the historical background to contemporary schooling as it relates to RE.

Types of contemporary schools

There is a diverse range of different types of contemporary schools. The situation is fluid, though the distinctions between types of school established by the School Standards and Framework Act 1998 (HMSO 1998) provide the point of departure for more recent legislation. The main division is between maintained schools, funded mostly through public funds, for example, through local and central taxation, and independent schools, which are mostly financed privately, for example, through fees and scholarships. Over 90 per cent of school-age children in Britain attend maintained schools.

Schools in the maintained sector may be divided into two groups: those receiving some funding from their Local Authority (LA) and those funded directly from central government. The partly locally funded schools are:

- community schools (once county schools);
- foundation schools (some formerly grant maintained schools (GM));
- voluntary schools, comprising voluntary aided and voluntary controlled schools.

The centrally funded schools are:

- City Technology Colleges (technically independent schools);
- Academies (publicly funded independent schools).

In addition, any maintained school can opt to become a *Specialist School*. Such schools meet full National Curriculum requirements, but have a special focus on a chosen specialism (typically one but can be two). They have a key role in revitalising education especially in disadvantaged areas.

Community schools are, in the main, established schools that are run and operated by LAs (many of them County Councils). Most foundation schools are former GM schools that opted out of LA control in order to achieve a greater measure of autonomy and self-government, and which now receive most of their funding direct from central government; foundation schools are now locally funded.

There are various types of *voluntary* school. These are schools founded by a charitable organisation, frequently but not exclusively a church in the form of a Diocesan Board of Education. Here funding and control are shared in a partnership between public and private charitable funds: as a rule of thumb, the LA pays for the day-to-day upkeep of the schools, including staff wages, while the charity contributes to more basic costs such as capital building projects. Most of these, especially in the primary sector, are *voluntary controlled* schools, where much of the control in the partnership passes from the charity to the LA. In the case of *voluntary aided* schools, the founding body retains most of the control but receives financial aid from public funds. In voluntary aided schools the foundation body has a majority on the governing body, but such is not the case with voluntary controlled schools.

Most voluntary schools are Christian church schools of either Church of England (Anglican) or Roman Catholic foundation, though a few involve other denominations such as Methodists. The most significant non-Christian voluntary schools were founded and are now run by the Jewish community. A recent and highly significant innovation by the Labour government has been the extension of voluntary status to previously private schools rooted in religious traditions other than Christianity and Judaism – Hindu, Islamic and Sikh schools, for example.

The foundation bodies of voluntary aided schools (but not voluntary controlled schools) retain a high level of control over their admission policies (though this is a matter that is now occasioning political debate in relation to the issue of social inclusion). Because the Church of England is the established national church, it has been committed to providing schools for the whole community rather than simply for its church community alone. Where Church of England schools are over-subscribed, links with the church may be a factor in admission policy, but many Church of England schools operate an open admission policy, opening their gates to all pupils in the local community whose parents want them to attend. This has led to the odd situation of a number of Church of England schools in which the pupil community is predominantly Muslim. For example, Sir John Cass Foundation School in inner London is a Church of England School, but has an 80 per cent Muslim intake. Roman Catholic and Jewish schools, by contrast, have tended to see their role in terms of service to their specific religious communities. These schools have generally tended not to be for everyone in the local community. It is not always so, but generally the key aim has been to provide an appropriate Roman Catholic or Jewish education in a faith school for every child from families that belong to that particular religious community.

City Technology Colleges (CTCs) are funded directly by the government and offer a wide range of vocational qualifications alongside A Levels or equivalents. They teach the National Curriculum with a specific focus on science, mathematics and technology. Most CTCs teach a longer day and several operate a five-term year. CTCs have developed close links with employers. Academies are publicly-funded independent schools, with the freedom to raise standards through innovative approaches to management, governance, teaching and curriculum. They are established in disadvantaged areas, either as new schools or to replace poorly performing schools, where other intervention and improvement strategies have failed. Academies are established by sponsors from the business, faith and voluntary sectors who contribute up to £2 million towards the capital costs of the new building. The remaining capital costs and recurrent funding are paid by the Department for Children, Families and Schools (DCFS). Partnership between sponsors, parents and other educational institutions is at the heart of an academy's role in raising standards. The DCSF's Five-Year Strategy is to provide 200 new academies, either open or in the pipeline, by 2010, including sixty in London.

The historical background

A short historical overview may help you to understand how the present schooling situation has developed. The first schools in Britain were not maintained by the state. Rather, they were founded and maintained by the churches and are traditionally known as independent schools because they were founded independently of government organisations. They have sometimes been closely associated with cathedrals. Examples are King's School, Canterbury, established in or about 598 AD, and St Peter's School, York, established in or about 625 AD.

The church continued to be the main provider of schools until the twentieth century, but the foundations of the present dual system of public education, grounded in partnership between church and state, were laid in the nineteenth century. Though the independent schools established by the churches became equated historically with a class-bound educated elite, the churches increasingly poured funds into schools for children from working-class families. Indeed, the notion of education for all regardless of ability to pay was a vision that originated in the Church of England. It was these schools that the government in the nineteenth century saw fit to contribute to financially. The first government grant for schools was in 1833. It was a grant to the National Society for Promoting the Education of the Poor in the Principles of the Established Church and to the British and Foreign Schools Society, a group of non-conformist Protestant origin and orientation. The first government grant for Roman Catholic schools was made in 1847.

The state only became a direct provider of schools following the Education Act of 1870. This Act allowed the establishment of Board schools, later to become County schools, alongside the flourishing voluntary church schools. The Education Act 1902 allowed voluntary schools to be supported from the rates.

The Hadow Report of 1926 recommended that separate senior schools should be provided for all pupils, thus introducing the distinction between primary and secondary education that remains today. Previously pupils attended a single elementary school before finishing school or moving on to Higher Education. The Church of England found it difficult to fund enough separate senior (secondary) schools. This was one matter that the Education Act 1944 sought to address, making the state the major post-war provider of new secondary schools. The dual system continued throughout the twentieth century but in the main with the state sector increasing and the voluntary sector decreasing.

The long involvement of the church in education partly explains their continuing involvement in RE, for example, their membership of Standing Advisory Councils on Religious Education (SACREs) and Agreed Syllabus Conferences (ASCs). Also the long-standing involvement of the churches in the provision of education partly explains the continuing place of RE and collective worship in schools, and the next section sets out the current legal position.

THE LEGAL FRAMEWORK

The legal requirements for RE

All maintained schools should provide RE and collective worship for their pupils, unless they have been withdrawn by their parents. RE in all community schools and all foundation and voluntary schools without a religious character must follow the Agreed Syllabus (AS) for the area. The AS is drawn up by the LA, taking advice from local bodies. The SACRE, a local body made up of representatives from faith groups, teachers and the LA, advise on RE and collective worship issues, whereas the ASC, a subset of the SACRE, produces or recommends new syllabuses. The 1988 Education Reform Act (HMSO 1988) requires that all local ASs must reflect the fact that the religious traditions in Great Britain are mainly Christian, while taking account of the teaching and practices of the other principal religions represented in Great Britain. The head teacher shares responsibility with the LA and the governing body for making sure that the RE requirements are met.

The precise nature of RE at a foundation or voluntary school depends on the religious character of the school. Whether a foundation or voluntary school has a religious character and the particular religion or religious denomination concerned is set out in The Designation of Schools Having a Religious Character (England) Order 1999 (HMSO 1999), or, for schools approved to enter the maintained sector after 1 September 1999, the religion or denomination designating the school.

RE in a voluntary aided school with a religious character must be provided in accordance with the school's trust deed or, where provision is not made by a trust deed, in accordance with the beliefs of the religion or denomination specified in the Order referred to above. Where parents ask for RE to be provided for any pupils according to the locally Agreed Syllabus, and it is not convenient for them to attend a school at which the syllabus is in use, the governing body must make arrangements. This requirement is lifted if, because of special circumstances, it would be unreasonable to do so.

RE in a foundation or voluntary controlled school with a religious character must be provided in accordance with the locally Agreed Syllabus for the area. However, where parents request it, provision may be made in accordance with the schools trust deed or, where provision is not made by trust deed, in accordance with the beliefs of the religion or denomination specified in the Order referred to above. This requirement is lifted if, because of any special circumstances, it would be unreasonable to do so. The governing body is responsible for ensuring that such RE is provided for not more than two periods in each week. The head teacher shares responsibility with the LA and the governing body for making sure that the RE requirements are met.

CTCs are required to make provision for RE which is broadly in line with community schools, and most follow the local AS. Some colleges and academies, however, sponsored by the Church of England, have voluntary status as regards their RE provision. Independent schools do not have to follow any Local Authority Agreed Syllabus for RE. Independent schools sometimes collaborate in the production of a RE syllabus, which is then used in a number of schools.

Finally, teachers cannot be required to teach RE except where the law provides otherwise. This would normally apply in a school with a religious designation.

The legal requirements for collective worship

The complex question of collective worship is considered in Chapter 11, consequently what is stated here is intended to be introductory.

The Education Act 1944 requires all schools to begin the day with an act of collective worship, involving all registered pupils unless withdrawal is requested by their parents. All pupils in each school had to be assembled together for this purpose unless the school premises made it impracticable to do so. The Education Reform Act 1988 continues to require collective worship to be practised daily but it removed the requirement for worship to be at the start of each day and for all pupils in each school to be gathered together. This means that the worship can now take place at the start of a day or later, and that there can be a single act of worship for all pupils or worship in different groups based on a variety of criteria, e.g. that of age and membership of a particular Year Group, but not that of religion.

The 1944 Act did not stipulate that the worship had to be Christian, though at the time this was assumed, as it was assumed that RE was Christian education. The 1988 Reform Act, however, was more explicit about the nature of the worship in (county) schools: collective worship 'shall be wholly or mainly of a broadly Christian character' (HMSO 1988, Section 7.1). Such worship will be of Christian character if 'it reflects the broad traditions of Christian belief, without being distinctive of any particular denomination' (Section 7.2): not every act of worship need be wholly or mainly of a Christian character 'provided that, taking any school term as a whole, most such acts which do take place do comply' (Section 7.3). Section 12 of the legislation established a procedure through which county (now 'community') schools can obtain a 'determination' that daily worship for specified pupils need not be Christian collective worship. This is applicable in cases where the family background of pupils makes Christian worship inappropriate. Collective worship in voluntary schools can be in the tradition of the religion or denomination which founded the school.

The legal requirements for school inspection

All maintained schools (community, voluntary, foundation) are inspected by the Office for Standards in Education (Ofsted). The legal basis for this is set out in the Education (Schools) Act 1992 and the School Inspections Act 1996 (HMSO 1992, 1996). When community schools are inspected, RE is inspected along with all other subjects in the curriculum. Among aspects included in the inspection are the quality of the teaching, the achievements and progress of the pupils, and the extent to which the RE meets the requirements of the relevant Agreed Syllabus. Collective worship is also inspected: for example, in terms of the degree to which it meets legal requirements and contributes to pupils' spiritual and moral development. Voluntary schools are inspected under Section 10 of the 1996 Act, but Section 23 of the Act deals with the inspection of aspects of the school that are conducted in accordance with the school's trust deed. In voluntary aided schools, this includes RE, collective worship, the ethos of the school and the contribution these make to the spiritual and moral education of pupils. In voluntary controlled schools this includes worship but not usually RE. With inspections carried out under Section 23, the governors are responsible for appointing the inspector: otherwise Ofsted oversees the appointment of inspection teams. The reason for the different arrangements has to do with the special nature of voluntary schools, in which the modern distinction between education and religious nurture (non-confessional and confessional RE) is not always sharply drawn, hence the need for inspectors with specialist expertise and training.

CONFESSIONAL AND NON-CONFESSIONAL RE

RE is not the same wherever it is found. It varies. Some of the variety is indicated by the qualifying words which are often attached to the words 'Religious Education'. One basic distinction is that between confessional and non-confessional RE. Confessional RE is that form of RE which nurtures and encourages pupils to practise and express religious faith. Non-confessional RE is that form of RE which does not aim to inculcate or nurture religious faith. Interestingly, contemporary debate in British RE has focused, not on the accusation that RE in community schools is a form of Christian confessional, but on the accusation that it is indoctrination into a form of secularism (Copley 2005).

Task 2.1 Strengths and weaknesses of confessional and non-confessional RE

Make a list of the strengths and weaknesses of a non-confessional model of teaching RE.

Make a list of the strengths and weaknesses of a confessional model of teaching RE.

Compare your lists with those of another student teacher and discuss their implementation in school.

RE in community schools

Confessional RE

The distinction between confessional and non-confessional RE has historically been controversial in British RE and in schools. *Working Paper 36: RE in Secondary Schools* (Schools Council), published in 1971, described the view of RE practised in county (now community) schools as 'confessional' and 'dogmatic', on the grounds that RE was inculcating and nurturing Christian commitment and belief. It concluded that religious nurture was inappropriate in any school and that an 'undogmatic' or 'educational approach' should be pursued instead (see Barnes 2002, for a summary and discussion of *Working Paper 36*). Looking back on this debate with hindsight it is clear that not all the arguments marshalled against confessional RE are as convincing as they appeared at the time. For example, it is not at all clear that confessional education necessarily compromises the development of autonomy in pupils. However, whatever case can be made for confessional RE, it remains difficult to justify the view that community schools, which are deliberately intended to accommodate pupils from different backgrounds and communities, should proselytise on behalf of one religion, when not all the pupils or their parents owe allegiance to this one religion. Christian Confessional RE may have been appropriate when all the pupils who attended the 'common' school were Christian, but it is inappropriate when the religious commitment of pupils is not uniformly Christian. Basically, the pluralist nature of society undermines confessional RE in schools where religious pluralism is represented and where the school does not purport to be aligned to any particular faith tradition.

Non-confessional RE

Non-confessional RE recognises that religious matters are controversial in society. It seeks to respect the variety of backgrounds from which pupils come. It wants to help them as they reflect on their own beliefs and values. This kind of RE does not prescribe the conclusions pupils should come to through their search. It is 'open'. Non-confessional RE is appropriate because it reflects the varied and controversial nature of the religions in British society. During the twentieth century there was a decline in church attendance and in the extent of the power and influence of the churches in British life. Early advocates of non-confessional RE believed that a holistic approach to education could not omit learning about religion, but they did not believe that RE should seek to secure commitment to Christianity or commitment to any other particular religion. This view accepts that RE should follow trends in society. As a result of immigration in the 1950s and 1960s, Britain became more a multi-faith society in the 1970s. The religiously plural nature of Britain is commonly regarded as justifying multi-faith RE in schools.

If society as a whole is unsure about where the truth lies in matters of religion, then its RE should reflect that openness or uncertainty. Thus, RE should include the exploration of different religions, so that pupils have the opportunity to consider the religious options available to them. To restrict the content to one religion would be to limit choice. Though the legislation for England does not stipulate the religions to be studied in community schools, it has been widely accepted that six religions should be included, namely Buddhism, Christianity, Hinduism, Islam, Judaism and Sikhism. Recently the *Non-Statutory Framework for RE* (QCA 2004) has extended the list to be studied by pupils to over 10 different religions and world-views. This has not been received uncritically by some within the profession who allege that it will both confuse pupils and result in superficial knowledge and understanding of religion (see Felderhof 2005).

Another reason that is advanced in support of non-confessional RE is that it accords the pupils appropriate dignity as human beings and particularly as vulnerable young people. This view emphasises that RE must be open, so that pupils are free to respond as they wish. Pupils come from a variety of backgrounds – some religious, some not, and with varying intensity. Some are trying to find their own way, which can mean facing the tricky question of how much to depart from the views held by family members. Being sensitive to the position of pupils means providing non-confessional RE in which there are no assumptions about the conclusions pupils may reach. To many people this kind of RE is particularly appropriate to community schools and those schools without a religious foundation. If you wish to teach this kind of RE, you need not personally practise a particular religion, though if you do have a commitment to one particular religion you are not disqualified, provided you accept the value of teaching about several religions in a fair, accurate and balanced way.

Non-confessional RE should not be mistaken for a 'neutral' kind of RE. It is certainly not neutral with regard to all values. The open approach values the recognition of variety in religion. It also values the dignity of pupils, with the opportunities and responsibilities they have as they review and develop their own convictions. Those who support non-confessional RE are unlikely to be content with racist or sexist responses from pupils, nor are they happy to accept underachievement or poor-quality teaching. The underlying philosophy is that RE is valuable for pupils, but this falls short of commending any particular religious position.

The limits of non-confessional RE

It is important to consider whether non-confessional RE is the only valid kind of RE for the wide variety of schools in Britain. Different kinds of schools provide different contexts for RE. A liberal democracy may be required to recognise that some parents wish their children to be educated in accordance with their religious beliefs, i.e., the parents' beliefs; and there is a legal right for parents to bring up their children in the religion of their choice. Some faith communities wish to operate schools in which the curriculum is based on religious values and principles, Christian, or Islamic or Jewish, for example. To prevent this would be to impose a vision of education on pupils that is not desired by parents and (perhaps) pupils alike. Moreover, many religious people affirm that faith schools are in a much better position to secure the realisation in pupils of positive personal and social values than 'secular' schools, which by their nature have to take account of a diversity of personal preferences and convictions that extend beyond that which is regarded as 'moral' by the different religions. Yet even if there are limitations to non-confessional RE, these do not overturn the essential point that RE in community schools should be accessible to all and therefore not confessional.

Task 2.2 Exploring 'open' RE

Observe an RE lesson with a view to unpacking its level of 'openness'. How is the agenda controlled? What limits, either explicit or implicit, are imposed on classroom interaction by either teacher, pupils or resource material? What ideologies, positive or negative, can you discern at work in the flow of the lesson? Is there any 'bottom line' at which the teacher must 'close' the lesson, e.g. the use by pupils of racist or other remarks that lack tolerance and sensitivity? What criteria can you use for recognising the need to draw a line under 'open' discussion?

Write a one-page report summarising your findings and file in your professional development portfolio.

RE in schools having a religious character

RE takes different forms in what are popularly called *faith* schools (but what are legally termed, according to The Designation of Schools Having a Religious Character (England) Order 1999 (HMSO 1999, 'schools with a religious character': for stylistic reasons both terms will be used). Different faith schools have different expectations of teachers (and pupils). Generalising is always risky. Roman Catholic schools usually want their RE teachers to be practising Catholics. Church of England schools normally want their teachers to have some sympathy with the aims of the school but they do not usually expect their RE teachers to be Anglicans. Though there are differences between Catholic and Church of England schools, there are also similarities in what they are attempting to provide and achieve, so the rest of this section explores them together.

What is the nature of RE in faith schools, how can it be justified and how 'open' is it? Most faith schools in Britain have a Christian foundation. Some are linked to particular denominations, mostly the Church of England or the Roman Catholic Church, but a few are linked to the Methodist Church. In addition, in recent years a number of faith schools from traditions other than Christianity have been granted maintained status.

The aims of faith schooling

Generally, the educational aims of faith schools with a religious character are related in some way to their foundation documents or their long-standing tradition of faith and practice. The beliefs of different religions each form a distinctive world-view. The main beliefs are about God, the origin of the created world, human nature and the way people can relate to God and each other, and human destiny. Those who consciously promote faith-based schools have in mind schools where the particular (religious) world-view influences the curriculum and ethos of the school and the nature and character of spiritual and moral development that is pursued. Sometimes the intention is that the world-view should influence the whole life of the school.

These basic aims inevitably affect the nature of the RE provided in faith schools, though it is incorrect to simply think of all such schools as confessional in the same sense. Many Church of England schools are confessional only in an attenuated sense (in the sense that Christianity receives public endorsement in the school but little attempt is made to nurture or convert pupils to Christianity), whereas Roman Catholic or Muslim schools are straightforwardly confessional and aim to nurture pupils into their respective religions. First, the RE syllabus may emphasise the beliefs, history and practices of the faith community concerned. Second, one of the aims may well be to encourage or secure some kind of faith commitment as understood in the faith community involved. Third, some of the leaders in the particular faith community may have more direct involvement in the teaching of RE than they normally would in schools without a religious foundation. Fourth, the position of RE teachers may be different from that of teachers in schools without a religious foundation. They may be expected to uphold and promote the beliefs of the faith community through participation in specifically religious school activities.

Perhaps one of the differences can be illustrated thus. Teachers in schools without a religious foundation are often encouraged to distance themselves somewhat from the beliefs and practices of the religions taught. There is a preference for saying 'Christians believe . . .' or 'the Muslim practice is to . . .'; whereas in faith schools it can be appropriate to say, 'we believe . . .' Of course, it is the case that in some faith schools (some Church of England schools, for example) not all the pupils are Christian and it is therefore not appropriate to speak inclusively of all pupils believing in some particular religious proposition or assuming that all value religious commitment. Plainly in a multi-faith context no teacher can repeatedly say 'We believe . . .' or 'I believe . . .' with reference to the key beliefs of each of several religions as they are explored.

Issues in faith schooling

There are a number of difficult questions that should be considered by those involved in a faith school. If you are thinking of teaching in such a school, you should continue to think through your views on these questions. One question is the extent to which encouragement to religious commitment is justified. This is a pertinent question for several reasons. One is the controversial nature of religious beliefs and the issue of their verification. Another question that arises is the point at which encouragement amounts to persuasion that is inappropriate and thus indoctrinatory. We may think of indoctrination as the attempt to secure allegiance to a particular religion without those concerned understanding why they should give such allegiance.

There is a practical or pragmatic reason why it is important to be clear about any justification for RE that is intended to lead to or encourage religious commitment. That is the question whether indoctrination works. If the faith community believes that coming to a particular religious commitment is necessary in terms of eternal welfare, it may tend to gear the whole style of RE towards that result. If a person is directed to heaven rather than hell, as a consequence of religious indoctrination, the lack of awareness of alternative religious beliefs and the absence of freedom may appear justified. But the point here is that, even in terms of the intended outcome, attempting indoctrination may be counterproductive. That is, quite apart from whether it secures genuine religious commitment (in a few), the attempted indoctrination may produce more opposition and unbelief than would result from a less restricted approach – a more open approach.

This may well come down to a question of theology or doctrine. If the faith community believes that mere conformity and insincere participation lead to salvation, then its proponents may well say that it follows that anything that keeps the young people within the faith community is better than allowing them to wander astray into some other set of fundamental beliefs. However, those involved in the work of faith schools are usually not content to manipulate pupils into mere conformity. They do not want to be seen as supporting hypocrisy, that is, as approving a public profession of belief that is not matched to inner conviction and commitment. To acknowledge that genuine faith has to be given voluntarily, and has to be based on understanding and conviction, is to open up the whole question of appropriate methods in RE in a faith school.

This key question comes into sharp focus when those in faith schools face the question of what approach to adopt towards pupils who begin to show they are no longer convinced of the truths held by the faith community, if indeed they ever were. In this context RE is required to adopt a less dogmatic and more open approach, if it is to be relevant to pupils. This does not mean the staff and governors renounce their commitment to the religious stance of the school; and it does not mean the RE teachers having to pretend the school is other than it is – a faith school. But it does mean that recognition needs to be given to those pupils who are still searching for answers and that such pupils are still valued by the community of that school. When RE teachers in faith community schools adopt this approach, far from betraying their calling, they are following it with great integrity.

This discussion demonstrates some of the differences between education and indoctrination. Faith schools have good reason to pursue education, including *educational* RE, rather than indoctrination, and indoctrinatory RE. Our discussion also shows how complex the matter of RE in faith schools is. This does not mean that the nature and role of RE in state schools are simple and uncontroversial! It does mean that those involved in faith schools need to think about the nature of nurture and the best means of its attainment.

Task 2.3 Evaluating religious nurture

Reflect on the questions below and then discuss with other student teachers:

- What is your understanding of religious nurture?
- Is it justifiable in state schools? Why?
- Is it justifiable in faith schools? Why?
- What reactions to religious nurture have you encountered? In school? In wider society?

- How might RE teachers help pupils with religious faith?
- How might RE help those who have no faith?

After discussion write a short paragraph response to each of the questions and keep in your professional development portfolio.

Task 2.4 Investigating the effectiveness of RE

On a large sheet of paper brainstorm all the factors you can think of that stifle the effectiveness of RE. You might represent these factors on a spider diagram or concept map (Capel *et al.* 2005: 264–5). Use different-coloured markers to cluster similar ideas together. Now rank your clusters in order of their relative influence on the quality of (your) RE teaching. How might these factors be addressed in your lesson planning? Repeat the exercise, this time addressing the issue of the factors that enhance the effectiveness of RE.

Compare your set of factors with those of another student teacher and identify differences and similarities that arise.

SUMMARY AND KEY POINTS

RE in community schools has to be non-confessional and open in order to cater for the different expectations and reflect the different commitments of pupils and their parents. This openness is not neutrality. For example, non-confessional RE recognises the value of both learning *about* religions and learning *from* religion. As far as we can tell, RE will continue to be part of the curriculum of schools and many of them will continue to need RE teachers who support RE that helps pupils explore several religions while permitting but not requiring adherence to any one religion.

RE in faith schools can have different expectations and aims. The RE in such schools is likely to pay particular attention to the religion to which the school is related historically. Religious nurture in faith communities, including any schools they operate, can be undertaken with integrity and professionalism. There are good reasons for not indoctrinating pupils in the sense of securing conformity without understanding or willing assent. This means making RE accessible to pupils with a range of opinions about religion, but without discounting the relevance and influence of the faith on which the school is based.

Being a schoolteacher is always a demanding task, and teaching RE in school is no exception. Helping pupils explore the fascinating and fundamental issues of life that are addressed in RE, though challenging personally and professionally, can be fulfilling. Different types of school may have somewhat different approaches to RE and collective worship, and the underlying rationale for these differences continues to elicit controversy and debate. This means there is a need for new reflective RE teachers who can contribute to ongoing debates.

FURTHER READING

Astley, J. (1994) *The Philosophy of Christian Religious Education*, Birmingham, AL: Religious Education Press. Astley subjects Christian RE to rigorous philosophical scrutiny and comes up with a clear justification of the value and importance of a distinctively Christian approach to education.

Barnes, L.P. (2007) 'Developing a New Post-Liberal Paradigm for British Religious Education', *Journal of Beliefs and Values*, 28(1): 17–32. Controversial and provocative critique of British RE that concludes by outlining a new model of British RE that focuses on effective strategies to challenge religious intolerance and develop respect for persons.

Barnes, L.P. and Kay, W.K. (2002) *Religious Education in England and Wales: Innovations and Reflections*, Leicester: Religious and Theological Studies Fellowship. Review of the history, philosophy and methodology of RE in England and Wales.

Copley, T. (2005) *Indoctrination, Education and God*, London: SPCK. Important study of the role of secular ideology in schools and in RE.

Copley, T. (2008) *Teaching Religion: Religious Education in England and Wales 1944 to 2007*, Exeter: University of Exeter Press. This book traces the developments in RE from 1944 to the present. It contains fascinating insights into the thinking of many religious educators and politicians active in the period concerned. It is a detailed and interesting account, likely to increase the understanding of anyone not familiar with the course of RE since the Second World War.

Parker-Jenkins, M., Hartas, D. and Irving, B. (2004) *In Good Faith: Schools, Religion and Public Funding*, Aldershot: Ashgate Publishing. A review of the recent growth of faith schools with an overview of the arguments for and against.

Part II

Teaching and learning

3 Developing programmes of study

Jo Backus

INTRODUCTION

This chapter focuses on the process of planning lessons and then schemes of work. The gradual evolution of your lesson plans and then schemes of work constitutes a crucial aspect of your professional development. The aim of this chapter is to guide you through the basic stages in the process of planning to teach: initial preparation, constructing lesson plans and evaluation after teaching the lesson, writing schemes of work. Alongside the approaches adopted in this chapter you must expect to encounter alternative approaches to planning and preparation of lessons and schemes of work, both in your institution of higher education (IHE) and in your school experiences. You should not be surprised by such diversity: in teaching, there is no one 'right' way of doing things. Part of your professional responsibility as a teacher is to be willing to adopt and adapt your own personal approach to the process of planning to teach. What follows, then, is an introduction to one possible way of proceeding.

OBJECTIVES

By the end of this chapter, you should be able to:

- explain the terms 'aims', 'objectives', 'progression', 'differen-tiation' and 'assessment' in relation to the delivery of RE;
- produce effective lesson plans;
- describe and justify your own personal approach to preparing to teach;
- construct schemes of work.

INITIAL PREPARATION

Background

The government document *Qualifying to Teach* sets out standards for planning and effective delivery of the curriculum (DES/TTA 2002). All courses in Initial Teacher Education (ITE) must conform to these standards although they may be enumerated differently within different courses. You should consult this document when engaged in planning.

Three sets of curriculum documents are essential for the planning and delivery of effective RE in the classroom. The first is the Agreed Syllabus, which details the major curriculum plan for all maintained and state schools at all Key Stages. Unlike subjects in the National Curriculum which have a single syllabus, RE possesses a range of syllabuses developed at local level. These syllabuses constitute the legal documents for the subject. They contain comprehensive accounts of the aims and objectives of RE matched to national legal requirements, and also indicate methodologies and content for effective subject delivery. The planned schemes of work that you find in RE departments, as well as a teacher's individual lesson plans, must by law draw on the relevant Agreed Syllabus for their rationale and content. A crucial task when you first arrive for your school experience is to identify which particular Agreed Syllabus the RE department is legally required to follow.

The second key curriculum document is the school's internal schemes of work. These adapt the general Agreed Syllabus plan into individual schemes of work which run for a given length of time. They provide a narrower window on the learning opportunities for pupils as well as an overview of content and resources.

Finally, there are the individual lesson plans, which itemise the learning opportunities, objectives (intensions), content and resources for the period of one lesson.

Task 3.1 School documentation

Obtain a copy of the local Agreed Syllabus for your experience school as well as the schemes of work you will be following for the classes you are teaching. These provide important background material for your lesson planning.

Before you can plan a lesson it is important that you know something about the class for which you are planning. This section is designed to enable you to learn about the classes you are going to be teaching.

Auditing the pupils

This aspect of planning involves the acquisition of an educational profile of the pupils in the class or year group under consideration. Three important elements should be considered here: (1) academic ability; (2) faith background; and (3) social context.

Information can be gained from a number of sources: frequently schools have an information folder available for student teachers and information on particular classes can be provided by the class teacher or year tutor. It may also be gained from observation of the class or discussion with their RE teacher and other relevant professionals.

Identifying the academic ability and special educational needs of pupils

Recognition of each pupil's age, aptitude and ability gives you important information to plan lessons to suit the pupils in question. Attention to the fact that all pupils have particular needs is an important aspect of planning and helps you to comply with school initiatives on inclusion. Policies on pupil inclusion cover educational needs, formerly identified as Special Educational Needs (SEN), and also cover those now designated as gifted and talented. This ensures that resources and methodology are sufficiently flexible to aid the learning of all pupils in the class. Contemporary Agreed Syllabuses for RE give helpful advice on the principles for dealing with inclusion in RE.

Consideration of pupils' backgrounds, religious traditions and world-views

Pupils always bring to their learning a set of assumptions and beliefs which are predicated on a particular faith or world-view. This is equally so for atheists, agnostics and religious believers. Though the pupils' beliefs may lack coherence and focus, they nevertheless play a significant role in the expectations and preconceptions pupils bring to the classroom. It is important therefore to ask how this background affects the learning process. For example, in some cases pupils may already have an affiliation to the particular religion being studied. Thus, materials chosen from a textbook on a religious tradition need to be broad enough to reflect what these pupils already know about their faith. You can also utilise their experience and knowledge to enhance the understanding of other members of the class.

Assessment of the impact on learning of the social context of the school

The social context of the school reflects on the range of the pupils' faith background and should inform planning. You need to be sensitive to the customs, practices and beliefs of the pupils in your class and therefore in planning lessons. If, for example, the school has a large Hindu community, arranging visits to local temples gives opportunities for dialogue between the classroom professional and members of the faith community in question, which can enhance the learning of the pupils.

Task 3.2 Constructing and implementing a class audit

Work with your fellow student teachers and/or your school-based tutor to construct a proforma that will aid the process of auditing a class you are preparing to teach. Ensure that an appropriate balance is drawn between, on the one hand, gathering sufficient data and, on the other, allowing the audit to become a burdensome task that distracts from its primary purpose of supporting your planning. The proforma ought to cover the following areas:

- the educational strengths, weaknesses, potential and (if appropriate) special educational needs of the pupils;
- a profile of the faith traditions and world-view stances of the class;
- the social and cultural factors in the school's catchment area that have a bearing on your planning.

Trial the proforma, analyse its strengths and weaknesses, and produce a revised version to take with you into your first teaching post.

Interpreting the Agreed Syllabus

In interpreting a syllabus, three key areas should be considered: (1) the aims, objectives and attainment targets for learning in RE; (2) the content of the syllabus, that is, the prescribed subject knowledge; and (3) the levels of attainment that pupils are expected to reach during their learning. Schools are legally obliged to teach from the local Agreed Syllabus.

The prescribed subject knowledge

The local Agreed Syllabus offers prescribed content that must be used as the legal basis of the schemes of work that are drawn up and used in the RE department. In following the guidance and instructions of the Agreed Syllabus, the schemes of work into which your lessons should fit are tailored to the specific needs of the pupils in the school. Also, they build on the strengths of the school staff. Even though specific content is prescribed, room is left for emphasis and originality; often there is a creative balancing act between giving pupils an opportunity to further their learning in Christianity with giving them an opportunity to increase their knowledge and understanding of other major world faiths.

Task 3.3 Analysing Agreed Syllabuses

Choose two Agreed Syllabuses for RE. Consider how these documents define what pupils are expected to learn in their RE and how the content is chosen for a Key Stage of your choice.

Analyse the similarities and differences between the two documents in terms of the following:

- aims and objectives;
- learning opportunities;
- levels of attainment;
- content

Discuss with a colleague whether you consider the differences to be chiefly practical or theoretical. Which is the better syllabus and why?

Levels of attainment

Most major RE curriculum documents provide specific levels of attainment that pupils ought to be achieving at each Key Stage (see Figure 3.1). These are indicative of progress and provide among other items the opportunity for teachers to consider the standards pupils are reaching at the end of the relevant Key Stages. They also aid the writing of levels of response mark schemes for key assignments that pupils may undertake. The syllabus may also give advice on the learning opportunities which could be used to enable pupils to demonstrate their development towards the indicated levels of attainment.

The *Non-Statutory National Framework for RE* (QCA 2004) sets the levels that pupils should (normally) be achieving at the end of each Key Stage in their RE. These provide useful descriptions against which pupils' work can be judged.

At the end of KS3 pupils typically achieve Level 6:

Attainment target 1: Learning about religion

Pupils use religious and philosophical vocabulary to give informed accounts of religions and beliefs, explaining the reasons for diversity within and between them. They explain why the impact of religions and beliefs on individuals, communities and societies varies. They interpret sources and arguments, explaining the reasons that are used in different ways by different traditions to provide answers to ultimate questions and ethical issues. They interpret the significance of different forms of religious, spiritual and moral expression.

Attainment target 2: Learning from religion

Pupils use reasoning and examples to express insights into the relationship between beliefs, teachings and world issues. They express insights into their own and others' views on questions of identity and belonging, meaning, purpose and truth. They consider the challenges of belonging to a religion in the contemporary world, focusing on values and commitments.

Figure 3.1 Levels of attainment in RE

Exploring the learning process

As well as focusing on an audit of the pupils, and the Agreed Syllabus, at the preparatory stage you also have to make decisions regarding the process of learning. You need to take account of at least five factors that come into play at this point in the process of preparing a lesson: (1) selection of teaching methods; (2) progression from previous work the pupils have undertaken; (3) differentiation in order to match the learning to pupil progression and preferences for learning; (4) integration of resources and information and communications technology (ICT) to enhance the learning process; and (5) assessment.

Teaching methods

Effective learning depends on effective teaching. Frequently whole-class approaches to teaching are adopted with a format of teacher talk, question-and-answer and written assignments. This can be a very self-contained format, enabling teachers to get through a content-heavy curriculum. One criticism, however, of this particular diet is that it is unable to engage the pupils as fully as might be expected.

It follows that using a range of teaching methods is an important part of your work as a teacher and therefore of your planning. Research has shown that as pupils learn in different ways, they need to be aided in their learning by teaching methods which suit their individual learning preferences. As Kincaid suggests:

> [W]hen the task is to impart knowledge and understanding it is quite in order, although not always appropriate, for the teacher to adopt a presentation style of teaching in which he or she either talks to the whole class or makes use of audio-visual techniques to get across a certain body of information. When the task is to help pupils develop the skills of investigating an issue, of finding information, selecting and sorting out what is or what is not relevant, and drawing conclusions from the information available, a presentational style is no longer useful. In these sorts of tasks pupils need to be active rather than passive, doing things rather than having things done to them or for them.
>
> (1991: 42)

In short, it seems that pupils need to be active learners rather than passive learners; and that talking to the whole class for too long is not good teaching (see the chapter on 'Active learning,' in Capel *et al.* 2005).

Task 3.4 Exploring teaching methods

On a sheet of A4 paper draw up a chart indicating the raft of basic teaching methods available to you in the classroom. You should base it on your personal experience of being taught, on your observations in schools and on conversations with colleagues in your IHE as well as methods identified in various texts. You may find it useful to refine your chart in the light of charts produced by your fellow student teachers.

Draw up a lesson plan. It may be either one you have produced yourself or the plan of a lesson you have observed being taught. Now rewrite the plan three times. Each new version should make use of a different selection of teaching methods. This activity is designed to make you more aware of the way in which the same learning objectives can be achieved using a range of different teaching methods.

Critically review your revised lesson plans with some of your colleagues. Ask yourself the following:

- What are the individual strengths and weaknesses of each lesson plan?
- What implications for learning are contained in each plan?
- How well do the learning objectives and teaching methods match up?

- What criteria are you using to evaluate the plans?
- Are there any specific methods that most attract you?
- Which methods are you likely to find most difficult to implement?

Progression

Ensuring progression in pupils' learning, where progression is interpreted as deepening understanding of an idea or concept, is a vital part of the planning process. Having accurate records of pupils' achievement over the course of the year, in previous years and throughout previous Key Stages is very helpful here. One question you need to ask yourself when considering this aspect of planning is 'How does the work in the lesson build upon and refine the learning of the pupils?' An important feature of progression is cognitive development: the knowledge and understanding that pupils acquire during their learning, especially their linguistic competence, conceptual understanding and thinking skills. The development of pupils' religious literacy includes their progressive understanding of technical terms and the ways in which these operate in religions discourse.

The progression of pupils' learning in RE is normally in terms of two broad attainment targets: 'learning about religion' and 'learning from religion'. These are commonly found in the Agreed Syllabuses (and are repeated in the National Framework) that you consult during your ITE course.

- Learning about religion includes enquiry into, and investigation of, the nature of religion, its beliefs, teachings and ways of life, sources, practices and forms of expression. It includes the skills of interpretation, analysis and explanation. Pupils learn to communicate their knowledge and understanding using specialist vocabulary. It also includes identifying and developing an understanding of ultimate questions and ethical issues.
- Learning from religion is concerned with developing pupils' reflection on and response to their own and others' experiences in the light of their learning about religion. It develops pupils' skills of application, interpretation and evaluation of what they learn about religion. Pupils learn to develop and communicate their own ideas, particularly in relation to questions of identity and belonging, meaning, purpose and truth, and values and commitments.

(QCA 2004: 11)

An example of how these are included in one Agreed Syllabus is given in Figure 3.2.

Both attainment targets normally carry equal weight and are meant to enable an open, philosophical approach to the subject matter as well as taking account of the spiritual, moral, cultural and social development of the pupils. Progression also involves the development of key skills and attitudes: investigation, interpretation, analysis, reflection, empathy, imagination, evaluation, critical argument, association, identification, expression, spiritual awareness, moral insight, etc.

Agreed Syllabuses adopt the two basic attainment targets 'learning about religion' and 'learning from religion'. These are then expanded to show how they apply and how they are to be used to guide teaching and learning. The example below is taken from page 14 of the 2004 North Somerset SACRE, *Agreed Syllabus: Awareness, Mystery and Value*.

1 Learning about religion

This includes the ability to:

- identify, name, describe and give accounts in order to build a coherent picture of religious beliefs;
- explain the spiritual dimensions of life;
- explain similarities and differences between, and within, religious practices/ lifestyles;
- explain the meaning of religious language, story and symbolism.

2 Learning from religion and human experience

This includes the ability to:

- reflect on aspects of human nature, identity, personality and experience especially in the light of one's own beliefs and experience;
- identify and respond to questions about the nature and purpose of life on earth;
- give an informed and considered response to religious and moral issues.

Figure 3.2 'Learning from' and 'learning about' religion

Differentiation

Pupils learn at different rates and in different ways. What suits one pupil in the way knowledge is managed may not suit another. This aspect of planning deals with the crucial question of differentiation, by which is meant the deliberate construction of learning to take account of the strengths and weaknesses of individual pupils and to cater for all levels of ability in your encounter with pupils. It is a hotly debated subject among RE professionals but, broadly speaking, there are a number of ways in which differentiation can be achieved. A clear indication that your lesson plan has been constructed with differentiation in mind is the presence of phrases such as 'By the end of the lesson all pupils will be able to . . .', 'Most pupils will be able to . . .', 'Some pupils will be able to . . .'. Such phrases will be augmented by the concepts, attitudes and skills that you feel pupils should demonstrate.

Consultation with the departmental staff to check whether what you have planned is appropriate or requires modification to fit the needs of all learners in the group is important. Decisions on how to differentiate learning can be difficult to make. On some occasions it is appropriate to provide specific resources for some pupils to aid their learning. On other occasions the whole class may benefit from common tasks that produce differentiated outcomes (see Figure 3.3). Different levels of support for the same task can be given to different pupils. Writing frames can be used with pupils, whereby prompts and aids, say in the forms of introductory sentences and sample

Many teachers find differentiation a difficult process to come to terms with, especially when faced with the challenge of simply producing lesson plans of reasonable quality. It is important that from the start differentiation becomes central to the planning process. The failure of a lesson is often due to lack of differentiation: giving pupils inappropriate undifferentiated work which is either too easy or too difficult is a recipe for disaster. A good start to taking account of differentiation is to work with each of the following two basic models.

Differentiation by outcome

Here pupils are set the same task to achieve, but the variety of levels they work at show their differing abilities. Such tasks need to be very well constructed, and pupils need to be given clear support and guidance, if you are to ensure that all pupils regardless of ability can access the task sufficiently well. 'Discuss the importance of prayer and pilgrimage for Muslims' is a question that could be answered, at an appropriate level, both by a lower-ability Year 7 pupil and by an A Level candidate. Here the learning process will be differentiated by the different outcomes.

Differentiation by task

By far the more difficult method of differentiation, though often the more effective, is differentiation by task. Here the teacher sets different pupils contrasting tasks on the basis of their ability. It may be done by offering the class a choice of questions, or grouping pupils into ability groups, with each group working on specially designed activities, or even by producing individual tasks for specific pupils. Essentially, this method identifies different tasks for pupils of differing ability. Pupils may be given the opportunity to opt for a particular task which they feel able to achieve, but then encouraged to attempt more difficult tasks as they progress.

Figure 3.3 'Outcome' and 'task': two basic models of differentiation

vocabulary are provided for them to expand. Different writing frames can be used with different pupils.

In many cases it is helpful to design specific assignments for pupils which bring together all the learning possibilities specified in the scheme of work, and which are meant to enable teachers to check whether their aims and objectives have been achieved. They also give a specific opportunity to check the standards the pupils are achieving at that time.

Further information on differentiation is given in Capel *et al.* (2005, Unit 4.1).

Resources and ICT

Consideration of resources and ICT are both vitally important in lesson planning. You need to avoid the trap of first writing your lesson plans and only then asking the question of how your teaching can be supported by resources and ICT. This 'supplementary approach' to lesson planning frequently leads to lessons that are disjointed and poorly resourced. Your use of resources and ICT should involve an 'integral approach' in which you begin the planning process with a broad range of resources already in front of you. Being able to refer to resources as you plan both stimulates the imagination and tends to produce an integral learning package (see Chapter 14 on the use of ICT).

Assessment

Finally, you need to consider the place of assessment in your lessons. You need to make sure that you have a clear and practical indication of how you intend to assess your pupils' learning, in terms of both their formative development and their summative achievement. Formative assessment refers to the use of assessment to identify strengths and weaknesses in a pupil's performance or attainment that can be used to guide and advance further learning, whereas summative assessment refers to final statements of a pupil's progress, usually expressed in the form of a mark or grade (further guidance is given in Capel *et al.* 2005, Chapter 6). Your lessons may also include self-assessment.

This range of information may seem daunting to you as you first start out. You may not be able to address it all in planning your initial lessons. However, by working with your tutors you should begin to make sense of the amount of background information you need.

LESSON PLANS

The lesson plan provides you with a detailed description of the heart of the teaching process: the individual lesson. Your teaching file should contain the school scheme of work you are following with each of your classes, immediately followed by the individual lesson plans, arranged in chronological sequence.

It is important for your lesson plan to achieve a balance between concrete practical issues and broader theoretical concerns. A lesson plan with clearly articulated learning objectives is useless if it fails to remind you to make sure that vital resources are present in the classroom. Similarly, a lesson plan that addresses all the immediate practical aspects of teaching while failing to be rooted in a clearly educational rationale is unlikely to support the learning process in any depth.

The content and structure of the lesson plan need to be clear and focused. There are a variety of approaches to lesson planning. Your tutors and teachers in school will use a variety of formats to write up their lesson plans. An example is provided in Figure 3.4, and the following ideas and suggestions are broadly based on that example. Another example is provided in Capel *et al.* (2005, Unit 2.2). Never forget, however, that it is your professional responsibility to create, own and develop your personal way of doing things.

Lesson plan: Green Street School Religious Education Department

Lesson topic			
Teacher		Room	
Class		Time	
Key Stage		Lesson sequence	

Lesson aim	
Attainment targets	1
	2
	3
Agreed Syllabus links	

Learning sequence			
Stage	Time	Activity	Teaching method
1			
2			
3			
4 [etc.]			

Resources	1
	2
	3

Figure 3.4 Sample 'lesson plan' proforma

Administrative information

The lesson plan is important not only as a preparation document and means of planning your teaching strategies: you also need to use it as a reference point and guide in the classroom. Consequently, you should include in it a range of basic administrative details: lesson topic; name, year group and Key Stage of the class; the date, location and duration of the lesson; and the position of the lesson in the sequence of lessons as set out in the scheme of work into which the lesson fits.

It is important to establish a routine for pupils in the classroom. The lesson plan should make clear the managerial aspects of the classroom situation. The lesson routines to be included in your plan should include: entry into the classroom; bringing pupils to attention; taking the register; issuing and collecting homework; dismissal procedures. It is likely that on school experience you start by following the established routines already put in place by the pupils' regular teacher, gradually developing routines of your own as your familiarity with the classes and self-confidence grow. As you become more skilled and confident in the classroom, so the need to articulate your lesson routines in your lesson plans begins to fade. Until you have achieved such a level of experience, however, it is probably best to heed the advice that lesson routines should be clearly articulated in considerable detail.

It is useful to have a seating plan or other aid to help you remember pupils' names, aiding interaction between you and the pupils. It could be included in your teaching file as a supplement to the basic lesson plan.

Lesson objectives and assessment

It is important that there is a clear match between the lesson plan and the overall scheme of work. Without this it is almost impossible to offer your pupils focused and progressive teaching. It means you must consider how the lesson and its objectives contribute to the overall aims of the scheme of work. Further, you should also consider the content which is to be taught, the teaching and learning resources, differentiation and assessment of the learning objectives.

The various lesson objectives, sometimes referred to as learning outcomes or intentions, serve to state clearly the specific learning that you want pupils to achieve during that lesson. Teachers use a variety of phrases to aid clarity when presenting objectives. One such phrase you will get to know well is 'By the end of the lesson pupils will be able to . . .'. This is developed by adding useful terms which indicate skills or knowledge components such as 'state', 'describe', 'identify', 'demonstrate an understanding of'. It is easy to allow such phrases to become mere rhetoric. However, a skilful lesson planner ensures that the plans serve to support teaching by reminding the teacher to focus on the essentials of the learning process. Once you become involved in the dynamics of classroom teaching it is extremely easy simply to forget the objectives you set for the lesson. In view of this you may like to follow the lead of many student teachers who have found it helpful to include in their plan, often in 'bullet point' style, an at-a-glance checklist of the key concepts, skills and attitudes that you wish your pupils to engage with during the lesson.

Clear and well-focused learning objectives enable you to see if you have delivered what you set out to do and also to see whether pupils have achieved what you wanted them to achieve. You can therefore use them in the process of monitoring and assessing pupils' learning. Your list of objectives should be limited to a realistic number, normally three or four. A quick check on the process is to ask yourself the question, 'If I describe the objectives to the pupils, will they understand what they are supposed to do and be able to achieve what is expected of them?' It is also helpful for pupils to be told the expected learning objectives for the lesson and what they can do to demonstrate achievement.

The learning sequence

Each lesson you teach needs to progress through a clear learning sequence. It needs a succession of activities, each planned to introduce and develop aspects of the objectives and the content you have specified, so that pupils can move through deeper or broader levels of understanding. A good lesson plan immediately draws attention to the progressive aspect inherent in the lesson. You may find it helpful to think of the lesson in terms of a series of numbered 'building blocks', each with its own time allocation, specified activity and teaching methodology.

Homework

Homework is important, but it should not become an end in itself; its use is to support and extend the objectives of the lesson. An effort should be made to devise home-work that develops skills or aptitudes in pupils that go beyond what can be pursued in the classroom: there is a place for small research projects, the opportunity for pupils to follow up their own interests, and so on. Naturally, homework must be planned and structured to ensure that it complements what is done in class.

Implementing lesson plans

The lesson plan is a plan, not a straitjacket, for learning. When starting to teach, most student teachers follow a lesson plan closely, but in time they learn to develop the skill and confidence to adapt what is taught in response to pupil reactions. This may mean moving the lesson in a different direction from that anticipated in response to issues that arise in the classroom. A good rule of thumb is to stick to the lesson plan as closely as possible, but be aware that there is no need to panic if you find yourself deviating from it. You should address technical items that may aid or hinder the delivery of the lesson.

EVALUATION

It is important to think of the planning process not simply as a journey from A to B but as an ongoing cyclical process. You need to be aware of the strengths and weak-nesses of your lessons just as much as you need to be aware of your pupils' progress. Only by developing a critical understanding of the strengths and weaknesses of your planning and delivery can you hope to refine and develop it for future use. Lesson evaluation should be formative, incorporating new information that forms the basis of the next round of lesson planning. It is important that, as soon as possible after the lesson, you note down a brief evaluation of the strengths and weaknesses of the lesson, together with any necessary administrative notes. You must develop ways of ensuring that your evaluation of a lesson (or later of a series of lessons) is not based merely on your own subjective impressions. Pupils can be asked for their opinion on the success of a lesson (or a series of lessons) or they may be invited to respond by completing a simple proforma that is appropriate to your needs and the pupils' level of education. Summative assessments also provide valuable information. If you fail to evaluate, you could find yourself falling into the trap of confusing good behaviour and enthusiasm on the part of your pupils with quality learning. Entertainment and education are not necessarily the same thing. The broad topic of assessment is outlined in greater depth in Chapter 6.

It may be useful to use the same proforma for evaluation as that used by your tutor, as it will identify the main issues and topics that need to be addressed successfully in a good lesson. Such evaluation forms an important part of the detailed assessment process which, by placing the lesson under scrutiny, allows your skill as a teacher to be enhanced.

Figure 3.5 suggests a framework for the personal evaluation of your lessons. Each of the criteria should be considered and the evidence that is relevant to their fulfilment adduced and considered. Although you may not wish to comment on all the evaluation items mentioned below after every lesson, you may wish to comment on a selection agreed between yourself and your tutor that reflects your development and progress.

PLANNING SCHEMES OF WORK

Different terms can be used to indicate the medium-term planning process. 'Schemes of work' is the term that is used in National Curriculum documents, and many RE Agreed Syllabuses are adopting similar nomenclature.

The schools' schemes of work set out the learning opportunities and objectives for pupils over a designated period of time. It may be a term, half a term or a more limited number of weeks. Developing schemes of work is an ongoing activity. It is one which gives opportunity for reflection on the learning that pupils have acquired as well as allowing for creative changes in the curriculum. For example, the partial failure of a lesson may lead you to refine the match between the content of a scheme of work and pupil needs. This flexibility means that account can be taken of new developments and fresh insights into the delivery of the topic. In your school experience you will be given schemes of work that have been developed by the RE department. However, you are likely also to be given the opportunity to reflect on the construction of these schemes as well as a chance to write your own for the specific lessons you are delivering.

Advice on planning schemes of work for RE can be found in a number of sources. Typically there is material produced within the Local Education Authority to support teaching and learning from a particular syllabus, which can be accessed through the WWW. Often Agreed Syllabuses overlap in content and consequently resources and materials supporting one syllabus can equally support other syllabuses. The QCA website contains further materials to enhance curriculum planning – assessment ideas and exemplars of schemes of work to support teaching and learning.

Communicating with pupils. To what extent does your teaching:

- establish appropriate relationships with pupils?
- use their names to facilitate a good learning environment?
- set clear and consistent lesson routines and expectations of behaviour?
- reflect concern for both the individual and collective needs of pupils?

Planning and evaluating. To what extent does your teaching:

- set clear lesson objectives?
- have a sound structure for the lesson?
- establish high standards and expectations of learning?

Teaching and class management. To what extent does your teaching:

- match teaching methods and content against aims and objectives?
- monitor pupils' progress and intervene to aid their learning?
- establish a purposeful learning environment?
- maintain appropriate levels of discipline?
- utilise a variety of teaching and learning strategies?
- deliver a lesson with good pace and direction?
- give pupils clear instructions so that they know what is expected of their learning?
- involve designing and selecting appropriate resources?
- consolidate learning by the use of recap and other similar methods?
- celebrate pupils' work and achievement through, e.g., displays of their work?
- demonstrate awareness of pupils' individual needs and prior learning?

Monitoring, assessing, recording and reporting. To what extent does your teaching:

- assess your teaching and learning effectiveness?
- make use of feedback to pupils to enhance their learning?
- use level descriptions or examination criteria for assessment?
- reflect a range of assessment techniques?

Developing and maintaining specialist skills. To what extent does your teaching:

- demonstrate a secure knowledge of your subject?
- cope with subject-specific questions?

Figure 3.5 A framework for evaluating lessons

The Non-Statutory National Framework for RE is a recent invaluable source of information (QCA 2004). It is the first national document of its kind and distils significant elements of good practice as well as including information relating to teaching and learning in the subject. It lays out what might be called the 'big picture' of subject content and delivery, although the Agreed Syllabus remains the legal document which governs the curriculum at this present time. The *National Framework* (QCA 2004) establishes an entitlement for all pupils and promotes public understanding of the nature and importance of the subject for pupil learning. It recommends that:

- Christianity should be studied throughout each Key Stage;
- The other principal religions represented in Great Britain (here regarded as Buddhism, Hinduism, Islam, Judaism and Sikhism) should be studied across the Key Stages. It is important that ASCs and schools ensure that by the end of Key Stage 3 pupils have encountered all of these five principal religions in *sufficient depth*.

(QCA 2004: 12)

Additionally, the *Framework* identifies the necessity that the curriculum should enable pupils to communicate and share their ideas 'without embarrassment or ridicule'. So that all pupils' voices are heard, it recommends the inclusion of opportunities for all pupils to study:

- other religious traditions such as the Bahá'í faith, Jainism and Zoroastrianism;
- secular philosophies such as humanism.

Pupils should also study how religions relate to each other, recognising both similarities and differences within and between religions. They should be encouraged to reflect on:

- the significance of interfaith dialogue;
- the important contribution religion can make to community cohesion and the combating of religious prejudice and discrimination.

(QCA 2004: 12)

The *National Framework* document provides helpful advice on a number of important areas to aid pupil learning. It recommends the cultivation of particular skills in RE which include self-awareness and the development of a realistic and positive sense of their own religious, moral and spiritual ideas, and respect for all. Open-mindedness is to be cultivated so that pupils are encouraged to remain willing to learn and gain new understanding. Cultivating the skills of appreciation of awe and wonder are intended to facilitate the development of pupils' imagination and curiosity together with their abilities to respond to questions of meaning and purpose.

The *National Framework* document sets out important expectations for learning and attainment that are explicit to a variety of audiences 'pupils, parents, teachers, governors employers and the public' (ibid.: 9). Drawing on expertise from professionals and faith communities, it lays out possibilities for schemes of work that enable continuity and progression in pupil learning.

Before writing a scheme of work you need to prepare the ground so that what you plan is well matched to the needs and abilities of the pupils. You also need to ensure that your scheme is coherent in respect of your pupils' prior learning: the technical term used to refer to the coherent development of the learning progress within and across schemes of work is progression (see section on progression above).

Preparation normally involves paying attention to the following:

- an audit of the pupils in order to identify prior learning experiences;
- a review of the requirements of the Agreed Syllabus;
- a consideration of the process of teaching.

Each of these items is now be unpacked in greater detail so as to give a clearer picture of what is involved in this aspect of the planning process.

WRITING A SCHEME OF WORK

One of the major weaknesses in the planning of inexperienced teachers is the desire to move too quickly to the second basic stage of preparation, that of actually writing the scheme of work. It is important not to forget the importance of working through the initial stage of preparation. Once you are ready to write your scheme you should bear in mind the following issues.

Selecting the format of the scheme of work

It will be clear at an early stage of your ITE course that there is no one universally accepted form that a scheme of work should take. The model(s) used in your school may be very different from the one presented to you in your IHE. It is important to make a balanced judgement in reaching a decision regarding the form your own schemes of work will take. A sample format is outlined in Figure 3.6.

Balancing detail and time

Teaching is always rooted in a series of constraints. You are unlikely to find yourself in an ideal situation. You must learn to make appropriate compromises. In terms of writing a scheme of work, it is important to pay sufficient attention to detail if the scheme is to have any value. However, you must also guard against the danger of finding yourself devoting too much time and effort to the scheme to the detriment of other important responsibilities. In the model scheme presented in Figure 3.6, for example, each section may contain merely a brief bullet-pointed reference to the key issues involved. Planning should be integrated with your teaching and its function should be to aid and support it.

Utilising information technology

You will find it useful to establish a standard proforma which you simply fill in every time you come to plan a scheme of work. Sensible use of word-processing technology is important here: by drawing up a proforma file, and then simply copying it and

Practical details			
Class		Day/Dates	
Year		Time	
Teaching room		Number of lessons	

Aims and objectives	
Scheme aim	
Scheme objectives	1 2 3
Agreed Syllabus link	

The context of teaching and learning	
Ability range	
SEN pupils/Gifted and talented	
Faith backgrounds	
Social context	

The process of teaching and learning	
Progression	
Differentiation	
Resources	
Teaching methods	
Cross-curricular links	
Links with elements of National Strategy	

The lesson sequence		
Lesson 1	Aim	
	Outline	

Lesson 2	Aim	
	Outline	
Lesson 3	Aim	
[etc.]	Outline . . .	

Assessment		
Pupil assessment	Assignments	
	Grade criteria	
	Methods	
	Recording	
Course assessment	Process	
	Criteria	
	Recording	

Figure 3.6 Sample scheme of work proforma

completing a duplicate form for each scheme of work, you save yourself an enormous amount of work, both because you are not writing out the proforma each time and because many of the details are repeated from scheme to scheme. It is important to impose a basic routine and structure on your planning at an early stage.

Relating the scheme to the Agreed Syllabus

It is not sufficient to do the right thing: it is also important to be seen to do the right thing! Your scheme of work must conform to the requirements of your Agreed Syllabus. The fact that it does needs to be made transparent. An Ofsted inspector should not need to spend an evening cross-referencing between your scheme and the Agreed Syllabus in order to be assured that your scheme is a legal one! The connections should be immediately obvious. One way of doing this is to insert in brackets references to the appropriate sections of the Agreed Syllabus in the actual text of your scheme of work.

Cross-curricular opportunities

Opportunities for exciting and interesting work for pupils can be achieved through working with other departments in the school on thematic projects, e.g. a historical survey of a town for pupils in Year 9 can be augmented and enhanced through an RE study of the religious buildings and communities that the town has maintained over time; or a Year 10 module on the topic of creation can be enhanced through joint work between RE and science departments.

Evaluation of a scheme of work

As well as evaluating single lessons, it is important to assess and reflect on the extent and manner in which the aims and objectives of the scheme of work have been achieved. The sequence 'preparation – developing schemes of work – creating lesson plans – delivering lessons – evaluation' ought to bring you full circle. Naturally evaluations of single lessons feed into this, but there are other sources of evidence and relevant considerations. A summative test at the end of series of lessons can reveal the real extent of learning and achievement. In addition, comparisons can be made with work of other teachers and classes.

You should always remember that learning to teach is an ongoing process, and that consequently the format of your scheme of work is likely to develop over the years.

SUMMARY AND KEY POINTS

The process of preparing to teach is not a simple skill to be mastered. Rather it stands at the heart of the teaching process. You must learn to accept responsibility for the methods and content of your planning and preparation, within the framework required by the Agreed Syllabus. This chapter has sought to stimulate reflection on this responsibility by suggesting one possible model of the planning process: initial preparation, constructing lesson plans and evaluation after teaching the lesson, writing schemes of work. It also introduced you to some key educational concepts which you need to take on board if your planning is to include effective aims, objectives, continuity and progression.

FURTHER READING

Kincaid, M. (1991) *How to Improve Learning in RE*, London: Hodder & Stoughton. A very useful text offering theoretical and practical advice and suggestions on how to improve the delivery of RE in the classroom. Topics covered include learning theory, the place of RE in the curriculum, assessment and the evaluation of learning.

Kyriacon, C. (2007) *Essential Teaching Skills*, London: Stanley Thornes. A clear, practical guide to the teaching skills you will need as a trainee teacher. Areas covered range from planning and preparation to reflecting on and evaluating your practice.

Training and Development Agency, *Professional Standards for Teachers in England from September 2007*, London, TDA. This contains the government's standards for all trainee teachers in all subject areas. You should familiarise yourself with the sections dealing with RE and ICT.

4 Pupil learning

Trevor Cooling

INTRODUCTION

This chapter reviews the way thinking has changed since the 1950s regarding what pupils should be learning in Religious Education (RE). In particular, it focuses on the sorts of attitudes that should be promoted and suggests that openness to learning from people who are different from oneself is a central aim for education in modern, multi-faith societies. This requires the development of strategies that overcome the negative perception of religion prevalent in modern youth culture. There is an ongoing debate in the literature on RE about how the subject matter studied in RE should be used to achieve this goal. Two influential curriculum development projects are reviewed to support the notion that the key skills are the ability to listen carefully to the believer's perspective and the ability to apply what is heard to the pupils' own world of experience. A particular emphasis is given to planning lessons based on understanding religious concepts, rather than just passing on information about the religions.

OBJECTIVES

By the end of this chapter you should be able to:

*   describe the main changes that have taken place in the philosophy of RE;
*   comment on the attitudes and skills that RE should promote;
*   understand the rationale of two influential curriculum development projects;

- evaluate the importance of concepts in RE;
- apply your thinking to the design of effective learning strategies.

THE CHANGING NATURE OF RE

Anyone wishing to understand RE might be advised to start by looking at the changes that have taken place in the philosophy of school dinners (a much neglected topic on most PGCE courses!). In the 1950s and 1960s, the philosophy was that schools knew what children needed and they were all expected to eat it. After all, it was good for them! Etched on my memory is a picture of awe-inspiring dinner ladies serving up slabs of (often yellowing) liver, adorned with anaemic cabbage and lumpy mashed potatoes swimming in a watery gravy. The typical dessert was a sea of tapioca ('frog spawn' in kid-speak), with a rudimentary blob of jam in the centre. All, I was assured, most nourishing.

Things began to change in the 1970s, largely because dealers in pig swill were doing so well. So dawned the age of the school cafeteria, with its philosophy that pupil choice should determine what was served in the canteen. No longer did schools feel it was appropriate that they *tell* pupils what they *ought* to eat. This was a matter of personal choice. The school provided the menu, the pupils chose; and so we moved into the era of beef burgers, beans and chips. Schools were to be the precursors of McDonald's.

Unrestrained pupil choice soon led to anxieties among school catering professionals. Maybe pupils were not always choosing what was in their own best interests? So we moved to the current philosophy of healthy eating where schools seek to guide pupils to ensure that the choices they make are good for them. The future health of the nation requires that we abandon the notion of unrestrained choice.

The history of RE provides a remarkable parallel to these changes. In the 1950s and 1960s it was widely assumed that the purpose of the subject was to induct pupils into the religious heritage of the nation, namely Christianity. The largely unquestioned assumption was that it was both good for them and good for the country that they learn about this. The approach was what we now call 'confessional'. Two things led to the widespread abandonment of this philosophy. First, teachers were sensitised to the dangers of indoctrination. Second, the nation as a whole began to wake up to the significant presence of people from other religions among its citizens as well as in the wider world. Teachers were also aware that the diet of poorly taught Bible stories, characteristic of the confessional approach of this period, was resulting in the educational equivalent of overflowing swill bins. Pupils were turned off. So, in the late 1970s, RE teachers increasingly adopted what came to be called the phenomenological approach, more popularly known as 'multi-faith RE', which emphasised the importance of pupils learning about a number of religions and choosing for themselves. The approach championed the academic, objective and respectful study of religion. It was widely assumed that this phenomenological study would automatically be more interesting for the pupils as it offered them a wider choice than the confessional Christian approach.

A significant number of RE textbooks currently in use in schools adopt this phenomenological approach. These often organise the content under themes that are supposed to be common to all the religions, such as 'sacred books' or 'rites of passage'. The assumption is that by emphasising what is common between the religions, pupils learn to respect people from a variety of different religious traditions. The aspiration is that pupils learn tolerance, become less prejudiced and realise the importance of making their own, autonomous choices in life through the study of a number of religions.

For a number of reasons, there has been growing dissatisfaction with the phenomenological approach. Two in particular are relevant to the theme of our chapter. First, the emphasis on pupils making their own choices in the matter of religion ignored the question of whether all the choices that could be made were equally acceptable. For example, does the teacher mind if the pupil decides to become a Satanist? Clearly there is the need for pupils to learn to make *discerning* choices, not simply *just* to choose. Second, there is a big question as to how relevant this amassing of knowledge about a variety of religions is to modern teenagers. The phenomenological approach was modelled on the university subject called *Religious Studies*. People who take this subject at university are fascinated by information about the world's religions. It is a big assumption, however, to think that 14–year-olds also feel this way. And are we *really* sure that learning information about the religions leads to less prejudice and more tolerance?

When the philosophy of the canteen moved from pupil choice as an end in itself to educating pupil choices, it was not a return to the idea that the school simply told the pupils what was good for them. So too, when the philosophy of RE moved beyond the phenomenological approach, it did not abandon the idea that learning about a number of religions was important in favour of telling pupils what to believe. It did, however, pay much more attention to looking at the contribution that learning about the religions made to the personal development of the pupils, in terms of the attitudes it generated and the relevance of the content for pupils in their own life experience.

Task 4.1 Identifying approaches to RE teaching

Find a number of different RE textbooks. Decide which of the following is the main approach adopted by each textbook:

- the confessional approach where the intention is to transmit the ideas of one religion to the pupils in the hope that they come to believe them;
- non-confessional approach to teaching one religion which aims that pupils should understand that religion, but doesn't seek to gain the pupil's acceptance of it;
- a multi-faith approach where the emphasis is largely on pupils acquiring information about the religions;
- multi-faith approach which requires the pupils to make judgements and which seeks to educate those judgements by encouraging pupils to reflect on them.

Discuss the strengths and weaknesses of the four approaches, as developed in the textbooks, with your tutor or another student teacher.

RELIGIOUS EDUCATION AND THE PERSONAL DEVELOPMENT OF PUPILS

The culture of our pupils

For a number of years I taught RE in a boys' grammar school. After a period of time I started to claim that I was in charge of the special needs work. What I meant by this was that I was working with able and articulate young people who seemed to find it impossible to undertake an intelligent study of religion. Many of them just could not see the point. In my current job I work with lots of RE teachers. I keep hearing the same message from them, and it is not just academically able boys that have the problem.

Perhaps one of the most important insights to come from that loosely defined movement called postmodernism, is that we are all, to some extent, products of our culture. Our pupils are shaped by the media, the norms of their peer group and the cultural air that they breathe. One thing is clear, religion is not a significant element in this cultural climate. Two researchers working in this field have this to say:

> What appears to be taking place is this. As young people leave the world of childhood, they are absorbed incrementally into the world of adulthood. Today much of this is characterised by the secular rather than the religious . . . In this sense to be irreligious is to be normal.
>
> (Kay and Francis 1996: 144)

Secularity is therefore the air our pupils breathe. Like fish which simply assume the water in which they swim, many of them unconsciously assume the norms of a secular approach. What does this mean for an RE teacher? I suggest there are two possible consequences, depending on the way secularity is understood.

First, secularity can express itself in *antagonism* and *anger* against religion. This is the atheistic response which sees religion as responsible for many of the evils in the world and regards it as an intellectual impostor, holding to untenable beliefs as a source of illusory comfort. Those who opt for religion are regarded as inadequate escapists, unable to cope with the realities of a godless world. Underlying this view is the influence of a philosophy commonly called *scientism*, the belief that 'real' knowledge is found in the realm of science and mathematics. Religion, with its incredible views on the supernatural, is held to be in direct conflict with it. Research suggests that scientism may be a widespread philosophy in modern youth culture (ibid.).

Second, secularity can express itself simply in *apathy* about religion. The influence of the philosophy of relativism, the idea that truth is a personal matter, has under-mined commitment to the big philosophies of life. Not only has religion suffered, but so have other all-embracing causes including political philosophies such as Marxism. There really doesn't seem that much point in campaigning for what after all is only a personal preference. Labelling oneself in terms of a big cause, especially a religious one, is simply not 'cool'!

This is not the whole picture, however. Commentators on the culture of modern youth also report a spiritual hunger, which, although it may be repressed by the pragmatic materialism of Western consumerism, is still a motivating force. The work of David Hay has been particularly influential in this regard (Hay 1990a; see Chapter 10 for further discussion). In extensive surveys he found convincing evidence that many people have deep spiritual experiences which have enormous personal significance and meaning, but which are rarely talked about with other people. The reason for this is an implicit secular censorship which makes people think that owning up to having had such experiences makes them appear abnormal. The truth is that they are in fact 'normal', but it is the conspiracy of silence that makes them appear abnormal.

The future of plural societies

Debates about the role of RE have been influenced by concerns about the future of religiously plural societies. The phenomenon of religious terrorism and the increasingly fragmented nature of society have naturally focused minds and raised the issue of how RE can contribute to better relations between the different ethnic and religious communities. These concerns originally came to prominence in the clash that took place between conservative Christians and the RE profession in the debates that surrounded the place of RE and collective worship in the 1988 Education Act (see, for example, Jackson 2004; Robson 1996). The Christian lobby worked hard to secure a predominant position for Christianity in the curriculum. The RE profession resisted, wishing to defend the multi-faith approach.

The details of this complex debate are not our concern now. What is important is that the attention of influential writers on RE was focused on a particularly harmful type of religious attitude, namely that which seeks to defend its position against that of others, sees other people from different religious traditions as a threat and adopts various strategies to diminish the influence of the perceived opponents. In a highly influential editorial in the *BJRE*, John Hull described this as 'religionism'. This operates on the basis of a 'name and shame' philosophy. You name people according to their religious affiliation and then seek to shame them if their affiliation is different from your own. Hull described the attitude of mind as follows: 'We are better than they. We are orthodox; they are infidel. We are believers; they are unbelievers. We are right; they are wrong . . . The identity which is fostered by religionism depends upon rejection and exclusion' (Hull 1992: 70).

Hull went on to suggest that one of the functions of RE should be to promote more open and healthy, less defensive attitudes. A similar argument was put forward by John Hick when he suggested that Christians should stop thinking of Christianity as the only true religion and adopt what he calls 'religious pluralism', the view that the different world religions are simply different ways of conceiving of God and that they are therefore all 'true' (Hick 1997).

Task 4.2 Exploring the religious attitudes of pupils

Observe a discussion lesson with a class of older pupils (Year 9 or above) and record the key contributions made by the pupils.

- Note down any examples of phrases used which seem to illustrate attitudes influenced by secularism or religionism.
- Are there any contributions which give evidence that pupils may have had spiritual experiences which are important to them?
- If possible, compare your findings with those of other students: do they concur with the national research you have read about in this chapter?
- Together decide how RE teaching needs to respond, if at all, to the changing cultural climate that your pupils inhabit.

The shift from a cafeteria of religions

What then is the implication of these two issues for pupil learning in RE lessons? In many people's minds it is that we can no longer be satisfied with pupils simply making their own choices on the basis of information supplied in the classroom, but rather that we, as their teachers, have to make sure that their choices are 'sound' and their attitudes are 'healthy'. I now examine two influential views as to what this entails.

First, David Hay has argued that RE should constitute 'de-indoctrination' (Hay 1990b). What he means by this is that teachers have to combat the negative effects of secularisation by adopting methods which affirm and encourage the deep spiritual experiences that are latent in most human beings (Hammond *et al.* 1990). Only in this way, he believes, can RE become relevant. Pupils are not going to learn anything from religion if they reject it outright as a waste of time. So, one of the tasks of RE is to undo the antagonism and apathy towards religion that is engendered by secular Western culture. In this way religion becomes relevant to pupils, so that instead of simply opting for the prevailing secular rejection of religion that is the norm within their culture, they adopt a more sympathetic attitude towards religious belief.

Second, John Hull argues that RE must oppose religionism. I was once at an RE conference where a teacher said 'I always tell my pupils there are no right or wrong answers in RE.' Her motivation for saying this was that she wanted to move away from the situation where her pupils viewed religion as something in which people had to believe that they were right and everyone else was wrong. Her idea was to combat the popular view of religion as involving tribal loyalties that brought one into conflict with those from other tribes.

It seems hard to object to any of this. Why shouldn't an RE teacher want to engender more sympathy for their subject content by challenging the anger and apathy generated by secular attitudes? Why shouldn't we oppose narrow and vindictive attitudes which cause disharmony in society? Any sound approach to promoting citizenship must surely do that. The problem comes when we remember why the confessional approach was rejected as a model for RE. It is widely accepted that it is inappropriate in a plural society that schools should tell pupils what religious beliefs they ought or ought not to hold. But if we, as teachers, set out to combat a secular approach, surely this in itself is a form of confessionalism? It is hardly acceptable to those who believe that secularism is right. And there are some very influential and intelligent secularists around, for example, Richard Dawkins. Furthermore, if we promote the idea that all religions are equal, is this not deeply offensive to many religious communities? For example, most Muslim parents are not going to be happy with their children being told that Islam is only one among a number of true religions. So how do we avoid confessionalism if we are to persuade our pupils of the relevance of religion and of the evils of prejudice?

To answer this, I suggest we have to distinguish between the imposition of a particular view and the encouraging of a more open approach. Secularism is harmful because it causes pupils to reject the possibility of a religious approach to life *without thinking seriously about it as an alternative view*. Secularism has made them deaf to other voices. It closes down the possibility of meaningful conversations between religious and non-religious people. Likewise, a religionist approach manifests a similar problem, because it drives us back into our own tribe. Both of these are clearly unacceptable in a plural society, because they lead to conflict and rejection of others and stop pupils benefiting from contact with other people from whom they might have much to learn. The health of a plural society depends on people being prepared to listen to each other, on them being willing to work together for the common good and on the ability to make concessions to other people out of respect for their aspirations, way of life and deeply held beliefs. Neither popular secularism nor religionism encourage this sort of 'conversational' approach (Jackson 1997). So the RE teacher can legitimately resist them in the pursuit of an educational approach which promotes responsible citizenship.

Wanting to encourage pupils to be reflective and open is very different from telling them what they *ought* to believe. Promoting a reflective approach helps pupils to become more critically aware of the culture that has shaped them and helps them to see the possibilities of learning something valid from other people. The shared characteristic of both popular secularism and religionism is the inability to comprehend the possibility or legitimacy of another point of view and the inability to reflect critically on one's own position. To tell pupils, however, that a secular approach is wrong *per se* or to tell them that they must believe that all religions are true is to move beyond what is legitimate. The difference can perhaps be illustrated by returning to the statement of the teacher at the RE conference. Instead of telling pupils that there are no right and wrong answers in RE, which is in effect to tell them that they ought to adopt relativism, I suggest we should explain that there is no agreement as to what the right or wrong answers are in religion. This is simply to ensure that they are aware that the existence of pluralism is a matter of fact that has to be accommodated in some way. It is not to tell them how they should respond to that fact.

LEARNING FROM RELIGION

The phrase *learning from* religion was coined to capture the aspiration that pupils should not just acquire information, but learn something about themselves; in other words, that their study of religion has outcomes in their own life and thinking (see QCA 2004: 34). The function, then, of RE is to encourage a more reflective approach to religious matters so as to create the context in which this can happen. The question then becomes how, practically, can we 'use' religion to achieve these goals? There are basically two extremes in approaching this question (with my apologies to Vikings and, particularly, to missionaries – for whom I have the greatest respect – for the parody).

The RE teacher as Viking

I once heard a lecture where it was said that the job of the RE teacher is to ransack the world's religions in order to find material that can be used to promote the personal development of the pupils. By this the speaker meant that RE teachers should not be too concerned about teaching religion from the point of view of the believer, but rather that they should look for gems that could be plucked out of their context in the religion and used for some other purpose. An extreme and facetious example would be using the New Testament story of Jesus feeding the five thousand to teach the importance of picking up litter (because Jesus' disciples picked up twelve baskets in the story). This has nothing to do with the significance that the story has for Christians. It rips it out of its Christian context to use it for another purpose, supporting the school's litter education programme.

The RE teacher as missionary

In stark contrast, this position views the religious content as sacrosanct, to be conveyed in a pre-digested form to unquestioning and passive recipients. The expectation is that just learning the religious material has a salutary effect on pupil personal development. It is therefore expected that the systematic learning of religious information, of itself, will produce the required outcomes. Certainly the confessional approach *as taught in some schools* would have been a classic example of this. (I hasten to add that there can be excellent examples of confessional teaching.) Less obvious perhaps is that the phenomenological approach fell into exactly the same error. It too assumed that information about religion taught to pupils would auto-matically have moral effects, in particular that it would make them more tolerant. The research evidence suggests that this may not be correct (Malone 1998).

Andrew Wright has suggested that the greatest danger of this position is that we represent religions as providing pre-packaged, simplistic answers to the great intellectual and spiritual challenges faced in life by human beings (Wright 1993). He suggests that the trouble with this approach is that it makes the religious life seem to consist of simplistic answers to complex and challenging questions. Wright argues that if we are going to produce pupils who have learnt to be religiously literate, we must introduce them to the *ambiguity* of the religious life. By this he means the awareness that faith does not necessarily give straightforward answers.

Neither the Viking nor the missionary approach constitutes an adequate model for the way in which religion might be used in RE so that our pupils learn from it. The first fails to do justice to the fact that each of the religions should be taught in a way that respects its integrity and is recognisable to a member of the faith community. To do otherwise is to fail to equip pupils with an important skill for life in a plural society, namely to be able to listen carefully to someone else so as to understand as clearly as possible the way things look from their perspective. This is essential if the blinding effects of both religionism and secularism are to be overcome. At the same time, we have seen that *just* reflecting the believer's perspective may well mean that the religious content remains largely irrelevant to the pupil. If our pupils are to learn from religion, they must be taught it in a way which overcomes its seeming irrelevance. Otherwise it is drowned out by the secular voices in our pupils' culture. How can these aspirations be achieved? In the next section I shall examine two approaches which seek to do this.

APPROACHES TO LEARNING FROM RELIGION

Ethnography and the Warwick RE Project

The Warwick Religions and Education Research Unit (WRERU) derives from the work of a team in the Institute of Education at Warwick University (Jackson 1997). A premise of their work is that understanding the faith of another person means entering, as far as is possible, into their way of life. The responsibility of the RE teacher is then to ensure that the representation of a religion given to the pupils through textbooks and in other ways is not distorted. They recommend ethnography as an ideal methodology to achieve this. By this they mean the direct study of individuals in the context of their own family and community life with a view to observing, and to a degree experiencing, what life is like for them. This 'conversational' approach, as Jackson calls it, leads to the undermining of stereotypes and a greater empathy for the life and aspirations of other people. Ideally the Warwick team would like pupils themselves to become field ethnographers, but they recognise the practical limitations. So it has published a series of textbooks, under the general title Interpreting Religions, which draw on their own extensive ethnographic research among young people from a variety of religious communities in England (Robson 1995; Mercier 1996; Wayne 1996). In one book, for example, we meet Kamran, a 13-year-old Muslim who lives in a terraced house in Birmingham, and learn about his daily life, beliefs and attitudes (Mercier 1996). Ethnography, the Warwick team believe, undermines secularism and religionism by bringing the pupil in the classroom into conversation with the young person in the faith community.

The Warwick team do not assume that creating this conversation is an easy task. They recognise the huge gap that exists between the secular culture of most pupils and the religious world of the young people in the textbooks. They see two separate tasks as being necessary. First, the pupils need to be sensitised to their own culture and the assumptions this generates. If they are not so sensitised, these assumptions inevitably distort their perceptions of the life of the young person in the faith community. Second, our pupils need to become aware of what Jackson calls the *grammar* of the young person's faith, by which he means the complex of practices, relationships and beliefs which constitutes the life lived by that person. In this approach, the pupil is encouraged to move to and fro, from their own perspective to that of the young person in the book, as a means of understanding where both they and the young person in the book are coming from. This is described as *building bridges* and depends on the teacher being able to identify concepts which are familiar to the pupil and concepts that are central to the faith of the young person and to bring them into line with each other. Thereby the pupil sees the relevance of the faith world to their own, often predominantly secular, world by examining concepts in the two worlds which relate to each other. For example, pupils are encouraged to think about the books which have a good influence on their own lives, when studying Muslim attitudes to the Qur'an (Mercier 1996: 25).

A final question is, how can the pupil learn something about themselves from the study of someone else's faith? The Warwick Project has coined the term *edification* to describe this. This is explained as follows:

> Engagement with another's way of life has the potential to make an impact on one's own thinking and attitudes. The WREP approach encourages students to do more than reconstruct the religious lives of others. It also encourages them to relate the material studied to issues which are of concern to themselves.
>
> (Robson 1995: 4)

> What might appear to be entirely different and 'other' at first glance can end linking with one's own experience in such a way that new perspectives are created or unquestioned presuppositions are challenged.
>
> (Jackson 1997: 130)

The Warwick team think that an encounter with someone else's life of faith should have an impact on one's own life. They regard one of the purposes of RE as being to capitalise on the opportunities for edification by planning specific learning activities which encourage it.

Theology and the Stapleford Project

Another project which takes a similar approach to the Warwick material is the Stapleford Project, based at the Stapleford Centre in Nottingham. It is close to my own heart as I have been involved in developing it for a number of years (Cooling 2000; Cooling and Cooling 2004). The big difference from the Warwick approach is the emphasis placed on the role of theological concepts in giving access to the faith of another person. It is this that is seen as the key rather than ethnography. The popular name for this approach is *concept cracking* (Figure 4.1). As with the Warwick Project,

As a practical classroom tool, the *concept cracking* approach has been broken down into four specific steps, which can be remembered using the acronym USER (**Unpack, Select, Engage, Relate and Reflect**). It can be illustrated by using the story from the New Testament where Jesus turns the traders out of the Temple in Jerusalem (Mark 11: 15–17).

1. **Unpack** *the concepts*
Before teaching any topic it is important to be aware of the different theological concepts that underpin it and are important to understanding its meaning and significance. If, as teachers, we are not clear about the ideas we are covering, our pupils certainly will not be. In the case of this story, the key concepts include anger, injustice, holiness, Jesus as God's son and judgement.

2. **Select** *one or two concepts as the focus for the lesson*
It is very important to focus your lesson on one or two key concepts that you are seeking to teach. Otherwise your pupils become confused. Let us tackle the concept of righteous anger in this example, to get across the idea when anger is justified and when it is not.

3. **Engage** *with the pupil's world of experience*
This is perhaps the hardest and yet the most important stage in the process. The key is to find parallels in the pupils' world with the concept of righteous anger. One possibility would be to ask pupils to give examples of instances when they have been angry. The purpose of the activity is not so much to pass judgement on the particular instances as to establish the idea in pupils' minds that there are right and wrong forms of anger and to begin the process of searching for criteria to distinguish between them. This builds the bridge between the pupils' world and the religious concept.

4. **Relate** *to the religious concepts and* **reflect** *on their personal significance*
At this point introduce the story from the New Testament. An effective way of doing this is to use the painting called 'Christ driving the traders from the Temple' by El Greco (contained in Cooling 1998) and to ask the pupils to comment on how Jesus' behaviour is being portrayed in the painting. In particular they notice that there are two groups of people, those who are the object of his anger and those who are being affirmed. A role-play could then be used in which pupils take on the role of members of the two groups and debate Jesus' behaviour. Finally, there needs to be a whole-class discussion in which the question of why Jesus thought his anger was justified is discussed. It should draw out themes like the importance of resisting injustice and exploitation, the holiness of the Temple and Jesus' special relationship with God that made his anger uniquely justifiable, as far as the Gospel writer is concerned. Pupils should be encouraged to express their own views, perhaps though the medium of a diary entry by someone who was present in the Temple, as to whether or not Jesus' anger was justified.

There are two important points to note from this example:

- Steps 1 and 2 represent important preliminary work that must be done by teachers to clarify our own understanding of the topic. This is very important as a way of giving a lesson a clear focus. However, the actual teaching often begins with step 3 in order to ensure that the lesson seems relevant to the pupils. Most lessons have to begin with an activity that is designed to build the bridge between the pupils' world and the religious topic.

(Continued)

> • This process accommodates both the concerns we have been discussing about pupil learning in RE. Considerable effort is expended on ensuring that the pupils overcome their initial negativity to Jesus' behaviour, so that they understand, as far as is possible, the Gospel writer's perspective. There is emphasis on the importance of listening as a skill in learning about religion. Considerable effort, however, is also expended on ensuring that the pupils learn something of personal relevance from the story. In this case they have reflected upon the difference between justified and unjustified anger in their own lives.

Figure 4.1 'Concept cracking': a working example

the theoretical background to the approach has been translated into a practical form in a textbook for use in RE lessons (Wright 1995).

A major premise of the project is that the alienation which most people experience when encountering religion is because the concepts which enable one to make sense of a religion are largely absent from the secular culture. It advocates the process of 'concept cracking' as a means of unpacking and exploring religious and theological concepts in the classroom. For example, seeing a picture of Muslims prostrate in prayer can, unfortunately, be a source of great hilarity to many Western teenagers. The difficulty is that they have no experience of the concept of submission to a higher being, which is being expressed through the body language of the Muslim worshipper. It is simply not part of a Western liberal view of life which emphasises rights and autonomy rather than duties and submission. So teaching about Islamic prayer remains a lost cause unless some way of allowing our pupils to get their minds round the idea of submission can be found. They may well end up with a page full of pictures and labels illustrating prayer positions in their exercise books at the end of a lesson on Muslim prayer, but unless they have some feel for their meaning and significance for Muslims, they might just as well have hieroglyphics on the page. Consequently, a key task for the teacher in teaching any religious topic is to identify the theological concepts which are integral to understanding the meaning and significance of that topic. Otherwise we could be teaching nothing but meaningless information.

Of course it is one thing to identify a key theological concept, it is quite another to teach it to teenagers. A lesson on the concept of submission hardly seems likely to grab their attention. However, like the Warwick approach, the Stapleford team argue that theological concepts have their parallels in the concepts that are part of the everyday experience of teenagers in modern Britain. An important part of our job as RE teachers is to look for ways of translating religious concepts into forms that make sense in our pupils' world of experience. For example, with Muslim prayer a key preliminary to understanding is to have been made aware of the importance of body language in human communication. There can be great fun to be had in a lesson exploring how, in our everyday lives, we use our bodies to say things. An interesting homework is to ask pupils to spot some of the more unusual things people say in this way! This can then be followed by a lesson where Muslim prayer positions are examined with this question in mind: What are these people expressing? This could be followed by pupils working out ways in which they could express homage through their own bodies. Can they conceive of situations when this might happen? Older pupils might like to consider these words from the marriage service: 'with my body I thee worship', or 'with my body I honour you' in its modern form. The important general point to note is that these learning activities are designed to convey a feeling of what the concept of submission means for the believer.

This approach is designed to overcome the alienation that many pupils feel towards religion. It certainly contributes to the process of *learning from* religion, by enabling them to listen to the believer with more empathy and thereby developing a key skill which eliminates the negative effects of secularism and religionism. However, it needs to go beyond simply enhancing their understanding of religion if it is to contribute to developing the pupils' understanding of themselves. Here is where the emphasis on concepts as the focus gives a particular edge. Initially it is very hard to see how looking at Islamic prayer positions can help a Western teenager who rarely, if ever, prays, let alone participates in corporate rituals of prayer. But once we focus the attention on the concept of submission expressed through the body, it opens up consideration of a wealth of parallel experiences. Do they ever consider submitting to anyone? What would make them willingly do it? Has our society got it right in viewing submission in a negative light? And so on. The following quote from a primary school RE specialist sums up the point:

> It is not the religion per se from which the child is learning, but rather from some of the key concepts, feelings, experiences, values and truth claims upheld and engendered by that religion, its faith and its communities.
>
> (Albans 1998: 4)

Task 4.3 Lesson planning using the 'concept cracking' framework

Select a topic from the RE scheme of work being used in your practice school. Now prepare to teach this topic conceptually by:

- brainstorming the various concepts that underpin the topic (Unpack);
- deciding what the key concept is which it is necessary for your pupils to grasp if they are to understand this topic (Select);
- identifying parallels for that concept in their own world of experience (Engage);
- developing bridges which can be used to enable the pupils to see the relationship between the key religious concept and the concept from their own world of experience (Engage and relate);
- considering how the students may be able to apply what they have learnt from their study of the religious concept in their own world of experience (Reflect).

IMPLICATIONS FOR THE CLASSROOM

Finally, we address the implications of these ideas for teaching and learning with reference to lesson planning, particularly for choosing activities, to using a variety of art forms and literary genres and to the importance of questioning.

Designing learning activities

One of the most alarming features of past research about the teaching of RE in secondary schools has been the revelation that the learning activities that pupils are given are often very ineffective. There are two major problems. First, it appears that many of the learning activities set do not move much beyond the level of information recall. Second, activities that pupils already have done in their primary schools are reappearing in the secondary school RE programme. For example, one Ofsted report on RE described its findings as follows:

> Many activities set at Key Stage 3 were widely used at Key Stage 2 and were quite unsuitable for most secondary school pupils. Pupils in years 4 and 7 were asked to make advent calendars. Pupils work in years 3, 6, 8 and 9 included a cartoon account of the six days of creation, usually followed by a picture of God sleeping in a bed on the seventh day. The only difference in outcome from both the tasks was in the quality of the art work . . . There were too many instances of filling in missing words.
>
> (Ofsted 1997: 29)

If this situation were to persist, the effect on pupil learning would be devastating. If pupils are already switched off religion, being given tasks to do which they carried out in primary school can only reinforce the idea that religion is trivial and irrelevant, just kid's stuff. To overcome this perception, the learning activities we set must be worthwhile and demanding. This means that we must plan activities which require the pupils to use the information they are learning in a way that enhances their understanding of the concepts that are the focus of the lesson (Figure 4.2). So in our Islamic prayer example, exploring the way humans communicate through body

---

Examples of activities applicable to a number of religions that get beyond simply regurgitating information on a topic, but which require the pupils to use that information to express their understanding are:

- Pupils work in pairs. Each one of the pair has to design three questions on the topic they have studied. The first is a factual recall question, the second is a question which probes significance and the third requires an application in a new situation. The pupils write answers to each other's questions and discuss their answers.

- Pupils imagine that an event or story that they have learnt about is to be made into a video. They have the job of writing the back cover blurb in no more than 100 words. The task is to highlight the most significant points to capture the potential viewer's attention.

- Pupils are asked to plan a new festival to celebrate an aspect of the topic they have studied. They must explain the symbolism and significance of their suggestions, justifying them from their studies.

Figure 4.2 Examples of tasks designed to develop religious literacy

language and then discussing how this relates to Islamic prayer generates a much greater understanding than simply asking pupils to draw and label the prayer positions. It also opens up opportunities for pupils to apply what they learn in their own lives. A key question to ask when designing learning activities is what sort of conversation between pupils is generated by the activity? If the answer is trivial conversation, then it is a fair bet that the activity is trivial.

Fortunately the National Framework for RE (QCA 2004) has set a new agenda for Key Stage 3 where challenging learning activities are at the centre of RE teaching. New publications are providing the resources to support classroom teachers in the development of thinking skills and in the promotion of learning (e.g. Baumfield 2002; Hookway 2004).

A further key question focuses on the need to ask ourselves what exactly is the purpose of each learning activity we set (see Chapter 3). Possible purposes could be:

- to acquire new information;
- to engage the pupils' interest and help them see parallels in their own lives;
- to explore the meaning and significance of the information;
- to stimulate the application of the ideas in the pupils' own lives (edification).

If we know exactly what we want to achieve, we can design our activities accordingly and are more likely to offer a range of different types of activity that helps to maintain the interest level of lessons. If we don't ask ourselves what the purpose of our learning activities are, the likelihood is that the pupils end up focusing on accumulating information. An important feature of lesson planning is to identify the purpose of the lesson and then identify specific learning outcomes: this provides the context and rationale for selecting appropriate classroom activities and tasks.

Task 4.4 Evaluating learning activities

Collect a range of examples of learning activities from your own teaching, from your observation of others' teaching and from books and other sources. For each, decide:

- What was the intended purpose of the activity? *List the learning outcomes.*
- Did it help the pupils to interact with the religious material so that their understanding was enhanced?
- How could the *activity* be improved to achieve its intended purpose better or to achieve a different purpose?

Asking the right questions

Asking questions is a very important teaching skill. As with designing learning activities, the key is to have thought through the purpose of asking a question. If we don't, we almost inevitably drift into asking questions which require no more than information recall. Consider the following questions:

- How would this person react if . . .?
- What would it mean if . . .?
- Can you think of a situation when . . .?

You find that questions such as these are needed alongside those which elicit information-based responses. Planning the questions you might use is a very important, but much neglected, part of lesson planning

Using a variety of languages

One of the difficulties with teaching religion is that it is easy to trivialise it by using straightforward descriptive language alone. The mystery and ambiguity, the trust and devotion, the paradox of truth, the vividness of spiritual experience that lie at the heart of most religion can vaporise as we seek to describe it. To be true to the nature of religion, we must use a variety of modes of expression that allow pupils to capture a glimpse of the indescribable. Story, poetry, art, music, drama and other art forms are integral to the nature of our subject (Cooling 1996).

SUMMARY AND KEY POINTS

Recent thinking on RE has emphasised the importance of pupils learning from religion as well as learning about it. Putting it another way, RE should contribute to the personal development of our pupils as well as increase their knowledge of the religions. This means that you have to develop strategies which move beyond the transmission of information about the religions to enabling your pupils to apply insights from what they learn to their own lives. In doing this there are two major obstacles for us to overcome: popular secularism and religionism. The key skills to be developed are that of being able to hear a person who may have very different views from our own and then being able to apply what we have heard in our own lives. Ethnography and a focus on theological concepts are suggested as two ways of achieving these goals.

FURTHER READING

Cooling, T. (2002) 'Commitment and Indoctrination: A Dilemma for Religious Education', in L. Broadbent and A. Brown (eds) *Issues in Religious Education*, London: RoutledgeFalmer. This chapter, in a text designed to be accessible for the newcomer to RE, reflects on the way in which the controversial nature of religion can be managed in the classroom.

Cooling, T. (2003) *Try Something Different: Approaches to Teaching and Learning in RE*, Nottingham: The Stapleford Centre. A short practical guide designed for the busy teacher which introduces the major approaches to RE which the classroom teacher is likely to encounter. Part of the REthinking series published by The Stapleford Centre.

Cooling, T. and Cooling, M. (2004) *Concept Cracking: A Practical Way to Teach Big Ideas in RE*, Nottingham, The Stapleford Centre. This short, practical guide to teaching theological concepts in RE, based mainly on Christianity, is published as part of the REthinking series by the Stapleford Centre. It should be read alongside Chris Wright's classroom text (1995).

Jackson, R. (1997) *Religious Education: An Interpretive Approach*, London: Hodder & Stoughton. This seminal book describes in detail the ethnographic approach developed by the Warwick RE Project. It deals with the theoretical issues that surround modern RE teaching as well as describing the practical responses made by the Warwick team in the development of materials for the classroom. The book should be read alongside the pupil textbooks (Robson 1995; Mercier 1996; Wayne 1996).

Qualifications and Curriculum Agency (1998) *Exemplification of Standards in Religious Education: Key Stages 1 to 4*, London: QCA. This highly practical book gives examples of learning activities in RE and illustrates the objectives that they are designed to achieve in both learning about and learning from religion.

Qualifications and Curriculum Agency (2004) *Religious Education: The Non-statutory National Framework*, London: QCA. This is a 'must read' text for student teachers. It outlines the widely agreed expectations for RE and is a shaping influence on syllabuses across the country.

Wright, A. (1993) *Religious Education in the Secondary School*, London: David Fulton Publishers. This book should be read by every RE teacher. It is a masterly sketch of the debates about RE. Wright puts forward an invigorating view of the subject based on the promotion of religious literacy.

The Stapleford Centre publishes an excellent series for student teachers called *REthinking*. Each book is 32 pages long and offers highly practical and up-to-date guidance on teaching and learning in RE. There are titles on thinking skills, brain-based learning, planning challenging lessons, differentiation, assessment and storytelling. Further details are available from www.e-stapleford.co.uk.

Part III

Classroom issues

5 The role of language in Religious Education

Ann-Marie Brandom

INTRODUCTION

Language is that which we use to communicate to others our needs, ideas, desires, values, stories, opinions or beliefs, and, as such, language is open to interpretation. Language is dependent on its context, on the emphasis given to the particular words used, and even the body language which accompanies human speech. Language communicates by identifying, explaining and expounding what is meant. Religious language is no exception.

The term 'language' is used in this context to refer to that which is both symbolically communicated and that which is spoken of in the religious world. It is fundamental to this chapter that such 'religious language' is understood in two ways: (1) as language which is reflective of the specific community from which it derives its authority; and (2) as language that is common to all religions. Having said that, it must be made clear that it is only through dialogue that we have the opportunity to discover the 'truth', the 'validity' or the 'meaning' of that which is being communicated in religious terms. It is to this end that the aim of this chapter is: (1) to encourage the definition and use of subject-specific terminology; and (2) to invite reflection on current trends in the classroom in the light of the necessity of using religious language.

OBJECTIVES

By the end of this chapter you should be able to:

- identify subject-specific religious language;

> - develop your own glossary of terms relevant to teaching each world faith and the philosophy of religion;
> - make such language relevant and challenging to the appropriate Key Stage you are teaching;
> - devise activities whereby religious language is used by the pupils in an accurate, informed and reflective manner;
> - identify which model of RE you wish to use in the classroom to promote effective religious dialogue.

RELIGIOUS LANGUAGE

The importance of religious language in RE

Many of you reading this now can easily recall an instance where a misinterpretation of language, either verbal or non-verbal, has led to an embarrassing and unnecessary incidence of confusion. All of us can recall such situations, and the RE classroom is no exception. Just as ambiguity exists in everyday language so it exists in religious language. Knowledge, understanding, ideas, beliefs, opinions and thoughts about religion need to be aired by your pupils using the appropriate religious language in order for clarity of understanding to take place. The role of language in the RE classroom requires time and scrutiny on behalf of the teacher in order to ensure that confusion is averted and the pupils use appropriate religious language in an informed and balanced manner.

The attention you pay to the use of religious language in the classroom can enhance the quality of each lesson you teach: it can inform the knowledge and understanding of the topics being studied for all levels of ability; it can enhance the calibre of discussion of each topic, both inside and outside the classroom; and it can facilitate a more structured approach to the ultimate questions in life, inherent within the nature of our subject. Only by giving appropriate attention to religious language can you hope to enable pupils to come to grips with and appreciate the complexities of religion in a positive way.

Just as you have been bombarded by a whole new vocabulary since you started your initial teacher education course and have begun to assimilate it as you go about your work in your IHE and school, so the same principle applies to the subject of RE for the pupils you teach. The religious language specific to RE requires skilled interpretation if your pupils are to learn effectively.

The notion of religious language is one which, whether your undergraduate studies were in Religious Studies or Theology, you have already spent at least three years coming to grips with. The fact is that you now have to enter a classroom where words such as 'reincarnation', 'forgiveness', 'spirituality', 'love', 'guru', 'sin', and 'divine' bring you face to face with challenges that are at the very heart of the task facing you as an RE teacher. One of the principles of hermeneutics is interpretation. In RE you must anticipate the different understandings pupils bring with them when they come to examine religious concepts. Such anticipation better enables you to help them to use such language with greater understanding and insight.

Religious language and the learning process

Effective teaching requires familiarity with the concepts of religion and with the interpretation of these concepts both within and beyond religious communities. This reflection on language allows you to develop a pattern of teaching in which your pupils are:

- presented with core subject material, language and concepts;
- invited to give initial reactions to the information;
- introduced to the variety of ways in which those both within and outside the faith community understand the language;
- encouraged to revisit the material in the light of this information and given the opportunity to reconsider their initial interpretations.

CASE STUDY

The Christian concept of 'miracle'

The issue of 'miracles' occurs in many instances in world faiths. Let us take the instance of miracles in Christianity. The word 'miracle' has popular connotations, as in the sentence 'It will be a miracle if England ever win the World Cup again (and don't we know it!).' However, the word functions differently in the context of the 'specialist' or 'technical' language of Christian theology. In Christian terms, 'miracle' clearly means more than an unlikely occurrence. It has to do with the interruption of the natural order of things by the supernatural. It is easy to equate this with mere magic, but the Christian understanding goes deeper. The significance of 'miracles' in the life of Jesus, from a Christian point of view, is that they reveal the nature of Jesus as both God and man, the incarnate Christ. They are a demonstration of the compassion of God and indicative of the establishing of the 'Kingdom of God'.

A consideration of miracles in Christianity demands that you deal with the concepts of the 'Kingdom of God' and that of 'incarnation'. This in turn naturally extends into an exploration of the nature of God, and the significance of each miracle in terms of the whole Christian world-view. But let's just concentrate on the word 'miracle' for the moment.

Once you have sifted out the central religious concepts involved in studying miracles, and have anticipated the pupils' reactions and initial understanding of the concept, you can identify how that concept is viewed from within the faith tradition. Miracles are a contentious subject within the Christian community and opinion, basically, may fall into two camps. There are those 'conservative' Christians who accept the miracles as historical events and even choose to believe that miracles still occur today, then there are the 'liberal' Christians who view the miracles as purely symbolic, a metaphor to enable us to understand God better. The contention within Christianity between those who are conservative Christians and those who are liberal Christians is intense, and your pupils need to be aware of this and be helped to engage with the debate. Pupils could consider the issue whether every single gospel miracle *really* happened and whether there are alternative explanations of the miracles. Conservative Christians typically interpret the miracles literally and liberal Christians interpret them symbolically.

You should then plan to examine the external views held on miracles. These range across a broad spectrum. At one extreme your teaching should refer to modern naturalistic assumptions that miracles simply don't happen, and that therefore Christianity, in its traditional form at least, is rooted in delusion and superstition. In contrast, you should also encourage your pupils to be aware of current postmodern suspicion of scientific authority, with its greater openness to 'spiritual reality' and refusal to dismiss Christian claims *a priori*. This may naturally lead into discussion of the relationship of religion to science.

Once you have introduced the topic and examined the actual core material in its appropriate context, your pupils can be introduced to the variety of positions which it is possible to hold on the subject of miracles. You should encourage them to identify, at a level appropriate to their ability, the key components of each position and explain why these different positions are justifiable ones. The pupils can then be invited to identify their own position within the range of options on the agenda and justify it. Class discussion on the truth, viability and ambiguity of the contrasting positions needs to explore why positions can differ and tensions can exist within the same faith community. The pupils can be taught how to reflect intelligently on the issue of miracles in a manner that is both sensitive to the deep-rooted importance of miracles in the Christian tradition, yet also critically aware of the controversial nature of the concept. In this way you are helping your pupils to examine the religious context of the miracles, to appreciate the diversity of the understanding of miracles from within the faith community and be aware of the external conflicts of interpretation. By encouraging such engagement with religious language you are developing the religious literacy of your pupils.

This case study emphasises the importance of language used to explain religious ideas. You need to ensure that your language is appropriate to the pupils you are teaching and attention to this feature of planning is one key to successful teaching. The case study and Task 5.1 may help you structure your lessons and promote intelligent inquiry by your pupils.

Task 5.1 Language: introducing religious concepts to pupils

Using the case study as a model, discuss with other student teachers how you would address the following teaching situations. How would you

- introduce the concept of 'annica' to your Year 9 pupils;
- introduce the concept of Brahman at Key Stage 4;
- teach 'Tahwid' to a Year 7 class?

Make any assumptions you need to set the context of a class, perhaps drawn from your school experience.

RELIGIOUS LANGUAGE IN THE CLASSROOM

Introducing a vocabulary

In 1994, the Schools Curriculum and Assessment Authority (SCAA) published a set of Model Syllabuses intended to support the work of those responsible for devising RE syllabuses at local level (SCAA 1994a, 1994b). SCAA included with the syllabuses a Glossary of Terms (SCAA 1994c). The purpose was twofold: (1) to offer teachers guidance on the meaning of key words as used in each religious tradition; (2) to standardise the spelling of such words. The Model Syllabuses accepted the importance for pupils of developing a working knowledge of key words and technical terms which are in use within each religious tradition. This emphasis upon language and the distinctive vocabulary of religion is also prominent in the *Non-Statutory National Framework of Religious Education* (QCA 2004: 18).

In the same way it is vital when you are preparing your lessons to identify the religious language you are about to use, to understand what it means yourself, and to take responsibility for ensuring that your pupils do likewise. To understand a word, however, you need to do more than learn a dictionary definition: genuine understanding is revealed in a pupil's ability to introduce such language appropriately into a conversation.

Time and effort must be devoted to defining the concept you are about to teach (Chapter 4 in this volume). You must be familiar with the material you are going to use in the classroom and identify the specific religious terminology. At the same time you must recognise the importance of presenting the terminology in a form suitable to the age and ability of your class. Avoid the trap of thinking that critical engagement with subject-specific vocabulary is a task open only to A Level pupils. All pupils you teach are capable of engaging with religious language provided it is presented at an appropriate level. Even if the concept is a complicated one, it does not mean that the pupils do not understand it. Their understanding depends upon your ability to break down both the concept and the language for them. Their understanding also depends on your expectations of them. It is a recognised fact in teaching RE that the pupils arrive in your classroom with their own world-view, your job is to help them to articulate and to reflect upon the basic language and concepts that best describe their particular commitment. The language and distinctive concepts of other world-views should be introduced, with a view both to facilitating an understanding of different viewpoints and to initiating dialogue between them. Pupils are also sensitive to your expectations of them, hence the need to reinforce what they already know as well as challenge them with new ideas and concepts (see Chapter 4, where you will find advice and tasks related to explaining and using religious concepts).

Task 5.2 Identifying the world-view of the pupil

Choose a small number of willing candidates from the pupils you teach. It need not necessarily be the whole class. If possible, select them from a number of different year groups. (You could usefully carry out the research among your fellow student teachers if you wish.) On a worksheet ask pupils the five questions listed below. In the initial stage you may want to ensure anonymity. There is no age limit for this activity, although you may need to revise the language to meet the needs of younger pupils.

- Who or what is 'God'?
- What is the purpose of your life?
- According to what principles do you live your life?
- What happens to you when you die?
- Why is there suffering in the world?

How do the responses fit into the following categories of world-view?

- specific confessional (Buddhist, Christian, Hindu, Islamic, Jewish, Sikh, etc.);
- liberal universalist;
- agnostic;
- atheist;
- postmodern non-realist.

By completing this activity pupils (or student teachers) may be able both to identify with a particular world-view and to recognise how their world-views relate to others. This in turn may help you to plan introducing pupils to an understanding of a range of world-views. Discuss your results/findings with other student teachers and go on to identify their implications for your planning for teaching.

Creating a glossary

The simplest thing is to ensure that you write the words on the board for all to see. The words should be there at the beginning of the lesson to allow you and the pupils to focus on them. Alternatively, write them up as you go along or have them written on the worksheet you give them. You have to decide whether you want the words to have definitions on the board or the sheets or whether you want to teach pupils the definition as you go along. The pupils should be encouraged to build up their own glossary of terms in their books and you should provide regular opportunities both in the lessons and in their written work to check the appropriateness of the usage. This procedure encourages pupils' confidence in the use of religious language and accuracy in lessons, particularly in discussion work. It may also familiarise them with the necessity of accuracy in terminology when there is ambiguity of religious understanding, as well as alert them to the possible ambiguity of religious terminology!

Task 5.3 Exploring approaches to religious language in the classroom

Observe three or four lessons on different religious topics and throughout each lesson list the subject-specific religious language used by the teacher and/or the pupils. Analyse the words you have listed in the light of the following questions:

● Are the pupils given a definition of specific religious language at any point in the lesson? Is the correct spelling taught?
● Does the teacher assume an understanding of the religious language?
● Can you assess whether the pupils understand the terminology being used?
● In what way does the teacher ensure that the pupils understand and use religious language appropriately?
● Is there a list up, either on the board or somewhere in the room, of difficult or new or significant religious words?
● Do the pupils have a glossary of terms in their books?
● Are the pupils encouraged to use the religious language in discussion, either with each other or in groups?

Write a summary of your findings focusing on the implications you feel you should draw for your own teaching and lesson planning.

Language at each Key Stage

Once you have recognised the need for such attention to the detail of language, you must be able to identify what material is relevant to each Key Stage. Given that there are so many textbooks written for each stage, it is important to familiarise yourself with the resources available on a particular topic. Information is available through your teaching practice school, your IHE, the local RE Centre, the local Advisory Service and specialist bookshops.

Task 5.4 Preparing to address language issues during your teaching

Obtain and familiarise yourself with a copy of the policy on the use of religious language in your RE department, if one exists.

Initiate your own personal glossary of key religious terminology.

Obtain for your records a copy of the *SCAA Religious Education Glossary of Terms*, published by the School Examination Council (SEC) in 1986; this material is now appended to some Agreed Syllabuses and is available on the WWW: http://www.learninglive.co.uk/teachers/re/religious_education/Syllabus.pdf.

THE HERMENEUTICS OF RE

There are a number of methodological models on offer for the teaching of RE (a representative number of which will be discussed below). As a professional RE teacher you have to decide what your aims are for your scheme of work and decide which model (or combination of models) is best equipped to achieve those aims. Each model adopts a particular view of the learning–understanding process, each has its specific hermeneutical programme to explain and interpret the nature of religion (basically hermeneutics is the science of interpretation), and each uses language in a particular manner.

The phenomenological model

The phenomenological model, popular in the 1970s and 1980s, and still alive today, requires the teacher and the pupil to be objective in the study of the topic in hand. Phenomenological RE is concerned with providing pupils with the skill and insight necessary to properly understand and think about religion. Pupils must examine religion by suspending their own judgement in order to appreciate the issues from the believer's point of view. In this way they are taught to gain a form of knowledge of the faith perspective which enables them to identify distinguishing characteristics of the faith, how it is celebrated and how it is unique to the worshipping community. Thus the pupils 'learn about' religion (Grimmitt 1973).

It is acknowledged that in order to understand religion it is not enough merely to know the 'facts'. Authentic learning requires giving the pupil the opportunity to learn what it is to 'step into the shoes' of a believer. It is important then to have knowledge and understanding of the factual elements of the feast of Passover in Judaism, but it is also important for a pupil to understand what it must actually feel like to be the Jew celebrating Passover. Empathy stands at the heart of phenomenological RE, and without it RE is reduced to mere rote learning.

To teach in this way requires neutrality from both the teacher and the pupil and is a direct reaction against the 'confessional' aims of RE. Rather than have syllabuses which train pupils to be good Christians, the phenomenological approach encourages pupils to identify commonalities in both religious language and religious experience. Indoctrination and bias are to be avoided. The underlying view of religion in phenomenology is that of the universality of truth: all religions are equal and should be examined objectively. This is significant because the emergence of the phenenological approach to RE surfaced at the same time as the new umbrella discipline of 'Religious Studies' won its place in higher education and at the same time as the multi-faith and multicultural nature of the UK was finally being recognised.

It is also significant that the phenomenological approach stems from an understanding of language as a means of identifying or labelling something. This model of language has its roots in empiricism. Empirical knowledge of the world is the result of our sense experience, and of our ability to use language to describe that experience. An extreme form of empiricism is logical positivism, a heavily influential (though now largely discredited) philosophical movement allied to scientism. For the positivist only that which can be verified by the senses, and then labelled through language, can have meaning. Consequently, any talk of God is quite literally meaningless: since we cannot experience God through any of our five senses, we have no way of verifying whether language describing such experience is true or false, and as a result we treat it as mere nonsense.

Positivism must not be confused with phenomenology, since the phenomeno-logical concern for empathy and the recognition of the essence of observed phenomena are far more sophisticated than positivist approaches to knowledge. Nevertheless the empiricist strain remains influential in the phenomenological study of religion. Study of religion has more to do with describing and empathising with religious culture than asking theological questions about the nature and reality of God. Smart (1973) listed the phenomenological description of religion under six categories: doctrinal, mythological, ethical, ritual, experiential and social. This struc-tured description allows appreciation of the commonalities of religious viewpoints and life stances. Strictly speaking, the essence of religious phenomena, that which holds them together and allows us to label them 'religious', is their concern for the divine or transcendent realm. Thus, when the first major phenomenological RE syllabus, the 1979 Birmingham Agreed Syllabus, included the study of humanism as a quasi-religious life stance, it actually departed from strict phenomenological descrip-tion. This is important, illustrating how easily phenomenological RE can slip into mere empirical description of religious and quasi-religious culture.

It is crucial in RE that the subject matter is approached from the child's horizon. This key insight reflects the legacy of the work of Goldman (1965) and Loukes (1961), and especially their insistence that effective learning must always link up with the experiences of the learner. Ideas, beliefs, opinions and thoughts about religion need to be aired by the pupils in our RE classrooms, using the appropriate religious language, in order for clarity of understanding to take place. The acquisition of the type of factual information advocated by the phenomenological model is important and necessary, but there is evidence to suggest that the focus on phenomenology as a model for delivering RE does not encourage the acquisition of higher-order thinking skills (Kerry 1980). If this is the case, pupils are not trained in skills to interact critically and reflectively with complex religious concepts and issues. Pupils become content with simple characterisations and binary opposi-tions: all religions believe in God; religion is either a force for good or a force for evil. The ambiguous nature of religions is overlooked, as are the differences between them.

The spirituality model

The emphasis on the 'experience' of the pupil as the starting point of effective RE, coupled with the awareness that badly taught phenomenological RE descends to the level of mere description, leads some teachers to pursue a 'spiritual' or 'experiential' model of RE. This model was comprehensively introduced to teachers of RE through the work of David Hay (Hay 1985; Hammond *et al.* 1990). Hay argues that the empirical world-view, so dominant in the phenomenological model, was not addressing the actual experience of many people in the world. If God could not be proved to exist, according to the logical positivist, then why was religion not dying out? Why did Hay's research (1982) suggest that 'experiences of the spiritual' were closer to being the norm than the exception to the norm? Religious and spiritual experiences flourish, Hay suggests, but we have lost the language that would enable us to explore and make sense of such experience. Yet the commonality of spiritual or religious experience led Hay to conclude that this experience is what makes us inherently human.

This thesis provided a new rationale for RE and gave the subject new impetus in the mid-1980s, one that flourishes today in many classrooms. The commonality of spiritual experience provides the perfect communal horizon from which to teach a form of RE that goes beyond mere description and penetrates to the experiential heart of religion. The evidence of the public acknowledgement of spiritual experiences gathered by Hay is believed to provide a ready-made defence of the validity of the subject. Thus RE functions to affirm and nurture spiritual experiences and also acts as a framework for understanding them. There is to be no suggestion by the teacher that these experiences should lead pupils to adhere to any specific faith system. The purpose of this model of RE is to acknowledge, share and experience the commonality of the phenomena of religious experience. The importance of beginning with the pupil's horizon remains paramount, as does recognition that each faith system is valid. If emphasis is going to be placed on the validity of the individual's experience of the spiritual, little validity is given to the integrity of worshipping communities. It is this factor which lays the spiritual model open to most criticism (Thatcher 1991). Despite criticism the spirituality model still has supporters, chiefly because it is regarded by some as reflecting government concern for the spiritual domain of education (see QCA 2004: 14).

The problem with this model, particularly in terms of religious language, is the danger of equating religious understanding with 'experience'. This means that feelings or emotions can dictate the religious content being studied. Thus spiritual RE is in constant danger of slipping over into 'emotivism', the philosophical doctrine that what I feel within is what is actually real. Take the example of the Jewish Passover. To understand the message of the Passover is to reflect on the freedom bestowed on the Israelites who were being held as slaves in Egypt. Simply to reflect on the abstract experience of freedom, though, cannot do justice to the Jewish understanding of the Passover, especially when viewed – as it now inevitably must be – in the light of the Holocaust. There is a limitation in dwelling on the experience of freedom, which prevents insight into what it means to be a Jew, to hold certain teachings as sacred and to live by those teachings. The danger in the spiritual model is that it ignores the importance of a coherent religious world-view which gives life and substance to an otherwise individualistic, abstract and merely emotive experience. A stress on emotive experience does not allow the question of truth in the religious context to be addressed, because truth here is by definition individual, not linked to an external system of authority.

This model thus builds on the expressive element of the phenomenological model and emphasises what it means for the Jew to celebrate Passover by equating this form of celebration with that which is familiar to the pupil. The perspective of the individual gives validity to the religious experience. This model can be traced back to Romanticism, a movement which threw off the constraints of a scientific world-view to focus on the meaning of what it was to be uniquely human, to think, to feel, to experience. The essence of the spiritual model of RE is to get underneath the outward phenomena of religion and focus on the spiritual experience (Chapter 10, in this volume). Language operates as a means of bringing inner experience to expression. To understand such language one must pass beyond mere words and enter the emotive worlds that are their real source. Consequently, lessons in spiritual RE are concerned to encourage pupils to use their imagination and their creativity, hence the importance of creative tasks (Hammond *et al.* 1990).

The critical realist model

Here we are concerned with a third possibility, moving beyond phenomenology and spirituality. Critical realism is a philosophy concerned to explore the true nature of reality. It accepts that there is a world out there open to investigation, and recognises that human beings are at least partially capable of being able to make sense of it. They do so through a range of interpretative methods, including – but not exclusively – natural science, that use language in a complex manner to achieve increasingly complex descriptions of a complex world.

When RE draws on critical realism it does so because it is concerned for religious truth, and believes that both phenomenology and spirituality, unduly influenced by a fear of confessionalism, have bypassed this crucial issue. It attempts to build on the best traditions of that which has gone before. The pupil's horizon does need to be the starting point of learning, factual information must be gained if pupils are going to discuss religion meaningfully, empathetic understanding of a person's faith and spiritual experience is paramount in these discussions, religion is a phenomenon common to all humankind whatever the components of the belief system, whether humanistic or religious.

The difference is that the world-view underpinning the critical realist model takes seriously all the claims to 'truth' made by the world religions and secular groups. These truth claims address that grappling with reality which is at the very heart of our existence. Such engagement with the universe leads to the construction of stories and narratives which seek to retell the story of the way things actually are in the world. Since there is a plurality of secular and religious narratives, we have to deal with the ambiguities of this quest for meaning and truth.

Pupils in the RE class are invited to define their current world-view and are given appropriate language with which to discuss, debate, question and thus understand it better. At the same time they must learn to engage with the narratives of alternative secular and religious traditions. The only way they have of finding their way through this maze of options is to develop the appropriate linguistic skills whereby they can enter into intelligent conversation with adherents of a range of world-views. Being religiously educated is all about developing religious literacy. Mere knowledge of religious culture, or mere sensitivity towards spiritual experience, important as both are, simply do not go far enough.

Some would argue that the critical realist model is too difficult and challenging for pupils, for it requires not only an emphasis on religious vocabulary but also on the differences within and between religions. But surely the time has come to focus on the complexities of religion and not to present idealised pictures of religions and relations between religions that are falsified by experience. We need to capitalise on the growing awareness pupils have of religious issues, which are increasingly commanding press attention, and on their experience of religious education in the primary school. The critical realist model chooses to deal with the explicit differences between religions, as pupils already know that there are differences. They know, too, that tension exists within the Christian Church; and that tension exists between the Sikh community and the Muslim community in Britain. They know that ethnic cleansing still goes on in the world. They deserve an opportunity to be more widely informed, to be able to understand 'fundamentalism' in all its guises in order to make an informed decision on religious issues. They already have a world-view on some of the most important ultimate questions in life. They deserve an opportunity to define their answers and recognise differences and similarities between themselves and others.

In the light of the three different models presented it is important to examine the use of subject-specific language in the types of lessons listed in Task 5.5. It is important to identify what measures are required to teach this type of language effectively. It is also important to note the aims of the various lessons and identify which type of lesson you wish to have and why. There is a sense in which the different models advance different interpretations of the nature of religious language: the phenomenological model tends to underline the similarities between religions and their vocabularies; the spirituality model tends to look to the experience behind religious language; and the critical realist model tends to focus on the actual vocabulary of believers and the beliefs they express in their use of religious vocabulary.

Task 5.5 Language use in the RE classroom: practical examples

Examples follow of how language may typically operate in each of the three models of RE. They are based on the delivery of the story of the creation of the world in Genesis 1 as it functions within the Christian community, since that was one of the examples cited by Ofsted of repetitious and unchallenging tasks. The examples are offered not as 'models' of how to teach but rather as snapshots of how the three approaches tend to address specific issues and ignore others. It is important to address each example critically. It may help to ask yourself the following questions for each model:

- What is the subject-specific language that requires definition?
- To what extent do the learning outcomes of each model reflect the understanding(s) of the concept of creation within the Christian faith community?
- Do the learning outcomes take account of conceptions of the story held by those outside the Christian tradition?
- Do the learning activities address the complexities of the debate within and outside the Christian community, and of Christian/non-Christian dialogue?
- Where does the issue of the truth of the Christian doctrine of creation receive an airing?

The phenomenological model

Learning outcomes:

- familiarisation with the facts of the Genesis story;
- knowledge of what happened on each day;
- understanding of the concept of 'myth';
- identification of the nature of this creation myth in comparison with others already studied;
- recognition of the importance of the story to Jews, Christians and Muslims.

Learning activities:

- reading Genesis 1;
- listing what happened on each day;
- for homework, getting the pupils to divide their page into seven sections and illustrate what happened on each day;
- in class discussion, getting the pupils to identify the similarities with and differences from other creation myths they have studied, thereby reinforcing their understanding of the concept of 'myth' and enabling them to recognise why this story is important to Jews, Christians and Muslims.

The spirituality model

Learning outcomes:

- familiarisation of the pupils with the facts of the Genesis story;
- knowledge of what happened on each day;
- understanding of the concept of 'myth';
- identification of the nature of this creation myth in comparison with others already studied;
- reflection on, and sensitivity towards, the wonder of creation.

Learning activities:

- reading Genesis 1;
- listing what happened on each day;
- for homework, getting pupils to: write their own creation myth; or produce a poem about how wonderful creation is; or draw up a poster for a wall display entitled 'The Mystery of Creation';
- in class discussion asking, 'What kind of world did God create?', 'What kind of world would you create if you were God?'

The critical realist model

Learning outcomes:

- familiarisation of the pupils with the facts of the Genesis story;
- knowledge of what happened on each day;
- understanding of the nature of the story as it operates within the Christian community;
- acknowledgement of the contention between liberals and conservatives within Christianity regarding the nature of the Genesis story;
- recognition of alternative, possibly negative, non-Christian interpretations of the myth;

(Continued)

- grappling with the truth of the story: what it says about who God is; what it says about the created order; what it says about human beings;
- appreciation of the different viewpoints the pupils bring to the lesson.

Learning activities:

- reading Genesis 1;
- listing what happened on each day;
- identifying what the story teaches about God, the created order and human beings;
- recognising the literary genre of the story, i.e. mythical poetry rather than bad science;
- introducing or eliciting the Christian interpretation(s) of the story;
- comparison with alternative non-Christian interpretations;
- exploring class opinions as to the veracity of the myth, and the origins of the universe.

You may feel that the tasks described in the critical realist model are too academic and do not reflect the expressive range and emotive nature of religion. However, engaging pupils in such intellectual stimulation can only succeed in bringing the subject to life. Looking from a contrasting perspective, I would argue that a primary reason for many pupils' negative attitude towards RE is indeed the result of a lack of intellectual challenge. Our pupils are bored not because religion itself is inherently boring but because the manner in which we as teachers present it, devoid of conflict, danger and intellectual stimulus, is inherently boring. In adopting the critical realist model you should soon discover that the nature of the informed discussion, which begins to take place in the classroom, spills out into the corridors because pupils are debating the nitty-gritty issues of life.

SUMMARY AND KEY POINTS

This chapter has attempted both to unpack the key issues surrounding the place of language in the RE classroom and to review some of the methodological models that are used by religious educators. Our focus fell on the different interpretation of religious language that each model presupposes. While a preference has been expressed for a critical realist model, this should not pre-judge your own evaluation of the issues. Each model has something valuable to contribute to religious education. It is your responsibility as a professional teacher is to adopt appropriate methods of teaching that enable pupils to develop their religious literacy.

FURTHER READING

Fisher, R. (1998) *Teaching Thinking: Philosophical Enquiry in the Classroom*, London: Cassell. Central to this chapter has been the notion of critical thinking as the process at the centre of RE. Although Fisher's book is not directly concerned with RE, the application of his work to the development of religious literacy is obvious.

Geaves, R. (2006) *Key Words in Religious Studies*, London: Continuum. Accessible and useful guide to religious vocabulary.

Grimmitt, M. (1973) *What Can I Do in RE?*, Essex: Mayhew-McCrimmon. This seminal work should not be passed over simply because of its relative age. It outlines the rationale behind phenomenological RE and provides many practical and stimulating examples of the place of language in the RE classroom.

Grimmitt, M. (ed.) (2000) *Pedagogies of Religious Education: Case Studies in the Research and Development of Good Pedagogic Practice in RE*, Essex: McCrimmon Publishing. Outlines a range of methodologies, implicit in which is their account of the importance and nature of religious language.

Hammond, J., Hay, D., Moxon, J., Netto, B., Raban, K., Straugheir, G. and Williams, C. (1990) *New Methods in RE Teaching*, Harlow: Oliver & Boyd. Stimulating and accessible, this ever popular book examines the practical means by which to engage with the spiritual-experiential model.

Wright, A. (1993) *Religious Education in the Secondary School: Prospects for Religious Literacy*, London: David Fulton. Another seminal work which is suspicious of much current practice in RE and advocates an RE rooted in the development of religious literacy.

6 Assessment in Religious Education

John Rudge

Assessment is a challenging part of your professional role. Provided you are prepared to grapple with it, and don't simply try to find the easiest way round it, it pays dividends in terms of your developing professionalism as a teacher of RE. But it is a complex area. Assessment is not an exact science and only certain things can be professionally assessed in schools. Unfortunately the culture of regarding assessment as testing pupils' powers of recall is deeply and traditionally ingrained in our schools, in examinations, and especially in the expectations of many of our pupils and their parents. We need to stand a long way back from this approach and take stock of what we really ought to be trying to do.

The thinking that underlies this traditional view of assessment runs something along the following lines: 'I am the teacher, and you are the pupil. I have the information you need to pass your test and get a good grade, and you haven't! I make up packages of information, and give them to you. You must learn them, as best you can, and then I test you to see if you remember what I have taught you. If you can reproduce the information I have given you, you get good marks and a high grade. Of course, if you have a good memory, you have a head start over the others, and quickly rise to the top.'

It doesn't really matter how sophisticated the information packages provided by the teacher actually are. It may be the names of five religious festivals or a summary of the development of Wittgenstein's philosophical ideas. Learning is reduced to lumps of information which are ingested and swallowed, without being digested, processed and recycled. It is a model of teaching and learning in which the pupils are of secondary importance, information is mistaken for knowledge, recall is substituted for understanding and the prize goes to those with cameras and filing cabinets for memories. Questions about the value of the information, about how pupils might use it to enrich their understanding, and about how it might help them to develop as learners and people, are neither addressed nor assessed.

It is essential, from the start, that you move away from this kind of thinking about teaching, learning and assessment, which views the teacher as the active ingredient and the pupil as the passive recipient, with assessment bolted on at the end. Your focus for assessment must be on *the quality of your pupils' learning*. That assessment is an essential part of pupils' learning should be self-evident. That is why the emphasis in schools is now on the idea of 'assessment *for* learning'. The reason it is given such prominence is that successful teaching and learning can take place only if you and your pupils are aware of what they are trying to achieve, how they are progressing, what they can do to improve and whether they are getting the most from you as their teacher. All these things depend on finding out how they are getting on and helping them to develop. That is what assessment is for.

The argument in this chapter is that if you keep a broad and open view of what assessment is and grapple with the issues, if you follow a few basic guidelines, and if you are both systematic and flexible in your practical approach to assessment, you quickly find that it is rewarding both for the pupils as learners and for yourself as a teacher.

OBJECTIVES

By the end of this chapter, you should be able to:

- be aware of the key issues surrounding assessment in RE;
- understand some of the principles of assessing pupils which you need to follow as a teacher;
- be familiar with practical strategies for dealing with assessment during your school experience, and beyond.

ASSESSING, TEACHING AND LEARNING

Why do we assess pupils?

Assessment may serve a number of purposes. The popular view, often central in the minds of pupils and their parents, is that we assess pupils to give them a mark and grade them by their results. That is what exams are for. It is usually called *summative* assessment, or assessment *of* learning, but it is not the only, or the main reason, for assessing pupils. As a teacher, your main focus should be on formative assessment, or assessment for learning; that is, assessing pupils in order to help them in their learning. There can be a number of helpful outcomes from assessing pupils. It could tell you where they are starting from, for example the learning they bring with them at the beginning of Year 7, or what they remember at the beginning of a lesson from their last lesson. It can help you in finding out what they have learned, for example, from a series of quick and progressively more difficult oral questions around the class at the end of a lesson. This procedure can help to establish whether pupils have made progress during the lesson, whether they understand, enjoy and benefit from your lessons, and what needs to be done to improve them. This in turn helps you plan the next lessons. Was the lesson too difficult? Were its learning outcomes met in full or in part? What was the quality of learning for pupils of *all* abilities? A formal task at the conclusion to a unit of work could give pupils a chance to see how much progress they have made, what they found difficult and how they could improve. It could give you a clear idea of pupils' progress over time, whether the topic really stimulated their learning, whether they are ready to move on to a more demanding topic or whether some further reinforcement of ideas is needed.

It is only formative assessment which benefits the pupils directly in their learning. It is usually focused on the continuing assessment of pupils' progress in the classroom at regular intervals, and deals with immediate issues they are exploring and their developing understanding of their work. Unlike summative assessment, it involves *feeding back* to pupils information, comments, judgements and suggestions which helps them recognise what they have done well, how much progress they have made and how they can improve and progress further. Summative assessments, like SATs and GCSEs, are not designed to help pupils learn but to inform other people – teachers, parents, employers, curriculum planners and policy-makers – about what pupils have achieved at a particular point in their development. The pupils do not receive feedback, though if afterwards they received their papers back, there may be a great deal they, and you, could learn.

It is worth remembering that the root meaning of assessment is derived from a Latin word which carries the sense of *sitting down beside*. That is an important quality for the teacher to reflect on. It implies that there is a kind of learning contract between pupil and teacher, that when teachers give feedback to pupils they are supporting them in their learning. It reminds us that, in assessing pupils' work, you are trying to encourage and reward positive achievement, however limited, rather than accentuating a sense of non-achievement. Only in that way can you begin to dismantle the culture of failure which can easily dominate the lives of pupils and put them off schooling altogether.

It is worth reflecting on how assessment *for* learning is used in your own Initial Teacher Education course, how you are assessed to help you learn to be a teacher. Before you even begin your course, your knowledge and understanding of religions and of RE are assessed to establish *where you are starting from*. That should help your tutor to ensure that the course outline is likely to meet your needs and ensure your progress, and to make *adjustments to their planned programme of learning*. You may be asked to complete a pre-course task to *bring you up to speed* and to assess *your ability (and willingness!) to learn*. When you complete a school-based task or write an essay or give a presentation, your tutor gives you *feedback*, in their capacity as a *critical friend*. When you are assessed through *observation* during school experience, you receive comments, criticisms and suggestions from your tutor. Your *progress* is assessed through *reviews, audits and tutorials*. You actually learn from these assessments. They are a means of helping you to make progress by *making judgements* about where you are up to, and *setting targets* for your further progress. Tutors in both your school and IHE are all the time making *informed* judgements about your progress and feeding them back to you. You are also being asked to *evaluate your own progress* as part of the assessment process. At the end of the course there is no formal examination, and no judgement is made about how you have fared in relation to your fellow pupils. However, a judgement is made – a very difficult *professional* judgement for your tutors and other examiners to make – as to whether you have *achieved the standards* expected of a newly qualified teacher. This decision is based both on your progress during the course and on your attainment by the end of it, and much of the *evidence* comes from the formative assessments made throughout the course.

It is worth noting the key words italicised in the last paragraph. They represent most of the key ideas associated with assessment for learning. When you are fully conversant with your role in assessing pupils, you should be able to translate all these (italicised) terms into actual classroom practice. You might reflect on this when you assess pupils in school, where the pressure always to be putting them in rank order can be very strong. The competitive interpretation of and approach to learning and assessment, treating competition with peers as a spur to learning, are highly debatable, both in its intention and its outcome, as well as in its value.

What are we assessing in RE?

You must be clear what achievement you are trying to assess in RE. You may think this is so self-evident that it should not need to be stated. It is, however, lack of clarity about medium-term and short-term goals, about lesson objectives and proposed learning outcomes, where many of the difficulties about assessment arise. Setting appropriate and focused objectives for learning in your lessons is one of the most important skills you need to acquire. If your objectives (expressed in terms of learning outcomes) are too general and ill-defined or much too demanding (or too easy), the rest of your lesson planning falls apart, and you become unclear about what you are trying to assess; and if you are unclear, then your pupils may also be unclear. It is always a useful and salutary experience to share your objectives with your pupils at the beginning of each lesson, preferably in pupil-speak.

Merely remembering information is not an adequate goal. Once the principle is established that education is about the pupils, about what is of value to them and about what contributes to their spiritual, moral, cultural and intellectual development, you have to come up with something better than mere rote memorisation. This brings us to the heart of the matter, and to some of the key issues surrounding the nature of education itself:

- What is this knowledge we want pupils to have in RE?
- What does knowledge mean, as a quality beyond memorised information?
- How does this knowledge help the pupils to understand? Is it the same as understanding?
- How do we expect this understanding to enrich pupils in their own development as persons? By accident, osmosis or design?
- Given that RE involves evaluation as well as understanding, how are we to assess whether they really have understood and acquired the ability and sensitivity to evaluate?

- How can we know that they know?
- How accurate and reliable is our judgement, and what is the evidence on which we base that judgement?

This is not an exercise in academic semantics. We have to begin here if assessment is to be a useful part of teaching and learning. However, the issues are the same right across the curriculum, so you must not feel that you are alone in trying to grapple with these issues, or that RE is in some way an educational oddity.

To clarify the achievements we are concerned with in RE, it may help to reflect on where the subject stands in relation to the kinds of achievements expected across the curriculum as a whole. These may be divided into three broad categories. The first deals with attainments we may describe as practical skills. These would include such things as reading maps, writing legibly and playing a scale on a musical instrument. These are skills of the *can do* type. A second group of attainments is concerned with the development of cognitive abilities, mainly of the *knowing and understanding* kind. These could include such attainments as knowing that the weather profoundly affects people's lives (science), or understanding the difference between change and progress (history). A third group of attainments is concerned with the development of *personal qualities, beliefs and values*. These could include such qualities as being sensitive to the living and non-living environment (science), or beginning to be self-critical about one's own beliefs (RE). A balanced schooling is going to include all three categories of attainment.

Which category of attainments comes closest to what we understand RE to be about? The answer is likely to lie somewhere in the second and third categories, with some differences of emphasis, depending on your view of RE. There is rarely anything in RE that corresponds to the kind of achievements in the first category, important though they are in other areas of the curriculum. Broadly speaking, those who see RE as essentially to do with the objective study of religions tend to emphasise cognitive abilities, while those who want to see the main purpose of RE as focused on personal development stress the third group of qualities. The new *Non-Statutory Framework for Religious Education* (QCA 2004) offers a fair and informed balance between the two.

It is important to recognise that the different categories of attainment presuppose different approaches to assessment. With the first category, interpreting assessment as *measuring and testing* is appropriate. It is not appropriate for the other two categories. One of the key issues in the National Curriculum has been the pressure from certain quarters to try to make the overall pattern of assessment conform to this measuring and testing model. It leads to the naïve conclusion that if you can't measure it objectively, it is of no value. However, this model does not fit all, or even most, of the curriculum. We need to broaden our concept of assessment, rather than reduce education to what can be measured and tested. The broader concept of assessment includes a variety of ways of finding out and gathering evidence, less precise and more subjective criteria for making judgements, the value of the teacher's own professional awareness, and the views of the pupils themselves about their own development and progress.

If we apply these principles to RE, the most straightforward route to defining what we are trying to assess in RE would appear to lie in keeping the goals simple, not trying to be too sophisticated. This can be done by seeing RE as concerned primarily, but not exclusively, with two broad attainments which, for the sake of argument, we refer to as 'understanding' and 'evaluation'. We consider each of these in turn.

Understanding in RE

For practical purposes, you may find it easier to use *understanding* rather than *knowing*. The point has already been made that knowledge, to have any value, has to refer to something more than (memorised) information. The information is only of value if it is placed in a context with other information, and organised to give it some coherence. Otherwise it simply remains a trivial pursuit. Once information has been contextualised, it is given meaning by being related to ideas and concepts which provide the basis for understanding. Understanding is shown when information from different contexts is used as an example or illustration to explain an idea or concept. In RE, the concern with meaning should be paramount. For example, in studying the five pillars of Islam in KS3, it is important that pupils grasp both the context of the practices within Islam and their meaning for Muslims. To do so, they need to relate the practice of the five pillars to the concept of *ibadah*, or service (to Allah). They begin to show understanding of the five pillars when they can explain how the practice of giving *zakah*, for example, reflects the principle of *ibadah* and purifies the wealth of the giver.

Assessing whether pupils have understood something, as distinct from simply remembering what they have been told, involves setting them a task based on a situation, context or example which is unfamiliar to them, so that they have to deploy and apply what they have learned in a new way. This 'unfamiliarity principle' is an essential foundation of good assessment in RE.

Suppose you want to find out what a group of Year 8 pupils have learned from a visit to a synagogue. What they get out of the visit depends, of course, on how you have structured the visit as an educational exercise, how you prepared them for the visit and the follow-up work you did in class afterwards, and what you intended the visit to achieve. You could test them by asking them the names of the various things they saw in the synagogue. Or you could ask them, in a general kind of way, to describe their visit. Both those tasks could produce little more than recall of isolated pieces of information. Yet even in their descriptions there is likely to be evidence of some understanding through their choice of what to describe, or how to describe it, or the way they make links between what they have seen and what they have already learned. They may even include personal reflections which go well beyond mere description and show some genuine insight. The problem is that the task is not demanding enough, and does not actually invite some of these responses.

If, on the other hand, following the visit and further work in class, they are given the task of producing a guide to the synagogue, for a group who have not yet made the visit, explaining what makes it a Jewish building, and what they may gain from their visit, we are moving closer to what we mean by understanding. Now they need to select and deploy some of the information they have gathered and apply what they have learned to a new situation. Of course they may remember that the reading desk from which the Jewish scriptures are read is called the Bimah, but such recall of information is not really the object of the exercise. Though interesting, the ability to label religious artefacts is not essential to an authentic understanding of Judaism. On the other hand, a focus on the synagogue as Bet Tefillah would enable pupils to show their understanding of worship in Judaism, and give them the opportunity to show how the furnishings and appearance of the synagogue – the 'pieces of information' – are linked together.

Evaluation in RE

The issues come even more sharply into focus if we include the development of personal qualities, beliefs and values within the scope of our view of assessment. The concept of evaluation is used as shorthand for the assessment of this very subjective element. It is an inadequate but useful concept provided it is used in its root meaning. To evaluate something is to assess its value: in the context of RE it has to do with pupils thinking about the value *for themselves* of what they are learning about the beliefs, values and actions of others. This is what 'learning *from*' is all about. It is a reflective quality.

There are some who object to using assessment in this way. One objection is that it is impossible to assess such a subjective area of the curriculum, however justified the goals may be in educational terms. Therefore, we should not even attempt to do so. It has, however, already been argued that we need to broaden our concept of assessment beyond measurement and testing, beyond the elusive quest for total objectivity. Formative assessment, which involves many different ways of finding out how pupils are progressing, and includes as much feedback as possible to the pupils, together with evidence gleaned from pupil self-assessments, is appropriate to these educational goals.

A second objection needs careful thought, especially in RE. Some argue that we should not assess this area because it concerns the personal beliefs, values and attitudes of the pupils. These matters are their concern, not ours. It is no business of ours to enquire into the private lives of the pupils. There are important issues behind this argument, and it is useful to have some ground rules to keep us from the pitfalls. It is not, for example, appropriate to assess matters which pupils may wish to keep to themselves. Pupils should never be pressed to disclose personal or private information, and no assessment or judgement should be made of their willingness or unwillingness to do so. It is also inappropriate to assess whether pupils' own beliefs and values are right or wrong. While discussion of these matters forms part of the ongoing debate of the classroom, they are not issues for assessment. This supports the principle that RE should be open to pupils of any religious persuasion or of none.

On the other hand, pupils' developing beliefs and values are an essential part of the material of RE, and in the classroom the pupils are encouraged to share their ideas with others, and to enter into discussion of often controversial issues. Without this dimension RE has no *existential bite*, and is robbed of its relevance to the pupils. A formative pattern of assessment provides a fitting context in which pupils' development in this area can be encouraged, provided that it is dealt with sensitively by a caring and thoughtful teacher. When it comes to making more formal judgements about the quality of pupils' work, teachers should base their conclusions on the evidence that pupils provide, from what they say or write or show in other ways. Even though they should not make judgements about whether pupils are right or wrong, they can give feedback on the quality and scope of the arguments they use, the range of evidence they put forward to support their viewpoint, and the clarity with which they express their ideas. These are proper matters for assessment, as they are for any educational discourse, and have now featured for some time in GCSE courses, for example. We should not be afraid that subjectivity enters into our judgements; the teacher's professional judgement enters into all assessments.

We might therefore envisage a situation where a group of Year 10 pupils has been addressing the issue of vegetarianism. Following discussion, guidance from the teacher, a visit from a local farmer and some work in small groups looking at various aspects of the issue, a task is set in which the pupils are invited to react to a picture of a Jain monk with a brief description of his particular beliefs and practices related to non-violence (which they have not seen before). The unfamiliarity principle is again applied. In assessing the responses, the teacher is not making comments about whether the pupils are right or wrong in their final judgements. The teacher comments on the clarity with which pupils have expressed their viewpoints, how far evidence and argument have been used to support their position, what examples or illustrations have been given to elaborate their viewpoint; and because this is an RE topic, the teacher also comments on the use they made of what they learned about the different religious and moral positions that they discussed in class, on how far they show awareness of viewpoints different from their own, and on the insight they show into the religious and moral dimensions of the issue.

Much emphasis has been placed on the 'unfamiliarity principle' in assessing both understanding and evaluation. This principle requires pupils to deploy and apply what they have learned to new situations, contexts or examples. It this way their learning is extended and new insights are gained.

As a student teacher, and subsequently throughout your teaching career, you need to keep returning to the issues raised in the first part of this chapter, and to rethink how you should approach them in the light of your practical experience. But you also need to be aware of some of the practical possibilities and constraints of the learning situation. These are examined briefly in the second part of this chapter.

PRACTICAL CONSIDERATIONS

Assessment and planning

In your own teaching, assessment must play a central and integral role. It begins with your planning. Whatever lesson plan outline you use, it must always include your objectives, what you want the pupils to learn or to achieve, and hence your objectives are the same as the learning outcomes: 'by the end of the lesson, pupils understand why the Buddha's enlightenment is important for Buddhists today' or '. . . be able to evaluate the view that desire is the cause of suffering'. Your learning outcomes or objectives, in contrast with your general aim for the lesson, which is broader, should be assessable. Whatever means you use, you should be able, on the basis of evidence, to make a judgement whether your learning outcomes have been achieved, for yourself and for the pupils.

Getting your learning outcomes and objectives right and ensuring that you have achieved them is a skill that comes gradually. It is probably best to start with simple, straightforward and uncomplicated outcomes for each lesson or unit of work, and to keep them few in number. What you want pupils to understand and evaluate is a good place to start. Every lesson should provide some opportunity for pupils to respond, that is, to say or do something that helps you to see whether they have achieved the learning outcomes. You should carefully evaluate your success in this area, by reflecting on your experience, and identifying the steps you need to take to improve. Rather than concluding that your lesson was 'good' or 'went well' or 'they seemed to enjoy it' (an important criterion, none the less), you need to ask yourself, on the basis of your evidence, whether your learning outcomes were the right ones or could have been more focused; whether the activities you planned were the best ones for your objectives. Did you in practice concentrate too much on one at the expense of the other(s)? Did you try to cram too much information into the lesson at the expense of your learning outcomes? A useful way to begin getting to grips with assessment is to study published assessment material. Task 6.1 invites you to look at your school's assessment policy and public examinations.

Task 6.1 Exploring your school's assessment policy

Before you start your practical teaching, familiarise yourself with the assessment policy and practice of your school. To help you do this, you could address these questions:

- What is the school's assessment policy?
- How is it applied to RE?
- How do other RE teachers assess pupils?
- What kinds of tasks are the pupils given to do?
- What sort of comments are put on their work?
- How do the assessments help them formatively?

You could also ask to see GCSE papers and marking schemes. Public examinations are no longer the secret they used to be, where an examiner would be lurking in the bushes to catch you out with a question which hadn't come up before, and to which only the examiners knew the right answer. You may find questions that vary in difficulty and are set according to prescribed and published criteria; and that there are rarely questions with simple right or wrong answers. Most examinations are now marked according to a published scale of 'levels of achievement', available to pupils and teachers alike, so that both know on what assessment is based. You can read more about this in Chapter 8 but it is worth absorbing the principles of assessment from the start.

You should also have a look at the Agreed Syllabus that is used in your area, to see if it gives any instructions or guidelines for assessment. Not all do. But most do indicate the achievements we should be expecting of pupils at each Key Stage, often in the form of statements of attainment. Statements of attainment are of paramount importance in developing your awareness of assessment in RE. They may be couched in general terms, but they should guide the planning of your teaching and your overall strategy of assessment. You should keep them in mind when you are planning how to develop a unit of work, and writing the objectives/learning outcomes for your lessons.

Tasks

The learning outcomes for each lesson contribute to the objectives you are trying to achieve over a longer period in a unit of work, which in turn contribute to the broad aims you have set for the unit. As a general rule, there should be at least one formal assessment task in each unit of work. 'Task' is a better concept than 'test'. It implies that the assessment is coherent and is given a context, and does not necessarily involve simply answering unconnected questions. The example given earlier, where pupils prepare a guide to a synagogue, represents this kind of task. As your skills develop, you should be able to make the contexts of the tasks more interesting and varied, at the same time ensuring that the substance of the task is likely to lead to the evidence of their understanding and evaluation that you are looking for. The 'unfamiliarity principle', through which you ask them to apply what they have learned to a new situation, needs to be introduced in each case.

Having set the task, you could break it down further to help them in their response. You could suggest some ideas for going about the task. You could give them an example outline. You could give them some questions to think about. You must check that they all understand what the task is! But you need to be careful that they do not take your example outline as the correct one, and that they do not regard your 'questions to think about' as a test. It is important to remember that we are not to use assessments to catch pupils out. We want them to have every chance to show what they can achieve.

Task 6.2 Planning for assessment

As you plan to teach a unit of work, prepare the outline of a task you could set the pupils to find out how well they have understood the topic. In your outline task you should try to include:

- interesting, stimulating or unusual context;
- material that enables pupils to show both their understanding and their ability to evaluate;
- the unfamiliarity principle: approaching the topic from a new angle;
- either some form of differentiation in the task itself or some indication of how you think different responses show different levels of achievement.

File the documents and results in your professional development portfolio as evidence of your ability to assess pupils (add further evidence as you gain experience to show your development).

Differentiation

Differentiation refers to the way in which teachers plan work for pupils of different levels of achievement and ability. Are assessment tasks appropriate to pupils with different aptitudes? What about those with particular learning difficulties? What about the very able ones who need stretching? It is important that they also have tasks to do which are not simply more of the same, but which challenge their under-standing and evaluative skills further. One of the ways of dealing with this issue of differentiation is through the way you teach the class as a whole, and individuals and groups within the class, through the resources you encourage them to use, and the speed at which you expect them to work. The teaching must benefit all the pupils, so that they all feel they are getting something out of it. Another way is to set different tasks, or tasks with different demands or expectations of pupils of different abilities. Another is to have the same process of learning for all the pupils, and to give them the same task, but in such a way that it produces different levels of outcome depending on the abilities of the pupils.

On the whole, it is this last method of differentiation which is most commonly used in assessment in a subject like RE. In differentiating by outcome, great care has to be taken in making sure that the task is accessible to all, and that it invites responses at different levels. The 'guide to the synagogue' task could be seen as appropriate for this purpose. Some pupils may simply describe what they saw, in a rather unstructured way. Others may offer some explanations. The most able may set their guide in the wider context of their understanding of Judaism and Jewish communities. But you would have to be sure that the task really triggered those different responses by giving some guidance – without giving them a model response. And you would need to think about those pupils in the class who found it difficult to express themselves through written work. Is there an alternative way in which they could offer a valid response? Perhaps they could respond through art work or through discussion!

Task 6.3 An exercise in participative assessment

During your early school experience, ask the class teacher if you can 'mark' a sample of pupil homeworks from the same class: do not write on their books but record your comments (and grade or mark if appropriate), then return the books to the class teacher to be marked. Compare your comments and results with that of the teacher and discuss the matters that arise.

Formal and informal assessment

You need to plan your formal task(s) at the same time as your objectives and activities, to ensure that they are coherent and consistent. Planning for assessment is essential in every lesson, and should be included on your lesson plan. Formal tasks are not, however, the only assessment you carry out during a unit of work. Assessment can take place in any context in any lesson. It can be done formally – for example, through a piece of written work which is marked – or informally – for example, through listening to a group of pupils discussing an issue you have raised, or through talking individually to a pupil. You are not, of course, 'testing' them, but you are listening for evidence of their understanding. Assessment can take place on any occasion when pupils express themselves in any way in relation to the stated objectives. Effective lessons always offer plenty of opportunities for expressing responses.

Listening carefully to pupils talking (assuming the talk is 'on task') provides a great deal of evidence as to whether your objectives are being met, and whether the pupils are in tune with you. The evidence is not structured but informal. That does not mean that it is merely accidental, even though some evidence can arise quite unintentionally. As your teaching skills develop, you can pick up all kinds of signals from the pupils that give you evidence about their understanding and evaluative abilities – and about your teaching when they are not on task! You learn to attune your ears to what is genuinely valuable evidence. This informal classroom feedback helps you to focus on the end of lesson plenary session and suggests questions to ask of the class. Such information also helps plan the next lesson. It may be useful to jot down ideas and evidence in a notebook as you relate and engage with pupils orally.

The device of a quick oral re-cap has already been mentioned. (Don't be too downhearted: it's probably a week since they last saw you.) There is no reason why you should not enquire whether they remember the name of the piece of furniture with three steps which they saw in the mosque or, come to that, what a *minbar* is. But good recap questions should be brief and get quickly to the heart of the matter, not focus on trivia. The questions should make them think as well as remember, for example, 'What do you think is the most important thing a visitor should know about a mosque?' To recap is a good way of using assessment diagnostically, and to reinforce learning.

Reference has already been made to another means of assessment which may at first seem a contradiction in terms. Self-assessment can play a useful and informative role in RE, especially in relation to some of the more sensitive aspects of the subject. It cannot be the only form of assessment but, used judiciously, it can produce valuable opportunities for feedback and gathering evidence, and provide a stimulus to pupils' thinking. It requires careful management by the teacher and you need to consult your tutor before venturing into this area of assessment.

Recording

Throughout this chapter the word 'evidence' has been used extensively. It is a key concept in the assessment process. It refers to the information we get from our assessments of pupils' progress. We need to retain some of that information, so that the conclusions we draw when we report to parents at the end of a year or a Key Stage are not just based on our memory, impression or intuition. Recorded evidence is essential for this purpose, and should ideally include information from a variety of assessment contexts.

Your starting point once again is the school and department's policy on record keeping, and to start with it is best to follow that guidance. Later on, there may be scope for experimenting. The traditional way is to have a 'mark book' and to record marks from formal written assessments during the year. You need to be careful that the process does not become an end in itself, so that you find yourself setting a test every two weeks so that your mark book is neatly filled up and looks impressive.

A better record would involve keeping in mind all the time the broad attainments you are hoping for in the pupils. What you need is good recorded evidence of those attainments. Of course, the results of formally assessed work provide some recorded evidence. But if you can regard a mark book as a flexible tool for recording evidence, you could use it for noting other evidence that might better contribute to an overall view of pupils' achievements. For example, you could keep (or, better still, keep a record of where to find) a pupil's best piece of work reflecting the attainments. Likewise, if you have carried out self-assessments, you could use a simple form to provide further evidence of achievement in more subjective areas. It is also worth leaving space in your book for recording more informal evidence that you may pick up at any time.

Let's suppose that Hussain is a quiet lad who doesn't say much in discussion. One day, in a discussion about marriage, he delivers a carefully worded and well thought out argument drawing attention to some of the advantages of arranged marriages and the disadvantages of 'falling in love', and he presents his arguments with evidence and with passion, and the rest of the class are stunned into silence. Here is probably one of the best bits of evidence you pick up during the year about Hussain's attainments, but it was unplanned and came out of the blue. You need to note that piece of evidence. If you don't, and all you have got are his test results, by the end of the year you may have forgotten his intervention, or that it was he who spoke out, and you have missed something important to the overall appraisal of his work. Alternatively, you may have noticed on a number of occasions that Kevin finds it very hard to listen to other pupils' opinions. He always tries to interrupt and not always coherently. That is also an important piece of evidence which can be noted in an appropriate way. Recording this kind of evidence does not imply that you are furiously writing down everything you hear in your mark book. It should be reserved for what is really significant, and experience guides you in how to discern that.

Reporting

Another skill closely related to the recording of evidence is writing reports. Your school tutor can guide you through the school's policy and practice, which can vary widely from school to school. Reporting includes giving a verbal report at parents' evenings. For this event you need to have your recorded evidence to hand. Your school experience should include an opportunity for you to write some reports, under supervision. Report writing is an art. You should ideally aim for a report which is succinct, based clearly on your recorded evidence, positive in tone, and tells the reader something about the pupil's attainment in RE, rather than just about whether they have worked hard and handed in their homework on time.

Task 6.4 Preparing a pupil report

Prepare a pupil report on two or three pupils in a class that you have taught for at least one unit of work. You might ask the class teacher if a parents evening is approaching and ask if you can draft such reports. Read the school's guideline on report writing and read also reports written by other teachers on (different) pupils. Share the contents of the draft reports with your class teacher. Use the reports as *aide-mémoires* if you attend the parents evening.

Levels of attainment

National Curriculum subjects now routinely use what are called *level descriptors* for reporting purposes. The level descriptions are paragraphs of prose setting out the kind of qualities and attainments likely to be shown by pupils of different abilities, arranged on a scale of levels, usually 1 to 8. The idea is that teachers look at the evidence they have collected, and then at the level descriptors, to decide which represents the 'best fit' as a description of what a particular pupil has achieved. RE is now moving strongly in the same direction, and this is being encouraged in most Local Authorities (LAs), but there is some catching up to be done here. Reporting needs to be based on how far, according to the evidence, you think pupils have progressed towards the achievements, using such categories as 'working towards' the attainments, 'achieving the targets' and, in a few cases, 'working beyond the targets'. In this way the descriptors also become a focus for target setting, because they indicate the kind of level of work expected at the next level. Much has been recently achieved in RE in developing level descriptors, and these are now part of the *Non-Statutory National Framework for RE* (QCA 2004).

Standards

One further factor you need to be aware of and thinking about is the concern for identifying and maintaining standards. The examination boards retain sample scripts from previous years representing various levels of achievement, or grades, so that they can compare standards from year to year. There is now a move in this direction to adopt a similar procedure in a more general way, so that schools have some idea of standards from year to year. It can be done in two ways. One is to take note of the guidance contained in published material, such as in the *Non-Statutory Framework for Religious Education* (QCA 2004). The other way, or an additional way, is to establish your own benchmarks in school, retaining some examples of assessed work which in your judgement are representative of particular levels of performance by the pupils in each Key Stage. You would probably need several years to build up and refine these

1.   Approach assessment as an essential part of teaching and learning.
2.   Encourage and reward positive achievement.
3.   Treat assessment primarily as a means of helping pupils to learn and to gather evidence of their progress.
4.   Always be clear as to what you are trying to assess.
5.   Base assessment tasks on the unfamiliarity principle.
6.   Remember that assessment can take place on any occasion when pupils express themselves in any way in relation to stated objectives.
7.   Base all assessment on professional judgement.

Figure 6.1 Seven basic rules of assessment

benchmarks, and such standards could never be absolute and definitive. They are simply another tool to help you to be as fair, balanced and consistent in your assessments and expectations as possible. (Inquire in your school experience school whether they have a bank of assessed work.) Of course, all assessment is based on professional judgement. Figure 6.1 states the seven basic rules of assessment.

SUMMARY AND KEY POINTS

The material in this chapter covers the basic requirements set out in the standards for Qualified Teacher Status (Training and Development Agency for Schools 2007) in relation to monitoring, assessment, recording, reporting and accountability, as they might be applied to RE. In addition, this chapter has highlighted some of the principles you need to bear in mind when you are assessing RE. The argument throughout has been that we need to break out of the narrow confines suggested by the processes of 'measuring and testing' into a broader concept of what assessment includes and entails.

Assessment is an aspect of teaching which should always be part of the ongoing cycle of curriculum development. It is so interwoven with the teaching and learning process that changes and reforms in one area inevitably impinge on the others. The challenge of assessment is that of responding to new pupils, new circumstances and to honing one's skills over time.

FURTHER READING

Black, P., Harrison, C., Lee, C., Marshall, B. and Wiliam, D. (2003) *Assessment for Learning: Putting It into Practice*, Buckingham: Open University Press. Explores assessment across the curriculum, and provide a useful starting point for RE teachers who want to develop a wider awareness of the matters raised in this chapter.

Capel, S., Leask, M. and Turner, T. (eds) (2005) *Learning to Teach in the Secondary School: A Companion to School Experience*, London: Routledge Falmer. Chapter 6 on assessment is a useful general resource.

Qualifications and Curriculum Authority (2004) *Non-Statutory National Framework for Religious Education*, London: QCA. Contains much that is relevant to assessment.

Torrance, H. and Prior, J. (1998) *Investigating Formative Assessment*, Buckingham: Open University Press. As the title suggests, this book looks in some depth at the possibilities and problems of formative assessment and provides a careful study of many of the issues that this approach raises.

Wintersgill, B. (2000) 'Task Setting in Religious Education at Key Stage 3: A Comparison with History and English,' *Resource*, 22(3). A brief but important account of HMI perceptions about the demands of RE tasks and their limitations in terms of suitability for KS3

7 Learning to teach Religious Education at Key Stage 4

Angela Wright

INTRODUCTION

> At Key Stages 3 and 4 one in five schools have raised pupils' achievement from satisfactory to good and at Key Stage 4 RE is the third most improved subject in terms of teaching and learning. On post-16 courses, RE stands out not only as the most improved subject, but that in which teaching and learning outstrip all others. There have also been significant improvements at Key Stage 4, which reflect changes in provision since 1997.
>
> (Ofsted 2005: 3)

Elsewhere in the same report it is stated:

> The motivation of gaining a qualification and the intrinsic interest of many examination courses has led to a major improvement to pupils' attitudes at Key Stage 4. Nearly 20,000 more pupils now take the full-course GCSE, while numbers entering for the short course have more than tripled. In turn, this has affected A-level entries, which have increased by well over 3,000. However, girls still outnumber boys in entering examinations and, in all examinations except AS, girls outperform boys.
>
> (ibid.: 3)

The improvements at Key Stage 4 Religious Education (RE) are significant. The numbers of pupils taking GCSE examinations in the subject have grown considerably; in 2004, Ofsted reported numbers having risen to around 400,000. This chapter charts recent developments in RE at Key Stage 4 and seeks to explain the reasons for the improvements in recent years. Issues over teaching and learning at KS4 are explored, in particular, effective planning and assessment. We look at how to ensure that 'teaching to the test' and preparing pupils for GCSE examinations embody excellent practice. The question of appropriate pedagogy is explored in relation to the questions of relevance, motivation and academic rigour.

OBJECTIVES

By the end of this chapter you should be able to:

- describe recent developments in RE at Key Stage 4;
- access the various options for RE available at Key Stage 4;
- translate, with guidance, examination specifications into effective and challenging practice.

RECENT DEVELOPMENT IN RE AT KEY STAGE 4

Legally RE remains a compulsory course of study at KS4 while also allowing for pupils to be withdrawn from the subject. Schools are responsible for ensuring that pupils' entitlement to RE is met in line with the expectations of their Agreed Syllabus. There was early recognition following the introduction of the National Curriculum and the new GCSE examinations in 1988 that RE needed to be brought as far as possible in line with other curriculum subjects if the subject were to be perceived as one which is relevant and academically rigorous. Much has been done since this time to address the 'Cinderella' syndrome which had hampered the subject for so long. The introduction both of new Agreed Syllabuses that required 5 per cent of curriculum time at KS4 and of the GCSE short course, which provided schools with a means by which pupils could receive accreditation through working with specifications which focused on relevant and challenging issues, raised the profile and the achievements of pupils in religious education. It is also particularly pleasing to note the increase and quality of teaching at GCE AS and A2 levels over the last few years. Fears that the short course specifications would fail to prepare pupils for GCE A Level study and indeed would have a detrimental effect on numbers have been unfounded. The introduction of the *Non-Statutory National Framework for Religious Education* sought to offer guidance for Agreed Syllabus Conferences to ensure the quality and coherence of RE across the country (QCA 2004). The content of the framework is exciting, innovative and raises the stakes in terms of assessment in RE, providing level descriptors and recognising that assessment remains an area of weakness for the subject. At Key Stage 4 the framework advises that pupils should be taking a public examination in the subject. There are available appropriate and challenging examined courses at Key Stage 4, which provide a coherent progression from work studied at Key Stage 3.

Current options at Key Stage 4 Religious Education

In your school experience school you may find one of the following options in RE:

- a GCSE for all pupils, following either the full or the short course;
- a GSCE short course for all pupils, with the possibility of 'topping' this up to a full course for those who choose Religious Studies (RS) as an option (examination RE at KS4 and post-16 is referred to as Religious Studies);
- a GCSE full course option, but with no other provision for those who do not opt;
- a GCSE full course option, either timetabled or 'twilight' after school, together with non-examination provision for all pupils (either as a discrete subject or as part of a carousel system, which may be discrete or integrated with Citizenship and/or PSHE);
- non-examination provision for all (either as a discrete subject or as part of a carousel system, which may be discrete or integrated within a Citizenship course and/or a Personal, Social and Health Education programme (PSHE).

GCSE Religious Studies, *not* Religious Education

When the GCSE short course was introduced, it was deliberately given the specification title 'Religious Education' rather than the 'Religious Studies' title of the full course. This was in response to the different focus of the new specifications from the traditional GCSE courses, looking at fundamental questions raised by religious belief and practice, embodied in philosophical enquiry into the nature and existence of God and the application of these ideas to ethical issues and ways of living. It was the nature of this content which offered something new, rather than any substantial difference in pedagogy. It is arguably possible to teach the content of both the full or short course specifications with an RE (simplistically characterised as prioritising 'learning from' religion) or RS (simplistically characterised as 'learning about' religion) bias depending on what you believe to be appropriate. The confusion and lack of coherence caused by the differently named specifications were overcome by the adoption of the title 'Religious Studies' for all GCSE specifications. The aims and assessment criteria were also amalgamated using the short course language. All GCSE Religious Studies, short course and full course, specifications now share the following two assessment objectives:

1   AO1 Describe, explain and analyse using knowledge and understanding.
2   AO2 Use evidence and reasoned argument to express and evaluate personal responses, informed insights, and differing viewpoints.

The specifications also recognise that although the assessment objectives are expressed separately they are not wholly discrete. The objective AO1 pervades AO2.

Selecting a specification

In selecting a particular GCSE Level specification it is vital to have all the key information readily available. The specifications, guidance, exemplification and examiners' reports are available online (see Figure 7.1).

AQA	www.aqa.org.uk
CCEA	www.rewardinglearning.org.uk/
EDEXCEL	www.edexcel.org.uk
OCR	www.ocr.org.uk
WJEC	www.wjec.co.uk

Figure 7.1 Awarding Bodies: web addresses

Before choosing or beginning to teach any GCSE specification, spend time exploring all that the Awarding Bodies can offer both you as teachers, and also your pupils. The specifications have resources, model answers, guidance for studying, support for you as a teacher and online help. They provide all the information departments need to enter pupils for the examinations. It is important to familiarise yourself with what is on offer from the various boards as this is a significant investment for you as a student teacher or NQT when you are beginning to plan and teach GCSE cohorts.

Task 7.1 Studying a GCSE specification for RS in your school experience school

Obtain a copy of the GCSE specification used in your school. Review its requirements by identifying the following:

- range of content;
- resources available, or identified elsewhere, in the specification;
- assessment structure and demands on the pupils.

Relate the course specification to the background of pupils in your school. Ask the staff in your RE department why this course was chosen and why others were rejected. Write a summary of this course indicating what you see as its attractive features and indicate any drawbacks you identified. Discuss the summary with your tutor.

Specifications for Religious Studies at GCSE level

All Awarding Bodies offer full and short course GCSE specifications. The specifications offer the possibility of 100 per cent examination or a combination of examination and coursework. The Awarding Bodies also offer an Entry Level Certificate for those who are not able to meet the requirements of a GCSE. (This is in line with the levels described in the National Framework of Qualifications; Entry level; Level 1 (GCSE grades D–G) and Level 2 (GCSE grades A★–C); see the QCA website, www.qca.org.uk). The content of the Entry Level Certificate covers the same material as the particular GCSE papers chosen and can therefore be taught alongside them. The GCSE specifications are based on the Common criteria and the criteria specific to particular subjects (see QCA website), which are prescribed by QCA, and are mandatory for all Awarding Bodies. The specifications for GCSE are also derived from the prescribed subject criteria for Religious Studies (QCA 2007) and meet the requirements of most locally Agreed Syllabuses. GCSE specifications for RS must reflect the fact that the religious traditions of the United Kingdom are in the main Christian, while taking into account other principal religions represented in the United Kingdom, thus meeting the same legal requirements as RE.

Both full course and short course specifications allow you to choose either the study of a specific faith, through belief and practice, or the study of texts, or allow for a study of Christianity alongside either one or two of the religious traditions represented in this country. These units tend to focus on the consideration of religious answers to philosophical and ethical questions. The specifications also allow for Christianity or one other principal religion to be studied alone in a systematic fashion; this enables schools with a particular religious foundation to adopt a specification which meets both their needs and the legal requirements. If a particular denomination is to be studied, it must be placed in the context of the broader religious tradition to which it belongs. Figure 7.2 offers an overview of the contents of the GCSE Religious Studies specifications from EDEXCEL and helps you identify these different options in the units and combinations available.

AO1 Describe, explain and analyse using knowledge and understanding (50 per cent).

AO2 Use evidence and reasoned argument to express and evaluate personal responses, informed insights, and differing viewpoints (50 per cent).

Figure 7.2 Weighting of assessment objectives

Task 7.2 Specifications for an RE course at Key Stage 4

Go to a number of the Awarding Bodies' websites (see Figure 7.1) and access their GCSE RS syllabuses. Summarise the material in the form of a table for full course and short course (comparatively) under the following headings: Content; Options; and Scheme and Form of Assessment. Note the similarities and differences. If you had a choice, which syllabus from which Awarding Body would you choose for the pupils you teach? Write a paragraph justifying your choice.

Coursework option replaced by 'controlled assessments'

In relation to coursework, the concerns expressed about the dangers of plagiarism, particularly through the internet, and too much 'support' being offered from both parents and teachers have now resulted in it no longer being compulsory. It is unclear at this stage to what extent coursework will be retained by some of the Awarding Bodies. It could be that all specifications will dispense with the need for coursework. However, QCA have identified that there is a specific issue of examiner shortage for Religious Studies, particularly given that the numbers of pupils taking the examination are growing year on year. The QCA has requested that the DfCSF funds QCA to look at ways to develop GCSE assessments in innovative ways, including the possibility of e-assessment.

The non-examination option

Without a doubt there are schools which still do not meet the legal requirements set out by the government and by their local Agreed Syllabus. You are unlikely to experience this during your initial teacher training, as IHEs are required to ensure that you have experience of both GCSE and AS and A2, if they are 11–19 training providers. It is perhaps enough to say that good practice can still occur in non-exam classes, but that this is not an easy task and perhaps represents an unnecessary struggle, if schools were only to afford RE the time, resources and staffing that it is entitled to. If you do find yourself in a situation in which you are teaching non-examination RE, use the opportunities that this offers. The GCSE specifications could still be used as a framework for devising innovative schemes of work.

Task 7.3 Non-examinable RE course at Key Stage 4

Read the case study below and list the strengths of the course identified by the teacher. In which ways might this type of course be suitable for the pupils in your school experience school? What might be the drawbacks? Write a one-page report and discuss it with your tutor.

Cath Brooke is an RE teacher in a school in South London. She works in a well-resourced department and in a school where RE is valued. She has been teaching a non-examination course for all pupils alongside a GCSE option group for several years. The course is successful and the girls really enjoy it. She puts much of the success of the course down to careful planning and resourcing. The modules of work are chosen because they are considered to be particularly relevant and interesting to the pupils. Examples are the role of women in religion and the portrayal of religion in the media. The problem of lack of motivation is not encountered with many pupils. Cath has her own thoughts on why this should be.

I think much of the positive pupil response is due to the fact that the pupils do actually enjoy the lessons. I acknowledge that the course is not an examined course as such (though work is still marked thoroughly but in a different way). Let me explain. The pupils have journals rather than books. Much of the work is discussion-based, but every lesson I give them an opportunity to make a written response to a key issue or question that we've been exploring. This response is often very personal, very much focusing on the 'learning from' elements of RE. In effect, I ask permission to share their work. I respond not with grades but with thoughts and ideas. I always try to be as positive as I can. It's ironic that this kind of writing often reveals clearly how well they have understood the topic we have been covering, without requiring them to write reams of notes. On my part the monitoring and marking are quite demanding. It is vital that they have responses from me. I also get them to do regular self-assessment activities, and also assessment of the lessons too. Their feedback is very useful in helping me to evaluate the various units of work and to make changes as I go along. The planning and resourcing of lessons also need to be spot-on. Imaginative and exciting activities, using artefacts, visits and visitors, conferences, videos, are all really important and its also important to give pupils the opportunity to be creative themselves. Personally, these lessons are some of my most enjoyable teaching experiences. We have flexibility. We avoid the pressures of exam work. The pupils really enjoy the 'space' these lessons offer.

TOWARDS EFFECTIVE PRACTICE AT KEY STAGE 4

Evaluating current provision

How do you go about developing the provision of RE at Key Stage 4? At this stage in your career you are unlikely to have much direct control over this beyond your personal teaching. However, once you gain your first teaching post you should expect to be consulted on the nature of provision, and once you achieve the status of head of department, you find yourself having to make vital decisions. Consequently, it is important to develop a critical awareness of the nature of the provision you encounter during your initial teacher education course.

Consider carefully what the department's philosophy of RE teaching is. What is their vision of RE? What pedagogical preferences are prioritised? How are 'learning about' and 'learning from' understood? What effect does this have on the teaching within in the department? You also need to think about external factors which dictate what goes on within the department. What are the constraints that limit the department – resources, timing, staffing? What are the expectations in the local Agreed Syllabus (or the faith syllabus, if your school is religious in its foundation) for provision at Key Stage 4? What is the nature of subject expertise held by teachers in the department? What would the pupils enjoy? How do you ensure progression from your Key Stage 3 schemes of work?

Task 7.4 Diagnostic evaluation of Key Stage 4 provision

This task can be carried out in one of your school experience schools. Its aim is to help you move beyond awareness of the nature and extent of Key Stage 4 provision for RE, towards a critical evaluation of that provision. Use this diagnostic table to identify the strengths and weaknesses of the provision.

Diagnostic table: analysing Key Stage 4 provision	
Positive factors	*Negative factors which I can change*
	Negative factors which I cannot change
Recommendations for future development	

Planning your schemes of work

At the heart of the planning process stands your ability to work with your examination specification, to ensure that you are taking account of the following:

- the most effective use of the time available;
- the best ways of dividing up the syllabus into, e.g. half-term modules;
- the nature of the content and how best to decide when to teach what, i.e. is there a natural progression from one subject to another? Are any of the content and its related concepts more difficult than others?
- the identification of aims and learning outcomes which are specific to each particular unit of work, and yet clearly linked to the overall aim and assessment objectives of the specification;
- the nature of the teaching and learning opportunities to be used;
- the opportunities for assessment, both formative and summative, unit by unit;
- the experience of practising examination questions regularly.

At this planning stage it is important to get Chief Examiners' reports from previous years for your particular specification to ensure you have a clear idea of what the examiners are looking for. They offer insight as to what issues and concepts pupils found most difficult and those questions which were answered well. This may affect your choice as to how much time to spend on any particular issue. Another important source to inform your planning is past examination papers, useful for ensuring your planning is accurate and for allowing you to build in appropriate examination practice throughout the course (see Task 7.5).

Working within your department at your school experience school, find out what the specification is for the GCSE cohort and produce a curriculum map, based on the following proforma. Identify:

- What is taught – the content of the specification, divided into half-term modules.
- When it is to be taught – the choice of when to teach what, and how long to spend on each aspect of the specification.
- Why it is to be taught – identify the aims and learning outcomes, by which you know that the specification has been taught in line with expectations.
- How it is to be assessed – identification of ways in which you build in both formative assessment and summative (end of module) exam practice (see Chapter 6 on assessment).

Once you are finished, compare your ideas with your department's schemes of work. How do they compare? Are there ideas that you can usefully share?

GCSE RE curriculum map: Year 10

Autumn term		Spring term		Summer term	
Module 1	Module 2	Module 3	Module 4	Module 5	Module 6
Title:	Title:	Title:	Title:	Title:	Title:
Aim:	Aim:	Aim:	Aim:	Aim:	Aim:
Learning outcomes:	Learning outcomes:	Learning outcomes:	Learning outcomes:	Learning outcomes:	Learning outcomes:
Content:	Content:	Content:	Content:	Content:	Content:
Assessment opportunities:	Assessment opportunities:	Assessment opportunities:	Assessment opportunities:	Assessment opportunities:	Assessment opportunities:

GCSE RE curriculum map: Year 11

Autumn term		Spring term		Summer term	
Module 7	Module 8	Module 9	Module 10	Revision	Examination
Title:	Title:	Title:	Title:	Title:	Title:
Aim:	Aim:	Aim:	Aim:	Aim:	Aim:
Learning outcomes:	Learning outcomes:	Learning outcomes:	Learning outcomes:	Learning outcomes:	Learning outcomes:
Content:	Content:	Content:	Content:	Content:	Content:
Assessment opportunities:	Assessment opportunities:	Assessment opportunities:	Assessment opportunities:	Assessment opportunities:	Assessment opportunities:

Think also about how the specification allows you to cover other areas of the wider curriculum such as 'spiritual, moral, social and cultural development' and citizenship education. In addition, you need to include Key Skills (level 2) in the teaching and learning opportunities afforded by the specification with which you are working; these are expected by QCA. These skills are communication, information technology, improving own learning and performance, problem solving and working with others (see www.qca.org.uk for more information on Key Skills).

Planning GCSE lessons during practical teaching experience

You have the opportunity to teach GCSE Religious Studies during your initial teacher education course. It is important to recognise the responsibility involved in this and to ensure you are fully prepared. So how do you go about such preparation? Here are some suggestions, which draw together many issues already raised in this chapter:

- Ensure you are really familiar with the units of the particular specification that are being taught in school. Look at the assessment objectives and consider how the teaching you have observed in school served to meet them. What place do end-of-module tests have? What opportunities are given for practising exam questions?

- When you know the particular content you are going to be responsible for teaching, ensure that you are confident in your own knowledge. Do the necessary reading to ensure this. It makes all the difference to your ability to teach effectively.

- Be aware that the content you are teaching may feature in either the examination or coursework (until 2009). What difference could this make to the way that you approach your planning and teaching?

- Look back at past examination papers and examiners' reports to identify what common misconceptions may be, what pupils tend to be able to do well and how to ensure that AO2 questions, in particular (evaluation), are made explicit and accessible to your pupils.

- Look at the technical language and phrases that are included in the specification and ensure that you include these explicitly in your teaching as they are likely to appear in examination questions.

- Investigate the resources in the department and those provided online, or recommended, by the exam board. Be aware in particular of any textbook which pupils are allowed to take home.

- Develop your own scheme of work, ensuring you are working with your tutor in school who has significant experience of teaching GCSE.

- In your planning, think carefully about how you are going to get an appropriate balance between the assessment objectives. It is possible that the specification may feel very content-heavy. Be aware that time in class together is precious and ensure that you balance recording information with meaningful exploration, investigation and evaluation of the content.

- Don't forget that GCSE pupils enjoy variety and experiences just as much as Key Stage 3 pupils. Be imaginative and innovative.

Task 7.6 Studying past papers

(This task can also be done with two or more student teachers leading to discussion of the analyses.)

An essential prerequisite for teaching GCSE is to familiarise yourself with the specification you are going to be teaching. Look at:

- aims
- assessment objectives
- content of chosen units
- examples of examination questions and coursework titles (if appropriate).

Now look at the Awarding Body's website and download relevant specimen papers and mark schemes. Identify from the examiner's reports what the issues were for the pupils studying the particular unit. What were the strengths? What common misconceptions or mistakes were made by candidates?

Brainstorm

- what the pupils need to know;
- what skills they need to develop – to show their understanding, their ability to use their knowledge and to evaluate it.

Now create another brainstorm, which identifies your ideas about the teaching and learning strategies you could employ to ensure content and skills are effectively integrated into your classroom practice.

How to use mark schemes

General guidance for examiners is offered and made explicit on the examination board websites. For each question on the examination paper there are points given. These are specified in brackets at the end of each question; often the Assessment Objectives (either AO1 or AO2) are specified as well. When paragraph answers are marked, they are given a level, from Level 1 to Level 5. Each level may have a range of 1 or 3 marks.

The task of ongoing formative assessment for the teacher is to make clear to the pupil how the assessment operates. The specification needs to be shared with pupils; in particular, the assessment objectives need to be clearly communicated and explained. This process works best if specific mark schemes are devised by you as the teacher, which interpret the general level descriptors for the assessment objectives, to level descriptors which are specific to the question being asked. Hence we move from generalisations to specific application of the levels. It can also be a very useful activity to encourage pupils to write their own mark schemes, given the general descriptors.

Through exploring this process together, the pupils are helped to understand assessment really clearly and to improve their exam technique.

It is important to know that examiners are encouraged to be positive in awarding marks where they are deserved, i.e. for any reasonable interpretation of the question.

Task 7.7 Analysis of a GCSE RS question

1. Consider the following question from a specimen paper on the OCR website:

   (a) *Describe the reasons Christians might give in support of their belief in God.* [8]

   (b) *Explain how believing that the Bible is the word of God might affect the lives of Christians.* [7]

   (c) *'There is no way of knowing what God might be like.' Do you agree? Give reasons to support your answer and show that you have thought about different points of view. You must refer to Christianity in your answer.* [5]

2. Now look at the mark scheme guidance for examiners:

   (a) *Describe the reasons Christians might give in support of their belief in God.* [8]
   Candidates could include personal religious experience; basic versions of the cosmological or teleological arguments (such as that we would not be here if there were no God); reasons based on the Bible; reasons based on social factors, such as believing because of being brought up in a Christian family or in a Christian country.

   (b) *Explain how believing that the Bible is the word of God might affect the lives of Christians.* [7]
   Answers might include the suggestion that Christians would read the Bible on a regular basis; that the Bible would be used for reference in times of difficulty; that the Bible would be a source of encouragement and hope; the Bible would provide Christians with ethical guidance; the Bible would be treated with respect and as a higher source of authority than other books. Candidates might also consider the effects of believing the Bible literally, and difficulties this might cause.

   (c) *'There is no way of knowing what God might be like.' Do you agree? Give reasons to support your answer and show that you have thought about different points of view. You must refer to Christianity in your answer.* [5]
   Candidates might write about the difficulties of knowing God who is ultimately beyond human understanding; the problems of 'knowing' a being who cannot be directly experienced through the senses. They might also argue that for Christians some knowledge of what God is like can be gained through the Bible and through the person of Christ, as well as through the individual experience of the believer.

3. Using the level descriptors for each assessment objective, write a mark scheme that is *specific* to this question relating to the nature of God in Christianity.

Explore your ideas about what could be included in a Level 1, Level 2, Level 3, Level 4 answer. Would the nature of the content differ? Try to write a Level 4 answer for yourself, to use as a model for pupils. How could you use this model question with pupils in class?

STEPS TOWARDS EFFECTIVE TEACHING AND LEARNING IN THE CLASSROOM

The vision

Religious Studies at GCSE is an opportunity to develop pupils' religious literacy. Its importance goes well beyond the piece of paper awarded to a successful candidate. Beware of 'teaching to the test' to the extent where pupils miss the point of studying Religious Education in school. You need to learn to live with this tension. It is important to use assessment for learning (AfL) strategies which encourage pupils to learn from each other, to become aware of the processes of learning in which they are participants and to become empowered to achieve in public examinations! It is significant that the vision offered by AfL in which pupils are empowered in their learning can also sit comfortably with a philosophy of RE which does not succumb to neatly packaged solutions to the issues raised by studying religion in the world. Instead a 'critical' RE demands a keen awareness on the part of pupils of the ambiguities and controversies inherent in the study of religion. They only need to watch the news or read a newspaper to be aware of these realities. The GCSE RE classroom should be a place to explore these issues with respect, trust and security, but it should also be a place dedicated to upholding the integrity not only of curious pupils but of those faiths, which are trusting the RE teacher to 'do good by them'. This we need to be keenly aware of as we also 'do good' by our pupils. This means that opportunity must be given for them to have a voice, as we challenge them to respond in an intelligent and informed way to the truth claims of the faiths studied.

Teaching and learning strategies

It is essential that pupils develop their knowledge of religious beliefs. Pupils learn and understand how beliefs can be practically applied to ethical and moral situations. The content of GCSE courses can be controversial and challenging for pupils to study. The understanding of these religious beliefs should inspire interesting responses from pupils and keep them motivated and keen to learn more. Pupils should be encouraged to develop their knowledge of faiths and this should be at the heart of the learning process. GCSE Religious Studies has a distinct subject content which is intrinsically dynamic and thought-provoking. Keeping the 'religious bit' in RS really matters as this is what makes the course interesting, and valuable to study. Let the religions and course content do the talking for you.

Ensure you make the content relevant to the world of teenagers. Use a variety of tasks and resources. Keep them fully engaged and involved in their learning. Focus on the different aspects of religion and make connections to the interests and experiences of pupils, e.g., to their interest in social justice and the well-being of others, and to the fundamental questions about life's purpose and meaning that all are required to consider. There is a need to create and foster a spirit of questioning, to develop verbal reasoning and allow pupils time to rationalise concepts. Get pupils involved in the application of religious beliefs to the moral and ethical dilemmas of today. The more they apply the beliefs and concepts they have studied to such dilemmas, the more familiar they will become with the religious ideals of different faith traditions. A good introduction to any unit of study is to get pupils to generate a list of questions relating to the topic. For example, on the subject of God, pupils typically come up with a range of questions relating to arguments for and against his existence, the image of God, qualities of God, and issues surrounding reasons for suffering.

A challenging GCSE curriculum should rightly be concerned with the development of pupils' thinking skills. Pupils should be encouraged to become critical thinkers and to process their thoughts and responses to religious ideals; it is essential that they can evaluate concepts effectively, and by developing their thinking skills pupils will not only enjoy the challenge of the subject but also should be able to enhance their abilities to analyse ideas, present relevant arguments and develop their own thoughts and responses to a variety of issues.

Pupils need to become familiar with the vocabulary of religions. This enables them to explore religious concepts in depth and be able to communicate religious ideas more effectively in examination conditions. Through investigating religious quotations, annotating them and assessing the meaning of particular quotations and expressing their own thoughts and responses, pupils are encouraged to become more religiously literate (see also Chapter 5, 'The role of language in Religious Education').

Providing differentiated work is also helpful in raising the motivation of pupils, as they are given opportunities to succeed and not to fail.

Formative assessment

Make sure you integrate principles of formative assessment (or AfL) into your GCSE teaching. Identify strengths and weakness in pupils' work and develop strategies both to maximise their success and to overcome their failings. This obviously requires time and attention, as written comments are invariably more helpful to students than a simple mark or grade.

In terms of the actual GCSE specification chosen as a course of study, it is important to communicate its expectations and requirements and to ensure that pupils feel informed about the journey they are undertaking. Understanding the outline, pattern and rubrics of the Awarding Body specification aids pupils' confidence and puts them at ease. Shared goals and intentions encourage and provide a sense of purpose.

Consider how to make provision for progress and achievement in your assessment system. It is important to reward the work of low achievers. Pupils need to recognise that they do not automatically achieve top grades, but need to work and apply themselves. Pupils should be working in line with realistic expectations of themselves. Predicted grades should be based on accumulated and extended evidence, though there is also a need for an optimistic view of each pupil, which holds high expectations for individual achievement. This can then be encouragingly communicated to pupils. It is important to create a sense of challenge that is appropriate to the level of ability of the individual learner.

Examples of good answers to exam questions should be presented to pupils, as well as advice on how deconstruct a question and assess what it means. Use class time to read out and share good answers from pupils. As a whole class, use the marking scheme to grade answers so pupils can understand the process of assessment and in turn understand what is expected from them in order to achieve high results, see Task 7.7.

If whole year groups are being put through a short course, then basic structures need to be in place to deal with the large number of pupils. Assessment methods that are quick, easy and effective need to be employed. Peer assessment can be helpful, as it exposes pupils to the ideas of their peers and allows them to participate in assessing and monitoring work. Regular verbal feedback in lessons also be a good use of time. End-of-unit tests using past papers give opportunities to grade work realistically in terms of ascertaining predicted grades.

The learning environment

Assessment for Learning literature talks much about the creation of classrooms as 'communities of enquiry'. From the outset think carefully about creating good class dynamics and effective teaching groups that work: consider the size of groups in relation to the space available; be respectful and positive to pupils; encourage participation; structure and pace the learning interaction according to the needs and aptitudes of the pupils, and so on.

SUMMARY AND KEY POINTS

This chapter has surveyed recent developments in RE provision at Key Stage 4. It celebrates the fact that significant progress has been made in teaching and learning. The range of options for teaching RE at KS4 has been explored. The importance of familiarising oneself with the content and expectations of specifications, particularly in relation to assessment, have been stressed. The chapter ends by outlining a vision for teaching RE at Key Stage 4 and the strategies by which such a vision can be realised.

FURTHER READING

There are no books written specifically on teaching RE at Key Stage 4. There are, however, a range of textbooks that relate to the Awarding Bodies' different RS syllabuses. These textbooks are listed under 'Support Material' that is available on the websites of the different Awarding Bodies (see Figure 7.1).

8   GCE A Level Religious Studies

Sue Cooke

INTRODUCTION

GCE Advanced Level (A Level) teaching is possibly one of the most exciting, stimulating, challenging and yet scary arenas for any classroom practitioner, let alone student teacher. Many of the greatest successes and failures in terms of results, lessons and activities can be experienced at this level. On the one hand, some of the most significant rewards can be experienced, since the pupils have chosen to study the subject and their level of response tends to be high. On the other hand, with the new modular system it is now easier to identify the strengths and weaknesses within a department. The numbers of pupils opting for GCE A Level Religious Studies (RS) is increasing each year as we reap the rewards of increased numbers taking the subject at GCSE. In 2005, it was the fastest rising subject and in 2006 the numbers taking the examination went up another 8 per cent. In order to meet the increased demand for the subject at GCE A Level, we need to ensure that teachers are fully prepared with a well-considered curriculum that maintains the interest and enthusiasm of the pupils. Where the previous chapter dealt with GCSE examinations and the next chapter deals with general religious education at 16-plus, our focus here is on RS at GCE A Level (the title RS identifies the examination subject, whereas RE is used of the non-examination subject).

OBJECTIVES

By the end of this chapter you should be able to:

- understand the terminology associated with GCE A Level RS specifications;

- understand how to begin planning and delivering an GCE A Level RS course;
- identify teaching strategies to use with GCE A Level pupils.

POLITICAL BACKGROUND

The focus on the teaching of RS at GCE A Level must be contextualised with reference to current government policy in this area. In 2004, Mike Tomlinson and his Working Group published a review of the 14–19 Curriculum (Tomlinson 2004). The Report proposed a radical reform of the present system, effectively challenging and providing a solution for the current divide between vocational and academic qualifications. In response to the commissioned report, the Government published a White Paper in February 2005 entitled *14–19 Education and Skills*. In the foreword, Ruth Kelly, the then Secretary of State for Education, paid tribute to the work of the Tomlinson Group and stated that the White Paper 'sets out a vision of what we want for children and teenagers, what we want them to learn, the skills we want them to acquire, but above all the values we want them to have' (DfES 2005: 3). The publication of this White Paper was an attempt to ensure that the trend towards low participation in post-16 education is significantly reversed over the next ten years. The overriding pressure to reverse this trend comes from England's poor performance in international league tables at this level.

THE CHALLENGE OF GCE A LEVEL RS TEACHING

Teaching GCE A Level RS can be a challenging task. Fortunately, in most schools GCE A Level groups tend to be smaller than the average class size and most pupils are reasonably enthusiastic to achieve good examination results. The smaller class size, however, brings its own set of issues. The smaller, more intimate environment, especially if there is only a handful of pupils, can make teaching difficult. It may be harder to instigate discussions and debate and get pupils to interact with each other. A teacher in training may be close in age to the pupils and this often leads to one of two scenarios. Either, the student teacher can feel intimidated by the group and finds it hard to teach because the pupils are similar in age. This is particularly the case when teaching more able pupils who are confident and assertive. Or, it can lead to the student teacher attempting to befriend the pupils and wishing to be liked by them. This lack of professional distance can make it harder for the teacher to discipline and assess pupils fairly.

One of the chief mistakes that student teachers can make when preparing GCE A Level lessons is to focus too much on the delivery of the content to the detriment of pedagogy. There is naturally more content to be covered in GCE A Level lessons, but this does not mean that teachers should resort to didactic lessons with an emphasis on note taking and lecturing. The transition from GCSE to GCE A Level is a large step for many pupils, one that is not made easier if teachers dramatically alter their teaching style and expect the pupils to be able to cope with a whole new approach. Moreover, GCE A Level teaching makes particular demands on the teachers if the content is to be related to the pupils' experience so that they do not simply learn for the purpose of examination success but also see the relevance of what is taught.

Task 8.1 Identify differences in the GCE A Level classroom

In your observation during your Initial Teacher Training course identify three or four pupils of RS GCE A Level. Ask them why they chose the subject at GCE A Level, what differences, if any, they have noticed in the teaching of GCE A Level RS from earlier teaching, and what the implications of this are for their learning.

Write a summary of your findings, identifying perhaps what your pupils think is the same and what is different when moving from GCSE to GCE A level. Does it suggest areas in which the pupils need help? Discuss your findings with your tutor.

WHERE DO YOU START?

Many student teachers will not get the opportunity to teach GCE A Level; your first experience of teaching A Level may well be as a practising teacher. For this reason, our discussion will presuppose that you are starting from scratch and that you have a free hand in choosing a particular option within an A Level Syllabus. Those who will teach or anticipate teaching A Level on their Initial Teaching Training course can skip this section and begin with the next section, 'Breaking down the specification'.

When planning to choose and implement a new GCE A Level course, or to bring about changes in an existing course, there are several key factors that need to be considered. First, it is vital to look at the different subject specialities within a department – there is little choice in opting for Buddhism if there is no-one qualified to teach it. Go with the strengths of subject teachers and where possible ensure that there are always at least two members of staff who can deliver the course. Having taken staff expertise into account, it is then important to consider subject combinations. A popular combination in many schools is 'Philosophy of Religion' with 'Ethics and Religion': this works well as similar skills are needed for the two areas and for most pupils it means that they are building upon knowledge already gained at GCSE. Similarly, if the religion studied at GCSE has been Hinduism, it may be more appropriate to continue studying that to a greater depth than to introduce a new religion. Finally, combining certain options may be inappropriate as the range of skills required may be too narrow or the material too remote from the interest and experience of the pupils, and so on. Judgements about appropriateness and coherence have to be made.

Second, look at the resources available in the department. When beginning a new course it is important to have proper resources. Similar measures must be put in place for the pupils, and it is also good to discuss curriculum changes with the school librarian. For some of the more popular topics at GCE A Level there are many excellent resources and textbooks, but for others there are fewer aids to teaching and learning available. Figure 8.1 presents a brief glossary of the terms used at GCE A Level. A lack of resources can put increased pressure on the teacher as there is no clear framework or books from which to work. This is a major consideration if there is an element of coursework.

It is helpful to define the terms that are commonly associated with GCE A Level teaching:

A2 – the second stage of the full GCE A Level, these modules can either be studied in conjunction with the AS modules or after they have been examined.

Advanced Level – this is awarded when a candidate has successfully completed the AS and A2 units of assessment.

AS – Advanced Subsidiary of GCE, often awarded at the end of the first year of study. It can be held as a qualification in its own right or further modules can be studied to gain a full GCE A Level

Modules – pupils study modules of work; by *successfully* completing a range of modules over their two years of study they are awarded a full GCE A Level.

Specification – this is produced by an Awarding Body and details the different courses and combinations on offer; a specification is often referred to as a syllabus.

Units – each module is examined by a unit of assessment which either takes the form of a written examination paper or assessed coursework. Some examination specifications now use the term 'unit' as equivalent to 'module.'

Figure 8.1 Terminology at GCE A Level

It is important to look at what the Awarding Bodies require: Do they have any compulsory units? Is there compulsory coursework? How do they examine the synoptic element? What weightings do they put on the different assessment objectives? Figure 8.2 details what three Awarding Bodies stipulate in terms of compulsory units, coursework and synoptic tasks.

Finally, if at all possible, talk to the pupils who are opting to study the subject at AS Level. Ask them what topics they would like to study and which combinations, explain why the current combinations exist and canvass their understanding throughout the course. Pupils are a vital resource.

The Awarding Bodies are (examples only):

AQA is the Assessment and Qualifications Alliance

OCR is the Oxford, Cambridge and RSA Examinations

EDEXCEL

	AQA		OCR		EDEXCEL	
	AS	A2	AS	A2	AS	A2
Compulsory units	Must study 2 units from a choice of 11	Must study 1 unit from a choice of 8 and Religion and Human Experience (Synoptic paper)	Unit 2760 Foundation for the Study of Religion and 2 others	No specific compulsory units, but they have to be chosen from specific ranges and there are several prohibited combinations	Range of options within unit	Range of options within unit and synoptic unit
Coursework	None	None	None	Option for coursework, but not compulsory – marked externally	Compulsory – internally marked and externally moderated	None
Synoptic assessment		Timed examination		Timed examination		Timed examination

Figure 8.2 The structure of a sample of GCE A Level specifications

BREAKING DOWN THE SPECIFICATION

Once you have chosen your specification and the modules/units that the pupils are to take, then you need to start planning the course. One of the first things to do is to find out when the Awarding Bodies offer the units of assessment for the modules your pupils are studying. Many Awarding Bodies offer January examinations for AS units in particular. If there is an option to take an assessment unit in January, it may be advisable to prepare pupils for this as this can reduce the pressure on them in the summer.

Once you have decided which modules the pupils are taking and when they sit the assessment units, you then need to break each module down into manageable sections and divide them into half-term blocks. Then plan each half-term block in more detail by writing schemes of work for each aspect of a unit. For example, AQA AS Unit D

'Religion, Philosophy and Science' has four key areas: 'Miracles', 'Creation,' 'Design argument' and 'Quantum Mechanics and a religious world view'. It would be more straightforward to plan each aspect separately and have four schemes of work rather than one overall scheme for the module/unit. When writing the scheme of work it is essential to look at what resources are available in the department. Crucially, you must look at past examination papers, mark schemes and Chief Examiner's reports as well as at the specification. These give the greatest clues as to what you need to teach, to what depth and from what angle. Use these to help you plan activities, notes and tasks for use with your pupils. Most Awarding Bodies now have material to help teachers online and you might ring the Awarding Body subject officer for further information about support material and teacher meetings. If possible, find out if any other schools in your area are doing the same modules so that you can share resources and ideas with them. Often RS departments are small and people can be working in isolation, so establishing links with other schools can help with resources and ideas sharing as well as helping to maintain morale.

Task 8.2 Analysing GCE A Level RE provision in your school

Identify the syllabus of the RS GCE A Level in your school experience school.
    Why was this syllabus chosen? Is this choice traditional or has a change been made recently?
    What resources do the teachers and the pupils have access to?
    How has the content been mapped for the year? Are schemes of work available?
    How have the assessment criteria been communicated to the pupils?
    How often do the pupils use the assessment criteria to assess their own work?
    What does the most recent examiner's report identify as key areas for consideration, and how are these highlighted in the departmental strategy for GCE A Level teaching?

    Record your findings and write any questions arising from this inquiry. Discuss this report with your tutor.

ASSESSMENT

There are two assessment objectives that are common across all syllabuses, although the weighting put on them at AS level and A2 level differs (and there is some room for flexibility by the Awarding Boards). It is important to look at this when planning your choice of board. If your pupils struggle with the more complex AO2 tasks, then it may be worth considering an Awarding Body where they place less emphasis on that objective. Additionally, remember to look at coursework requirements and how they propose to examine the pupils on the synoptic elements of the course.

Assessment Objective 1 (AO1) – Select and demonstrate clearly relevant knowledge and understanding through the use of evidence, examples and correct language and terminology appropriate to the course of study. *In addition, A Level candidates should demonstrate knowledge and understanding of the connections between different elements of their course of study.*

Assessment Objective 2 (AO2) – Sustain a critical line of argument and justify a point of view. *In addition, A Level candidates should relate elements of their course of study to their broader context and to specified aspects of human experience.*

Table 8.1 shows the weightings that some of the Awarding Bodies give to the two different criteria: As well as producing specific mark schemes for examinations, each Awarding Body also has sets of level descriptors for grades at AS and A2 and these are applied in conjunction with the mark schemes in order to determine pupil achievement. The Awarding Bodies often employ 'trigger words' that are used in examination questions. It is helpful to teach these to your pupils so they know whether a question is targeting AO1 or AO2. These trigger words indicate to pupils what the examiner is looking for and whether examples and/or illustrations are required within the answer. Aiding your pupils in the understanding of this process provides them with a clearer idea of what is expected and stops them from leaving out essential information or including irrelevant material.

Table 8.1 Awarding Body weightings of the two attainment criteria (%)

	AQA		OCR		EDEXCEL	
	AS	A2	AS	A2	AS	A2
AO1	75	60	66	64.6	70	60
AO2	25	40	34	35.4	30	40

Raw marks and uniform marks (UMS)

All AS and A2 papers are given a raw mark. These raw marks from the examiners are then converted to points on the Uniform Mark Scale (UMS) so that results from different options and units can be added together to get the final grade (even if they were taken at different times). The minimum number of uniform marks needed for each grade has been agreed by each Awarding Body across every subject and are set out in Table 8.2. From Table 8.2 it can clearly be seen that if a pupil has already

Table 8.2 Awarding Body mark distributions

Grade	AS	A2
A	240	480
B	210	420
C	180	360
D	150	300
E	120	240

achieved an 'A' at AS level, then they have automatically achieved at least an 'E' at Advanced Level. Similarly, if pupils finish their AS level with full UMS, then they already have achieved at least a 'D' at Advanced Level. It is possible for a pupil to achieve full UMS without having achieved full raw marks and one raw mark may earn a pupil more than one uniform mark. It is important to look at pupils' UMS as well as their raw marks when determining whether or not a pupil should re-sit a module.

How uniform marks are distributed between different units is decided by the Awarding Bodies, but – as Table 8.3 shows – 300 have to be allocated to AS units and 300 to A2 units.

Table 8.3 Distribution of UMS across a sample of Awarding Bodies

Awarding Body	Distribution
AQA	Each AS unit has 100 UMS attached, the two A2 units have 90 UMS each and the synoptic unit is worth up to 120 UMS.
OCR	As AQA
EDEXCEL	The two AS units, the A2 unit and the synoptic unit are all equal worth: 150 UMS each.

The standardising of marks to UMS means that it is easier for teachers to be able to compare relative performance of pupils between different modules. In the past it was hard to compare raw marks as grade boundaries varied between units. Now, however, it is clear to see in which units pupils excel or struggle. This information can be used in a variety of ways:

- It may indicate a teacher who is struggling with GCE A Level teaching as the UMS for their unit is continually below comparable units taught by other teachers.
- The module being taught may not be suitable for your pupils and there may be value in choosing a different module.
- The combination of modules chosen may not work well together.

Resolving the second and third issues can be relatively straightforward with a change in curriculum, resolving the first may be more problematic.

Table 8.4 shows how differences in UMS can be seen. It is clear from Table 8.4 that, on average, pupils are achieving less in AS Unit 2 and A2 Unit 7. These two units are linked and based on the same topic. If this pattern is repeated from a following year, or is repeated again next year, then decisions have to be made about how to support the teacher to deliver more effective lessons, or perhaps the department has to choose a new topic to be part of the course.

During the year it is important that pupils spend time writing essays if they are to practise their skills for the examinations. They need to be given essays to write at home, but it is equally important to spend time writing essays together in class and they need experience of producing essays under timed conditions. Below are

Table 8.4 An example of pupil attainment

Pupil	Unit 1 Religious Experience	Unit 2 Old Testament	Unit 6 Religion and Science	Unit 7 Old Testament	Unit 11 Philosophy of Religion	Unit 12 Synoptic Paper	Total	Grade
A	84	83	90	60	78	120	515	A
B	64	54	64	48	69	120	419	C
C	82	48	66	46	54	64	360	C
D	76	73	82	36	72	120	459	B
E	66	58	72	21	74	64	355	D
F	98	67	78	72	75	96	486	A
G	96	68	92	58	33	112	459	B
H	68	85	75	72	65	120	485	A
I	78	65	77	66	71	120	477	B
J	100	97	100	90	90	116	593	A
UMS Available	100	100	100	90	90	120	600	
2007 Average	81	70	80	57	68	105	460	B
2006 Average	77	73	80	57	70	75	432	B

Note: The pupil marks are all standardised marks.

some ideas of what can be done to help increase your pupils' confidence in essay writing:

- To begin with, do not expect your pupils to write whole essays, just give them sections of essays to do as you cover the relevant part of the specification. The jump from GCSE to GCE AS level is quite daunting for some pupils and they may panic at the thought of writing long, complex essays.
- Encourage your pupils to write plans for their essays and, if possible, take them in and comment on them before they begin writing their actual essays.
- If possible, give your pupils sample essays for their topics. It is good to work together as a class, writing sample answers or even just parts of essays. Pupils must not rely solely on these for revision. Too often pupils believe that if they learn them off by heart and regurgitate them in the examination when they see a question that compares in any way to one that they have practised, they will achieve a good grade.
- Ask your Awarding Body if they produce a pack of sample essays – most boards can supply you with sample 'B' and 'D' grade work. Going through these with pupils helps them to understand more about the standard that is expected.
- Allow pupils to mark their own essays and do some peer-marking. This familiarises them with the expectations of the Awarding Body. It also helps them see new ways of phrasing and presenting material.
- Make sure your pupils are familiar with the level descriptors and trigger words for your Awarding Body.

> **Task 8.3 Analysing examination questions**
>
> Choose a recent examination question from the syllabus, answer the question and use the assessment criteria to grade your answer. You could always invite the pupils to do this for you and provide constructive comments for you.
> Identify and record the implications for your teaching and how you might advise your pupils entering a GCE examination.

Synoptic module

The synoptic module, which covers material across different units, is a very important module for pupils who are completing an Advanced Level in RS, not least because it carries a minimum of 20 per cent of the total marks. The point of the synoptic module is for pupils to show a deeper understanding of the material covered in all the other modules and to make relevant connections between the modules. Pupils also need to show evidence of wider knowledge and understanding than that covered solely in other modules. As well as some discrete teaching for this module it is important to show pupils relevant connections and material when completing the other modules.

Advanced Extension Award

This is a completely separate qualification that should be offered to the top perform-ing GCE A Level RS pupils. It is offered by EDEXCEL Examination Board but the nature and range of the questions offered mean that any pupil can take and pass the paper regardless of which board and modules they have completed. It is a three-hour paper divided into two sections where pupils answer one source-based question and complete one essay. For each section there is a wide range of questions. It is a complex paper that really is only for the most able pupils, but it provides an excellent enrich-ment activity for 'Gifted and Talented' pupils. It also indicates a higher level of potential for any pupils applying to the top universities or for the most competitive degree courses. While it requires extra preparation, there is no additional material that pupils need to learn in order to complete the paper. They do, however, need to have an extensive and mature knowledge of the material that they have covered within their RS course. In this examination pupils achieve either Distinction, Merit or Fail, but their success or failure in this paper does not affect their GCE A Level in RS at all.

GETTING PRACTICAL

Once the specification and modules have been chosen and you have got your head around the implications and practicalities of the assessment system, it is time to begin the more enjoyable part of actually teaching the pupils. At this stage there are a few more things to remember:

- Get to know your group. You are likely to see you GCE A Level class more than once a week and they are likely to be smaller in size than your other classes, so it is good to get to know them.
- Plan a range of activities for them. Remember, these pupils have only just finished GCSEs a few months ago where they have had highly structured lessons with lots of different activities. Too often at GCE A Level teachers become focused on producing endless handouts and giving lots of notes as the focus switches from pedagogy to content. There is plenty of content to get through, but the pupils still need to experience a whole range of teaching strategies (suggestions can be found in the next section).
- Allow the pupils to lead the learning. GCE A Level pupils have chosen to be there and are more likely to be more enthusiastic about the subject and bring their own questions to the subject. It is important to allow time for them to lead the line of questioning sometimes and when possible allow them to prepare and present material to the rest of the class.
- Be flexible with your pupils. Sometimes your lesson may not work out as you have planned, but this does not mean that valuable learning has not taken place.
- Make teaching and learning different from GCSE. This is especially important if you are continuing with topics they may have covered at a more basic level

at GCSE. Pupils do not want to feel that they are just doing more of the same.

- Do not rely on lecturing. Few GCE A Level pupils can sit and listen to the teacher for extended periods of time.
- When note taking, encourage pupils do it in a way that suits them. Where possible, set alternative options for how tasks can be carried out. As long as all pupils have all the same information recorded, it often does not matter which format it is in.
- Remember that your pupils may have different learning styles and one task may not always suit all pupils. In a small class being aware of who needs more practical activities and who needs clearer explanation and more structured learning can make a difference to their confidence in learning and, obviously, their final results.
- Think about differentiation: there is a range of ability within your class. For example, it may be appropriate to give more able pupils original texts of key philosophers or preparation material for the Advanced Extension Award if more time needs to be spent with less able pupils.

Task 8.4 Profiling and assessing pupils at GCE A Level

Select three pupils from your GCE A Level group who represent top, middle and low ability in the group. Write a pen portrait for each of them documenting their strengths and areas for development. When you next take in a piece of their work, examine it for:

- detail (in terms of knowledge, understanding and length);
- structure (in terms of progression and clarity of points);
- critical reflection (in terms of evaluation skills in presenting and assessing religious material and arguments).

Feed back to each one of them your comments on their work. Invite them to set one target for their next piece of written work. Ensure that you keep a record of this target. Review their work with the original essay, your comments, their target and the next piece of work. What is the outcome for each pupil?

Teaching strategies

It is important to make GCE A Level lessons diverse in order to keep all pupils engaged and sufficiently challenged. Below are just a few ideas of what can be included.

- *Video and other media* – excellent resources when they are used to complement teaching. Short, powerful clips of film or television programmes can be excellent lesson starters. They do not have to be specific RS programmes either: there are many documentaries available that link well to ethical issues, particularly medical ethics. However, if you look closely you can find RS-related themes in most programmes – particularly soaps! If you can find a clip where people are debating some form of ethical dilemma, stop the clip before discovering what they decide to do and ask the pupils how they think they should proceed and what decision they would come to.

- *Dialogue* – pupils at GCE A Level still like to role-play and perform. Pupils can devise dramas based on ethical issues or set up discussions on particular topics between members of different religions.

- *Quotes* – as well as using original texts with pupils, use brief but interesting quotations. These provide an excellent way into topics as you ask pupils what the implications of the quote may be and whether they agree with it or not. There are many excellent online websites that have hundreds of quotes on them and most can be searched for statements on specific topics (for instance, www.quotationreference.com/main.php, http://www.quotations page.com/).

- *Music* – pupils love listening to music and when it comes to this area they can often be your greatest resource and ideas bank. A piece of music can be a great starter for a topic. For example, many of U2's songs have spiritual and ethical messages, Billy Bragg has written many songs about war and John Lennon's 'Imagine' is an all-time classic for RS lessons. If you're feeling very creative, allow pupils to write and then perform their own songs or to write new lyrics to an old tune – it can produce some amazing work.

- *Images* – a powerful tool in many classrooms. From many websites, particularly online news websites, challenging pictures can be downloaded and shown to pupils. Try creating a PowerPoint of images linked to suffering and setting them to music as a way of introducing forms of suffering to a class. On a more light-hearted note, many greetings cards have religious cartoons on them and can make for an effective lesson starter – they can be downloaded from different internet sites. Pupils can also collage pictures on a theme and annotate them with notes and responses as a way of creating group presentations.

- *Newspapers* – ask pupils to bring in any articles they find in newspapers linked to what you are studying and create a file of resources. Look at articles and editorials from two politically different newspapers when a key event or medical issue is reported. Allow pupils to discover the different ethical, medical or social arguments represented by each source. This can also be done using online newspapers that can be accessed through the internet.

- *Seminars* – allow pupils to prepare and present information to each other. They cannot be expected to present whole topics and do all the teaching on them, but pupil presentations can be an excellent plenary method and are a good way of ensuring that pupils have really understood all the material you have covered in a topic.

- *Debates* – popular in most GCE A Level classes, debates are a good way of getting pupils to discuss and effectively engage with material they have covered. They are excellent for the development of pupils' evaluative skills as they are able to both present and defend their views. To be successful, debates have to be planned and cannot just be done when you haven't had time to prepare a lesson. Try asking pupils to debate 'in role'. For example, when studying the Teleological Argument, recreate Hume's dinner party and, inviting them to transcend time zones, ask pupils to argue as one of the key philosophers, e.g. Paley or Swinburne. As well as familiarising them with the argument, they also have to be aware of who may challenge them and who they must be prepared to challenge.

- *Quizzes* – an element of fun and competition is always good and quiz questions can be set as a homework activity. Just make sure that pupils hand in questions and answers. This is a good way of getting pupils to revise material.
- *Sample questions* – as already explained, it is important to spend time helping pupils prepare essays by practising them in class.
- *Activities/games* – when possible, try and create games and activities for pupils. Sometimes, it may be possible to adapt a game or activity that you are used to using with younger pupils. Try taking all the premises for Aquinas' first 'Three Ways' and putting them on separate pieces of cards and asking pupils to reconstruct the arguments, the same could be done for the Augustinian and Iranaean theodicies. It sounds like a simple task, but pupils can find it hard and it does force them to really grapple with the format and logical progression of the arguments.

This is just a small selection of ideas and not every idea can be used in every lesson or even every week, but if every idea was used at least every half-term then pupils have a more varied set of learning experiences.

Developing good practice at GCE A Level

Good practice does not occur automatically, and teachers can learn much from the example of other teachers and from other school subjects. Here are some ideas that model good practice.

- Mark end-of-module essays according to the assessment objectives from the examination board, applying the assessment criteria. Communicate this mark scheme to pupils. Get them to use the same criteria to grade each other's answers as a form of peer assessment.
- Collect a good, middle and lower examination response as indicators for pupils. Have a folder of exemplary essays on different topics to critique, model or support an individual pupil's understanding of the topic.
- Consider ways of giving quality feedback to pupils (e.g., written feedback can be expanded during an personal interview with the pupil).
- Create a list of suggested targets for improving examination answers. Create a self-assessment sheet that allows pupils to record grades and set targets for improving their performance. Give pupils opportunities to comment on their strengths and areas for development.

- Set up a glossary with pupils in their folders, or create a glossary for each unit, or create a crossword using key terms and word matching exercises. These are also good for classroom displays.
- Ensure you give pupils the opportunity to offer their own opinions, beliefs and responses as well as 'hot seating' individuals to play devil's advocate with the topic.
- Create revision exercises for the end of each unit.
- Make explicit links with other subject areas to give pupils the opportunity to connect ideas meta-cognitively.

GENERAL RS WITHIN THE SIXTH FORM

All maintained schools of whatever type (see Chapter 1, 'The place of RE in the curriculum') have a statutory responsibility to provide RE for all pupils up to the age of 18. Unfortunately, many schools fail to meet this requirement for pupils who are not studying GCE A Level RS. There are two main ways in which this entitlement can be met. Schools can have one-day RE conferences where they invite guest speakers and have talks, seminars and workshops all based on a key theme. Alternatively, RE can be delivered through other areas of the curriculum such as General Studies, PSHE or even through Critical Thinking. The key point here is to ensure that it is clearly RE and not just some sort of social or ethical studies. Most of all, it needs to be contemporary, relevant and challenging.

SUMMARY AND KEY POINTS

Relax and enjoy your teaching and your pupils' learning at this stage. GCE A Level lessons can be some of the most enjoyable and it is important not to become so focused on results that you forget to enjoy the experience of teaching the pupils. Teaching and learning should be focused on the assessment aims and the syllabus content. Keep an eye on your Awarding Body's website and watch out for any new publications or INSET opportunities that they are offering. Remember to review your teaching and allow the pupils to assess how well the course is going and what is and is not working for them.

FURTHER READING

Abbot, I. and Huddlestone, P. (2004) 'The Curriculum: 14–19', in V. Brooks, I. Abbot and L. Bills, *Preparing to Teach in Secondary School*, Maidenhead: Open University Press. This chapter provides a comprehensive overview of recent governmental policy and practice in this area.

Dearing, R. (1996) *Review of Qualifications for 16–19 Year Olds*, London: SCAA This text contains the original recommendations for reform at post-16, subsequent policy can be traced back to this report.

DfES (2003) *14–19 Opportunity and Excellence*. London: HMSO. DfES (2005) *14–19 Education and Skills*. London: HMSO. Both reports seek to develop a more integrated approach to the 14–19 curriculum and to chart a course to educational excellence for all pupils.

Giles, A. (2002) 'Religious Studies at Post-16', in L. Broadbent and A. Brown (eds) *Issues in Religious Education*, London: RoutledgeFalmer. This chapter examines the philosophical underpinning for Religious Studies and offers a provocative way forward for teachers of GCE A Level.

Ogden, V. (1997) *The Role of Religious Education at 16–19 in the Ascendancy of Work-related Learning and a New Framework for Post-compulsory Education*, Abingdon: Culham College Institute. This is a report prepared on behalf of the Sir Halley Stewart Trust into the nationwide provision of post-16 religious education, together with a critical analysis of the relevance and potential of RE as a general entitlement.

9 Establishing and enriching Religious Education at 16-plus

Vanessa Ogden

INTRODUCTION

According to the *Non-Statutory Framework for Religious Education* (QCA 2004), post-16 Religious Education (RE) focuses on the higher levels of religious knowledge and understanding and upon the critical skills that enable pupils to assess and evaluative religious beliefs and practices; and all pupils in maintained schools are required to follow a post-16 course in RE. Some will pursue A/AS Level Religious Studies, but the majority will not. This chapter seeks to support your work in these two areas, though the emphasis will fall on non-examination RE (post-16 examination RE is considered in Chapter 8). It provides information to facilitate planning, suggestions for teaching and learning strategies and practical examples.

OBJECTIVES

By the end of this chapter, you should be able to:

- have a solid grasp of the field of education post-16 and be able to anticipate its potential changes, to your advantage, in planning;
- argue convincingly for the importance of RE in post-16 education;
- contribute to the teaching of a vibrant, challenging, exciting and diverse RE programme at post-16 level.
- plan several types of post-16 RE courses and be aware of their limitations.

RE IN THE CONTEXT OF POST-COMPULSORY EDUCATION

This section provides information about the field of education beyond 16 and RE's position within it. It helps you to understand the legal and statutory requirements governing pupils' post-16 entitlement to RE and it sets out some of the developments of the new framework which influences its provision. This information should help you to plan for the development of post-16 courses in religious education.

The legal and statutory requirements for RE at post-16

RE is a statutory requirement of the curriculum at post-16 for every pupil in grant maintained, voluntary aided and county maintained schools, as well as city technology colleges and academies. Both the 1944 Education Act (HMSO 1944, Section 25.1) and the 1988 Education Reform Act (HMSO 1988, Section 7) legislate for the inclusion of RE throughout the schooling of young people in England. Of the colleges, only sixth-form colleges are required by law to provide religious education under the regulations of the 1992 Education Act; tertiary colleges and other colleges of further education are exempt from offering a full entitlement.

In many schools and colleges across the country, however, provision of the full complement of post-16 RE is chequered. The reasons for this are complex and derive principally from the historical development of RE as regards both its pedagogy and its status. Issues of post-16 funding tied to recruitment and retention of teachers combine with this to undermine the provision of RE in this sector. The fact that post-16 non-examination subjects are often under-resourced also contributes to the poverty of provision of religious education at this level. However, there is a sea change in post-compulsory education with the enhancement of vocational studies, the implications of which are exciting for the RE practitioner.

The new National Qualifications Framework

The creation of a new National Qualifications Framework to provide parity of esteem between the academic and vocational curriculum was initiated in the spring of 1996; Sir Ron Dearing made proposals for a new framework for qualifications at post-16 in a document entitled *Review of Qualifications 16–19* (Dearing 1996). Although not radical, it suggested a measured change leading to the rationalisation of qualifications under one overarching certificate, while retaining the three distinct pathways of achievement that already existed: General Certificate of Education (GCE) and Advanced Level (GCE A Level); General National Vocational Qualification (GNVQ); and National Vocational Qualification (NVQ). These three were termed by Dearing 'subject-based education', 'applied education' and 'vocational education' respectively. The review also directly referred to the need for a spiritual and moral dimension to post-16 education (ibid.: 125ff.). These proposals were, in part, adopted by QCA. The 'New Qualifications Framework' was established and Awarding Bodies for all post-16 qualifications were required to make spiritual and moral dimensions of learning implicit in their syllabi or specifications. However, the suggestion that one over-arching diploma should be introduced to accredit the framework was at that time shelved.

In October 2004, Mike Tomlinson published *14–19 Curriculum and Qualifications Reform*, another review of the qualifications framework, which this time incorporated Key Stage 4 as well as post-16 education. He sought to rationalise the whole curriculum and routes to qualification from 14–19, seeking to provide enhanced fluidity between each of the three pathways by bringing them together under a unified framework of one diploma to be awarded at four levels: Entry, Foundation, Intermediate and Advanced (for further information, refer to Tomlinson 2004). All qualifications could be awarded at one or more of these levels, allowing pupils greater flexibility to qualify within a 'mix and match' credit-based system. Tomlinson also suggested that pupils could take different periods of time to qualify at particular levels to suit their needs (ibid.: 11). More radically, Tomlinson proposed that a range of opportunities should be developed for the accreditation of common knowledge, skills and attributes (CKSA) such as personal awareness, problem-solving, creativity, team-working and moral and ethical awareness (ibid.: 6).

For a number of reasons the government adopted the Tomlinson recommendations only in part and many of the more flexible elements of his proposed curriculum structure that draw in RE, such as CKSA, were dropped from the White Paper. Nevertheless, some exciting prospects for compulsory RE at post-16 can be drawn from the enhancement of the vocational curriculum. Currently there is no opportunity for discrete qualification in RE within the applied education and vocational education pathways. The accreditation of discrete RE is confined to the A/AS Level pathway which excludes a very large number of the young people now engaging in post-16 education. This is a fundamental problem and it requires all the creative resources of RE practitioners to find ways of offering post-16 pupils a full, accredited entitlement. The new National Qualifications Framework has the power to do this, in that it creates opportunities for practitioners to offer relevant and vibrant RE which, in a modular format, can be tailored towards the diverse needs of all pupils at this level (see Figure 9.1).

The accreditation of post-16 RE

Accreditation is of fundamental importance to the success of a post-16 education programme. Those studying at post-16 are less likely to value learning which does not add to their chances of gaining employment or a university place. This is understandable; most are governed by the pressures of an increasingly competitive post-industrial and global job market. It is vital, therefore, to consider the public accreditation opportunities available at post-16. They currently exist within the following awards:

- the A/AS Level in Religious Studies, General Studies or Critical Thinking;
- relevant units of GNVQ, currently being replaced by BTEC and Advanced Vocational GCEs;

Subject-based pathway in education and training Post-16
GCE A Level and/or AS level:

● Religious Studies, General Studies, Critical Thinking
● Units to Level 3 in Key Skills: communication, information technology

Applied education in education and training Post-16
General National Vocational Qualification, currently being replaced by BTEC, Advanced Vocational GCEs, in a broad vocational area such as:

● Business
● Health and Social Care
● Art and Design

Key Skills: communication, information technology
RE can be accredited as integral to GNVQs, or as discrete parts of key skills.

Vocational Training Post-16
National Vocational Qualification in a specific vocational occupation such as:

● Banking Services
● Funeral Services
● Animal Care

Although GNVQ is currently being replaced, it is set out here as an example while the specifications for new BTECs are being written: it functions well as an illustration and it can easily be adapted.

Figure 9.1 Opportunities currently available to accredit RE at post-16

● the Key Skills qualification (particularly communication and personal skills working with others);
● certification of other achievement, which can be provided internally by the individual school or college, or externally by Awarding Bodies such as the Award Scheme Development and Accreditation Network, that run general programmes of study sometimes related to Key Skills (ASDAN is a Qualifications and Curriculum Authority approved awarding body offering a number of programmes and qualifications to recognise and develop personal and social development skills which can contribute considerably to a person's employability);
● work which contributes to certificated recognition of spiritual and moral development opportunities.

Accreditation through GNVQ, BTEC, Advanced Vocational GCEs and Key Skills qualifications is the least-explored opportunity in post-16 RE for those for whom GCE A Level is inappropriate, or for those who have chosen not to sit it, and so the next section devotes some space to a consideration of these as methods of public recognition for study undertaken as part of the general entitlement to RE.

THE GENERAL ENTITLEMENT TO POST-16 RE

This section is devoted to an examination of the options available to teachers regarding pedagogy, content and structure when planning a course designed to offer a general entitlement to RE at post-16. It is appreciated that at this stage of your career such advice may appear redundant, in that student teachers typically do not gain experience of post-16 RE or are required to choose and develop a course of study at this level. However, the material may be helpful to those considering employment in certain sectors of education where you will be expected to choose and develop post-16 courses that allow for an element of RE.

It is intended that you should select from the material presented here; though many of these ideas can be used without the accreditation option, there are a number of possibilities available for the accreditation of RE through GNVQ, BTEC, Advanced Vocational GCEs and Key Skills qualifications (see Table 9.1).

Table 9.1 Accreditation possibilities through Key Skills, GNVQ and BTEC

Opportunity	Module/Unit	Assignment task
Key Skills	Communication	Seminar and business presentation through RE assessing use of image, communication of information and response to questions, etc.
	Information Technology	Preparing databases in RE: preparing documents for RE using desktop publishing, etc., use of the internet for communication and information gathering.
	Personal Skills: Working with Others	Exploring belief and practice and their effect upon life and work within a local faith community
GNVQ Advanced/ Vocational GCE	Equal Opportunities and Individuals' Rights	Religious attitudes and moral responsibility
	Interpersonal Interaction	Conflict and resolution in belief and practice between practitioner and patient, e.g. participating in or advising on abortion, dealing with confidentiality, child abuse, etc.
	Psycho-social Aspects of Health and Social Well-being	The effects of life in modern society upon the individual, her/his belief and practice, and interaction with health and social well-being
	Health and Social Care Practice	Respecting belief in planning care programmes, or promoting and protecting health and social well-being

Table 9.1—*(Continued)*

Opportunity	Module/Unit	Assignment task
	Educating for Health and Social Well-being	Human responsibility and initiatives in health and social education, e.g. healing the sick, the hospice movement, dealing with controversy, etc.
GNVQ Advanced/ Vocational GCE	Business in the Economy	Faith community and its influence locally, nationally and globally, e.g. co-operatives, langar, zakah, etc.
Business & Finance	Marketing	Spiritual and moral issues in advertising and influencing customer choice; what makes for successful long-term marketing?
	Human Resources	See example in Table 9.2
	Production and Employment in the Economy	Religious attitudes to employment and the importance of work, prohibited work, service, the spiritual life, e.g. the 'Protestant work ethic', dealing with unemployment, etc.
	Business Planning	Ethical considerations

Pedagogy

It is important to recognise that before offering any post-16 RE programme you must establish your pedagogy. You need to ensure that your course is founded upon educational aims that sustain the rigour and integrity of RE, and that these are not compromised by the process of tailoring your course to the needs of accreditation.

Task 9.1 Post-16 provision

Look at a post-16 course being taught in your school experience schools or one taught in another school. Look at the aims of the course and the pedagogical approaches adopted. Compare these with the aims and pedagogy of another course in another school in which a student teacher is placed on school experience.

The local Agreed Syllabus, the non-statutory National Framework for RE (QCA 2004) and the publication *Religious Education 16–19* (SCAA 1995b) should inform the development of aims. Bear in mind that: (1) aims need to be relevant to the whole-curriculum aims for post-16 education; and (2) that there is a direct progression from work with pupils at Key Stage 4. It is imperative that pupils should build on the conceptual understanding they have gained in previous Key Stages; they should also develop their use of the tools of interfaith dialogue in RE, theological and philosophical reflection, and religious language, thus aiming to further their religious literacy. Pedagogical approaches which further this aim encompass both systematic and thematic teaching in addition to an experiential element to learning, which involves faith communities themselves.

Content

The content of courses should reflect the aims of RE, rather than merely attempt to fit performance criteria and syllabus specifications of vocational qualifications. In a maintained school or a City Technology College to an extent the choice of content is limited by the law. The 1988 Education Reform Act (ERA) requires such schools to 'reflect the fact that the religious traditions of Great Britain are in the main Christian, whilst taking into account the teachings and practices of the other principal religions represented in the country' (ERA 1988, Section 7). In addition, the course should be in accordance with the local Agreed Syllabus.

As with your aims, content should also build on progression in learning from Key Stage 1 to Key Stage 4, thus reflecting the complexity and diversity of post-16 RE. It should not be repetitious of elementary learning: it should be developmental, capitalising on the pupils' increasing awareness of social, employment and personal responsibility in a plural, diverse and often conflicting context. Pupils should learn:

- about the importance of religion in directing belief, action and behaviour;
- how to critically analyse information and articulate their own beliefs;
- about world religions in the context of faith communities;
- the significance of such religious commitment for all aspects of life in Britain: personally, socially, occupationally and globally.

Structure

The structure and style of your course are determined by a number of practical management issues, and these are inevitably affected by the kind of accreditation which you can offer if you do decide to pursue that route. You may find that your course has to be run through a programme of day conferences. This circumstance has implications for grouping, staffing and budgeting. The following are the key issues that you need to consider.

Resourcing

Inevitably, you have to operate on a tight budget, which limits the kinds of activities which you can do. Also, you may find that there are very few appropriate resources for RE at this level.

Timetabling

If the subject's allocation achieves the government recommended 5 per cent minimum of timetable time, then you should expect a timetable allocation of one hour per week or six one-day conferences per year. This gives you scope for developing assignments which can be accredited through general studies, vocational education routes, and so on. If, however, your allocation is restricted to less than this, opportunities for accrediting RE are more limited.

Staffing

There are strong arguments that only specialist staff should teach RE units, as with other subjects, particularly since many staff have had no significant RE themselves on which to draw. The confidence of non-specialist staff may need to be boosted by INSET, since the quality of teaching makes or breaks a post-16 RE programme.

Size of groups

If you are working with a large sixth form you may find that you have large teaching groups: particularly if you are structuring a conference-based RE programme. You should carefully consider your teaching strategies and the kinds of activities which are manageable with the group size you have. Obviously the smaller the group, the greater the opportunities there are for pupils to express their own opinions and engage in more intimate learning strategies.

The ability of pupils

You should also be aware of the ability level of your pupils; groups may well be of mixed ability. If you have prior knowledge of your pupils, use it to gauge the level of work. You need to pitch your teaching accordingly and to differentiate just as you would do in other Key Stages.

Task 9.2 Structural issues in post-16 RE

Either in your school experience school (or another school if your school experience school does not teach RE post-16), discuss with your school-based tutor how these structural issues have influenced the courses offered. Compare your findings with those of another student teacher in another school.

Teaching and learning strategies and assessment

The final success of any course/programme in upholding the integrity, rigour and vibrancy of RE rests with the teaching practices employed in the classroom. This is the key to sustaining the motivation and interest of pupils. The talents and tastes of a group are important and should always be considered when planning teaching and learning activities. The teaching and learning strategies set out in Figure 9.2 could also be considered.

These strategies could be directly related to assessment tasks. It is helpful if preferred methods of assessment in vocational education and training mirror those which

- Make a video.
- Audio-visual resources.
- Plan and deliver collective worship.
- Business presentation for the National Record of Achievement.
- Courtroom drama.
- Debate.
- Visiting speaker.
- Plan and organise a charity event with informative publicity about the religious principles involved in caring for those in need.
- Display on a religious theme, e.g. the 'misinformation' of Islam in the media.
- Plan and run an awareness week, e.g. on disability.
- Plan an ethical advertising campaign linked to local business.
- Produce a magazine on moral issues or local faith communities news.
- Produce a photo-story.
- Pupils plan and organise their own conference.
- Carry out a survey on religious belief in the school.
- Use puzzles and games.
- Pupils give seminars to other pupils.

Figure 9.2 Ideas for teaching and learning strategies at post-16

are already common practice in RE (see Chapter 6 on Assessment). In vocational education, pupils must produce portfolios of evidence to demonstrate their ability to apply the knowledge they have gained in a practical context, a context which it is not always possible to reproduce for them, particularly if the training is classroom-based. Evidence in a portfolio might include outcomes from many of the teaching and learning strategies suggested above: artwork; extended writing; survey; interviews; video-recorded role-play or drama; newspaper work; display; a fully documented record of an event such as a disability awareness day; business presentations, and so on.

It should be remembered that writing assignments for accreditation in vocational qualifications is technically challenging. You should work closely with a staff team involved in teaching the vocational curriculum before venturing to set up your own. You must familiarise yourself with vocational teaching and learning styles, course specifications and assessment procedures. Records of continuous diagnostic feedback to pupils on their work need to be well documented. Pupils must be able to show written evidence of how they have planned their work, and how in their assignments they have covered the performance criteria and range of skills specified to be attained by each element of the unit. You may consider in the future taking an assessor training qualification which helps you to understand how pupils' evidence of work and your records of this should be presented in order to qualify for a vocational qualification.

The model which is presented here (see Table 9.2) shows how RE applies to vocational education and how it can be accredited through performance criteria in already existing qualifications. It does not claim that vocational qualifications in Business can be taught entirely through RE; it merely demonstrates the links that

Table 9.2 A suggestion for vocationally accredited RE post-16

Vocational Qualification in Business at Level 3 *Current GNVQ Mandatory Unit: Human Resources*	
Topics covered	*Related areas in RE*
Rights and responsibilities of employers/employees	Valuing the individual: what makes us human; reverence for life; where does responsibility for others come from? What is the extent of our responsibility for others to help them fulfil their human potential?
Legal and ethical constraints influencing the behaviour of public/private sector	Valuing the community: the concept of service; stewardship; the needs of the community versus the individual; the common good; leadership and power
Ways to uphold the rights of employees/employers including the role of trade unions and staff associations in negotiating conditions of service and resolving conflicts	The relationship between belief and way of life
The changing nature of roles and the challenges of introducing and implementing changes at work	Conflict and resolution
Interviewing and appraisal	Inter-faith dialogue

enlightened employers would deem appropriate in relation to their responsibilities for the workforce. In this case, again for reasons already described, a GNVQ specification has been used as an illustration that is easily adaptable.

The new framework has brought with it a fresh perspective on teaching and learning opportunities in the general entitlement to RE. Courses can be created which are relevant, rigorous and stimulating and the potential exists for accrediting your courses through GNVQ, BTEC, Advanced Vocational GCE, Key Skills or internal certification. This approach allows you to address a diversity of abilities and a range of interests, from the theological and scholarly to the socially concerned. The next section looks at A Level.

Task 9.3 Comparing learning, teaching and assessment

Either in your school experience school (or another school if your school experience school does not teach RE post-16) look at the teaching and learning and assessment of these courses. Compare your findings with those of another student teacher in another school.

RELIGIOUS STUDIES A LEVEL

This section begins to explore some of the practical matters involved in planning and implementing an GCE A Level course in religious studies. A more detailed discussion of GCE A Level teaching can be found in Chapter 8. There are obvious differences between those approaches which are appropriate for the general entitlement and those appropriate for GCE A Level: with the general entitlement, schools have a much freer hand for course design and assessment. GCE A Levels have specified content, and the qualification is mainly by written examination. To some extent, GCE A Level is the easier to plan for and manage precisely because it is more restrictive; content, assessment criteria and examinations are set externally.

The professional challenge

To take on responsibility to teach A Level, either at A/S or A2, is to commit yourself to a substantial amount of preparation and marking of a rigorous kind. Underestimating the challenge of teaching A Level risks the achievement of your pupils: your own preparation should be academic and subject to refined critical scrutiny; your teaching strategies should be re-evaluated continuously; and your pupils' progress checked at every stage. You need to read academic journals, textbooks and papers, as well as creating pupil resources, and you need to familiarise yourself with the conferences and lectures which are often held across the country for post-16 pupils. Helping pupils to become adept at constructing reasoned, logical and well-written essays under pressure takes up a significant part of your teaching time. There are a number of approaches that you should consider which help to support your work at this level.

GCE A Level is sometimes described as the 'gold standard' by employers, principally because it is regarded as a rigorous test of academic ability. As well as the ability to write incisively, it examines how well a pupil can manipulate knowledge and understanding to support a well-informed, theological and philosophical exploration of specified areas of in-depth study. The assessment objectives include the notion that candidates should deal with critical scholarship, and demonstrate understanding of the reasons for diversity in response, judgement and practice of both corporate and personal religious activity. The use of technical religious language in candidates' writing and extensive quotation are expected as a matter of course.

Task 9.4 Observe an A Level lesson

Discuss with a member of staff teaching GCE A Level the professional challenge this provides and how they deal with this. Observe the teacher teaching a GCE A Level class.

Choosing your syllabus and papers

The selection of examining board and syllabus is important: the choice influences the success of the candidates in the final examination. When choosing a syllabus, the teacher should think about content and the style of examination and how well these suit the candidates. Select your units of study carefully and base your choice on several criteria: candidates' prior knowledge of the topic; the number and quality of appropriate resources and textbooks available for study; and your own expertise. Examination papers can vary in layout and the kinds of questions which are set; they can be general or specific; it is wise to obtain a variety of samples and discuss these with post-16 pupils before making a selection. Some may have an optional coursework element which helps candidates who find a straight examination difficult. Reflect upon the assessment criteria for marking and how your candidates, given their abilities, best address these in their responses to the style of question set.

Awarding Bodies also vary in the support which they offer to teachers who are entering candidates for examination with them. Some are very approachable and provide INSET, supplementary notes, examiners' reports, resource lists, guidance on marking and a subject officer who can be contacted. You should be quite demanding of them; they are paid by your school or college for each candidate you enter. Also, it is worth asking the Awarding Body to put you in touch with an experienced teacher of the syllabus, so that you can gain advice and have the opportunity to discuss the practical implementation of the syllabus.

Task 9.5 Syllabus choice

Look at a range of syllabuses for GCE A Level and discuss with the teacher in charge of GCE A Level Religious Studies (either in your school or another school) the syllabus used and why that syllabus was selected over others.

Candidates with mixed ability

It is likely that your pupils are of mixed ability, although not to quite the same extent that you would expect to find in teaching groups at Key Stage 4. However, the differences between candidates become polarised at A Level because of refinement of the criteria for achievement and the skills required for the attainment of each level. Be aware that you still need to differentiate work; some of the language can be extremely difficult to comprehend for many pupils, particularly at first while they are making the transition between GCSE and GCE A Level.

Task 9.6 Improving vocabulary

Identify some of the difficult language in GCE A Level Religious Studies and then try to add to the ways listed to help overcome difficulties with language: use of glossary sheets and/or dictionaries; modelling concepts with drawings, charts or posters; simple learning and testing of words; peer tutoring. When you have the opportunity, try these out in practice.

For pupils who are of marked ability, you need to ensure that they are continually challenged to extend their powers of written argument and analysis, and to apply their knowledge and understanding to support their evaluations.

Schemes of work

Planning for an effective GCE A Level course should involve writing a comprehensive scheme of work which takes account of timing and the spread of content. Once time has been allocated to each topic area, allowing space for teacher-led revision, careful thought should be given to assessment tasks and how they relate both to the assessment criteria of the syllabus and the content. Tasks should be planned which effectively develop pupils' examination techniques and all the skills which they need. These should be included in the scheme of work, together with the assessment criteria, and then teaching and learning activities should be planned to correspond to these. In this way, the criteria for assessment are made explicit to pupils throughout their course of study. A revision course should be planned at the same time, revision booklets created, along with specimen question and answer manuals which pupils can borrow.

Teaching and learning strategies at GCE A Level

There is sometimes an assumption that with GCE A Level Religious Studies we leave behind any learning that does not centre around note-taking and textual reading. While those teaching and learning strategies are fundamental to GCE A Level, if they are used exclusively, study becomes monotonous and religions lose their richness and vibrancy. There is no doubt that good pedagogy engages pupils in learning through a variety of methods That said, candidates do need to assimilate comprehensive factual information, and a pupil's staple diet of learning should include plenty of reading around the subject. It is important to issue pupils with bibliographies and web addresses so that they can read and develop their research skills independently.

Pupils also require thorough coaching in essay writing techniques. Using a model for the structure of an essay that pupils can easily identify with, such as a 'hamburger model' is very helpful. In this model the 'bun' relates to the introduction and conclusion, which are similar but not identical, and which when read together should form a summary and evaluation of the main arguments deployed in the essay. The layers of meat represent the main arguments, while the salad, cheese and onions represent the factual information and quotations used to support the arguments. Finally, pupils can be shown how to add the 'relish', in other words, you teach them how to polish their writing – through appropriate quotations, references to scholars, and so on. This is a simple model for pupils who have never encountered academic writing before; there are others which you can construct to suit your own candidates.

There are a variety of different teaching and learning strategies that can be interwoven with textual work and writing. Being more practical, they support the intellectual challenge of GCE A Level by giving pupils models – visual images – on which to 'hang' much of their conceptual learning and improving motivation. Such strategies include using audio-visual resources such as video and music; exploring artefacts; engaging visitors from the faith communities or organisations; arranging trips; inventing games; organising quizzes and using prizes as an additional motivator; asking pupils to teach seminars; using independent learning through research and field work; encouraging pupils to attend conferences and to subscribe to magazines such as philosophical journals for sixth formers. The non-textual resources available within the faith communities, museums and art galleries are many, and they provide pupils with a real opportunity to have a direct engagement with the subtleties and intricacies of belief in a diverse and conflicting society, and a role in bridge-building and inter-faith dialogue. The effective use of creative strategies stimulates the class-room interaction and debate necessary to help refine skills of logical argument, as well as making lessons lively. Combining this with continuous constructive feedback and positive reinforcement contributes to the enhancement of pupils' confidence, and consequently their performance in the final examination.

SUMMARY AND KEY POINTS

As a future practitioner it is your duty to know how to develop stimulating and relevant courses, which are rigorous and which protect the integrity of the subject. Within this brief, there are exciting possibilities which have the potential to regenerate RE's contribution to post-16 education. Already there exist opportunities to create new perspectives on the links between RE and the world of employment and public life.

RE at post-16, like many other subjects, has been traditionally offered at GCE A Level and provided as a general entitlement in much the same style. As the new National Qualifications Framework develops, a new vision of the future of post-16 education is emerging, characterised by fluidity, flexibility and diversity. The potential for more dynamic and more inclusive RE within such a framework is considerable and exciting. RE can offer diverse modules of a subject-based or vocational character: permitting pupils to study the subject in a variety of contexts at a number of levels according to individual needs and requirements.

Some modules could reflect traditional GCE A Level content. Some could aim to develop critical thinking skills through philosophy or epistemology in relation to theistic and non-theistic belief. Others could concentrate on religious issues that affect the workplace or national and global public life, such as human resources or international team-working. Others could explore the religious dimensions of community life and citizenship, and so on. This new perspective on post-16 religious education reveals a wealth of learning opportunities that enables it to fulfil its key role as a significant contributor to social and economic capital, and as an investment in the enrichment of the individual, community, social and working life. RE post-16 is concerned with belief, and with the cultural, creative, transformative, critically reflective and cohesive dimensions of the social world; and these are the qualities that enable societies to prosper and develop.

FURTHER READING

Grimmitt, M. (1987) *Religious Education and Human Development*, Great Wakering, Essex: McCrimmon. This book examines the contribution of RE to human development and how learning in RE itself develops within the individual.

MacGilchrist, B., Myers, K. and Reed, J. (2004) *The Intelligent School*, London: Paul Chapman. This text provides a useful general pedagogical context for classroom teaching, with balanced critical analysis of current theoretical trends and valuable discussion for practitioners seeking to create a vibrant learning environment.

Ogden, V. (1997) *The Role of Religious Education at 16–19 in the Ascendancy of Work-related Learning and a New Framework for Post-compulsory Education*, Abingdon: Culham College Institute. This is a report prepared on behalf of the Sir Halley Stewart Trust into the nationwide provision of post-16 religious education, together with a critical analysis of the relevance and potential of RE as a general entitlement. The report discusses the aims of post-16 RE and its future character.

QCA (2004) *The Non-Statutory National Framework for RE*, London: QCA. Covers all aspects of RE up to the age of 19.

SCAA (1995b) *Religious Education 16–19*, London: Schools Curriculum and Assessment Authority. An influential discussion paper which makes suggestions for appropriate provision for RE at post-16. Now dated but still interesting.

Tomlinson, M. (2004) *14–19 Curriculum and Qualifications Reform*, London: HMSO. While many of the proposals in this document were not included in the subsequent White Paper, the text provides an understanding of the issues surrounding the academic divide and draws up a structure for radical change. It acts as an interesting, comparative perspective on what education post-16 might become.

Web resources

http://post16.reonline.org.uk/ Provides a range of resources, chiefly directed to A Level subjects.

Part IV

Religious Education and the whole school

10 Spirituality in the classroom

Clive Erricker and Jane Erricker

INTRODUCTION

This chapter aims to introduce the concept of spirituality as it is variously understood and currently debated in society and in education. It discusses the legal requirements for addressing young people's spiritual development in state education, the guidelines produced by the Office for Standards in Education (Ofsted) and the documents produced by the School Curriculum and Assessment Authority (SCAA – now the Qualifications and Curriculum Authority (QCA)). The SCAA documents present different understandings of the nature of spirituality and the relationship between spirituality and religious belief with reference to the development of spiritual education in state schooling. This leads us to consider the ways in which you may address spiritual development in practice within your teaching, the curriculum and RE.

OBJECTIVES

By the end of this chapter you should be able to:

- be familiar with the legal requirements, directives and guidelines for the development of spirituality in education;
- debate the issues around the different approaches to the nature of spirituality and its role in education;
- begin to identify ways in which spiritual education can be implemented in the curriculum.

SPIRITUALITY, EDUCATION AND THE REQUIREMENTS OF THE 1988 EDUCATION REFORM ACT

The 1988 Education Reform Act identified spiritual development as one of the main aims of state schooling, which should underpin the curriculum. The national system of education is to be one that both

- promotes the spiritual, moral, cultural, mental and physical development of pupils at the school and of the society, and
- prepares such pupils for the opportunities, responsibilities and experiences of adult life.

(HMSO 1988: 1)

These aims were restated in later documentation and in two official government circulars that followed the Act: Circular 3/89 and the subsequent Circular 1/94 (DES 1989: 4; DFE 1994a: 9). These documents (1) reinforced the concern of the 1988 Act to ensure that spiritual development reassert its presence in education, and (2) confirmed 'the government's commitment to strengthening the position of Religious Education and collective worship in schools' (DES 1989: 4).

Circular 1/94 further stated that

> The Government is concerned that insufficient attention has been paid explicitly to the spiritual, moral and cultural aspects of pupils' development and would encourage schools to address how the curriculum and other activities might best contribute to this crucial dimension of education.
>
> (DfE 1994: 9)

This emphasis on the importance of addressing spirituality caused some concern in the teaching profession generally (which thought of it as inappropriate to 'secular' subjects), though it was received more positively by religious educators who saw it as confirming the role of religion in education. In order to clarify some of the problems concerning the nature of the provision required, further directives and guidelines were produced by Ofsted.

Ofsted guidance on inspection

In its latest guidance documentation, *Promoting and Evaluating Pupils' Spiritual, Moral, Social and Cultural Development* (Ofsted 2003), Ofsted identifies three different components of spiritual development:

- the development of insights, principles, beliefs, attitudes and values which guide and motivate us. For many pupils, these will have a significant religious basis;
- a developing understanding of feelings and emotions which causes us to reflect and to learn;

- for all pupils, a developing recognition that their insights, principles, beliefs, attitudes and values should influence, inspire or guide them in life.

These three components are then put together to produce the following definition of spiritual development:

> Spiritual development is the development of the non-material element of a human being which animates and sustains us and, depending on our point of view, either ends or continues in some form when we die. It is about the development of a sense of identity, self-worth, personal insight, meaning and purpose. It is about the development of a pupil's 'spirit'. Some people may call it the development of a pupil's 'soul'; others as the development of 'personality' or 'character'.

> (ibid.: 12)

You should recognise that it is the school's provision for spiritual development that is the subject of Ofsted inspection rather than the pupil's spirituality. It is the job of the school to facilitate the spiritual development of pupils, and it is the job of the inspectorate to ensure that appropriate provisions are made; it is not the job of the inspectorate to assess the spiritual development of pupils.

One of the criticisms directed against earlier documentation by Ofsted on spiritual development in schools was that it did not supply any specific assessment criteria or identify how spirituality should be addressed in particular curriculum contexts. Earlier documentation was also criticised for stressing the importance of the development of the individual and the uniqueness of what is meant by spirituality to each individual rather than how schools and institutions can nurture spiritual development. The new 2003 Guidance addresses these criticisms by listing the characteristics associated with the spiritual development of pupils and by indicating what schools can provide to encourage spiritual development (Figure 10.1).

SCAA: The official position on spiritual and moral development

In 1995 the government, through SCAA (now the QCA), produced an important discussion paper, entitled *Spiritual and Moral Development* (SCAA 1995a). This prepared the way for a major conference the following year and subsequent publications related to spiritual and moral development in schools (SCAA 1996a, 1996b). These documents are foundational to the interpretation of spiritual development and to the form of its implementation in schools today. Through these discussion papers SCAA raised the profile of spirituality, while linking it to morality and values in education. This connection with morality is continued in *The Non-Statutory Framework for RE* (QCA 2004), where it is asserted that 'Religious education provides opportunities to promote *spiritual development*' (ibid.: 14) through:

- discussing and reflecting on key questions of meaning and truth such as the origins of the universe, life after death, good and evil, beliefs about God and values such as justice, honesty and truth;

Pupils who are developing spiritually are likely to be developing some or all of the following characteristics:

- a set of values, principles and beliefs, which may or may not be religious, which inform their perspective on life and their patterns of behaviour
- an awareness and understanding of their own and others' beliefs
- a respect for themselves and for others
- a sense of empathy with others, concern and compassion
- an increasing ability to reflect and learn from this reflection
- an ability to show courage and persistence in defence of their aims, values, principles and beliefs
- a readiness to challenge all that would constrain the human spirit: for example, poverty of aspiration, lack of self-confidence and belief, moral neutrality or indifference, force, fanaticism, aggression, greed, injustice, narrowness of vision, self-interest, sexism, racism and other forms of discrimination
- an appreciation of the intangible – for example, beauty, truth, love, goodness, order – as well as for mystery, paradox and ambiguity
- a respect for insight as well as for knowledge and reason
- an expressive and/or creative impulse
- an ability to think in terms of the 'whole' – for example, concepts such as harmony, interdependence, scale, perspective
- an understanding of feelings and emotions, and their likely impact.

Schools that are encouraging pupils' spiritual development are, therefore, likely to be:

- giving pupils the opportunity to explore values and beliefs, including religious beliefs, and the way in which they affect people's lives
- where pupils already have religious beliefs, supporting and developing these beliefs in ways which are personal and relevant to them
- encouraging pupils to explore and develop what animates themselves and others
- encouraging pupils to reflect and learn from reflection
- giving pupils the opportunity to understand human feelings and emotions, the way they affect people and how an understanding of them can be helpful
- developing a climate or ethos within which all pupils can grow and flourish, respect others and be respected
- accommodating difference and respecting the integrity of individuals
- promoting teaching styles which:
  - value pupils' questions and give them space for their own thoughts, ideas and concerns
  - enable pupils to make connections between aspects of their learning
  - encourage pupils to relate their learning to a wider frame of reference – for example, asking 'why?', 'how?' and 'where?' as well as 'what?'
- monitoring, in simple, pragmatic ways, the success of what is provided.

Source: Ofsted (2003: 13–14)

Figure 10.1 Ofsted's interpretation of spiritual development

- learning about and reflecting on important concepts, experiences and beliefs that are at the heart of religious and other traditions and practices;
- considering how beliefs and concepts in religion may be expressed through the creative and expressive arts and related to the human and natural sciences, thereby contributing to personal and communal identity;
- considering how religions and other world-views perceive the value of human beings, and their relationships with one another, with the natural world, and with God;
- valuing relationships and developing a sense of belonging;
- developing their own views and ideas on religious and spiritual issues.

Task 10.1 SCAA and the debate on spiritual education in schools

Obtain copies of *Spiritual and Moral Development* (SCAA 1996a) and *Education for Adult Life* (SCAA 1996b). These represent early attempts by SCAA to give meaning and substance to the notion of spiritual development in schools. Review each document and identify:

- what changes you observe between the two documents;
- whether the changes would be helpful to you as a teacher in implementing spiritual education alongside moral education;
- what specific principles, in approaching spiritual and moral education in the classroom, you think you need to employ to conform to the SCAA model;
- whether the SCAA approach is deficient in any respects, in relation to addressing children's spirituality or as guidance for classroom teaching.

Keep a record of your responses to each question for discussion in your tutor group.

THE NATURE OF SPIRITUALITY: SPIRITUALITY, RELIGIOUS BELIEF AND EDUCATION

This section considers the positions of six writers concerned to establish the approach that should be taken towards spiritual education: Jack Priestley, David Hay, Adrian Thatcher, Dennis Starkings, Clive Erricker and Andrew Wright. They are representative of the main interpretations of spirituality and spiritual development that are influential in schools.

Jack Priestley: spirituality as a dynamic process

Jack Priestley notes in his Hockerill Address of 1996 that the key moment in the use of 'spiritual' in modern education was its appearance in the 1944 Education Act, preceding 'moral, mental and physical' in the first sentence of the Act's preamble; he goes on to argue that it owes its presence to 'a simple piece of archiepiscopal jiggery-pokery' (Priestley 1996: 2; cf. HMSO 1944). Priestley explains this by relating how the author of that part of the preamble, Canon J. Hall, the Chief Officer of the National Society (NS), was chosen for the post by Archbishop Temple to gain 'the confidence of local authorities, directors of education and the teachers in their organisations' in seeking a partnership between church and state schools (Priestley 1996: 8). When Hall was asked why he had used the word 'spiritual' rather than 'religious', he replied, 'Because it was much broader . . . If we had used the word religious they would all have started arguing about it' (ibid.: 8).

Priestley also relates how the word 'spiritual' was defined as 'a meaningless adjective for the atheist and of dubious use to the agnostic' (ibid.: 2), in a 1977 report on the 11–16 Curriculum (DES/HMI 1977). Priestley observes that such views often flew in the face of, or were simply ignorant of, relevant educational research. This, as we shall see, is not an uncommon phenomenon.

The most significant points to note about Priestley's observations are: (1) how the notions of spiritual and religious are overlapping but distinct; (2) how contentious the word spiritual is in modern society; and (3) how the notion of the spiritual has a particularly ambivalent place in relation to the curriculum. Priestley's own position focuses on the way we talk about education. Drawing on the philosophers Ludwig Wittgenstein and Alfred North Whitehead, he argues that the language we use to speak of education imprisons us in an impoverished conception of it. We have reduced education to a thing we call 'curriculum' rather than understanding it as a process which is creative and dynamic. It is for this reason that we have such trouble placing spirituality in education, since

> to dwell on the spiritual is to emphasise the subjective, to dwell on the process of being and becoming. Discussion of the curriculum, however, centres around knowledge. Knowledge is seen as objective, something which exists outside of ourselves but which we can take in through learning and contain through memory. That is one of the key dangers of reducing education to curriculum and one of which we have suddenly become aware again. The documentation of the past decade has been depressing because of its limited vocabulary. It is dominated by notions of teaching and learning. There has been precious little attention paid to thinking, creating, imagining, becoming.
>
> (Priestley 1997: 29 ff.)

The emphasis in Priestley's understanding of the spiritual is not related to a particular faith stance or the distinction between the religious and non-religious. Priestley even refutes the need for definition in an attempt to open up our understanding of the possibilities of education once it is understood in its fullest (spiritual) sense of being a life-giving process.

David Hay: challenging the secular suspicion of spirituality

David Hay has been an important voice in addressing the spiritual in education prior to and since the 1988 Education Reform Act. You will find his most recent research into children's spirituality in the next section, but his concern with our suspicion of the spiritual in an age in which secularity dominates is a key theme in his earlier writing.

In 'Suspicion of the Spiritual: Teaching Religion in a World of Secular Experience' (Hay 1985) he argues that there is a detachment from the spiritual in the teaching of RE. He attributes it to a hermeneutic of suspicion: a scepticism towards religious experience that has developed from the reflections on religion of dominant thinkers such as Marx, Nietzsche and Freud. Here religion is equated with neurosis and alienation rather than being perceived as a positive influence on the lives of believers and society as a whole. The powerful metaphors associated with this view place God beyond or above the world: when coupled with our consciousness acting as an instrument of unintentional indoctrination, this results in people suppressing and keeping their experience secret, in so far as it contradicts 'official reality', 'for fear they be thought stupid or mad' (Hay 1985: 141). Such religious and spiritual experiences, according to Hay's empirical research, are far more common than institutionalised affiliation to religious institutions would suggest (Hay 1982).

Hay contends that religious education has distanced itself from faith, without which the understanding of a believer's experience of the sacred is impossible, and aligned itself by default with secularism. He states: 'We root science education in direct experience and I believe we should strive to do the same with religious education, [otherwise] it will be impossible for them to get a genuine grasp of the nature of religion' (Hay 1985: 144). Thus prayer, meditation and contemplation become the foci of religious education because they are 'the heartland of faith' (ibid.: 143).

We may say that, whereas Priestley is concerned with the way in which education has erased the spiritual because of its cognitive concern for curriculum knowledge, for Hay it is the character of modern industrial society and its anti-religious sentiment that have caused the spiritual to be omitted from the very curriculum subject in which it should be central. In this respect Hay's views bear some similarities to those of our next figure, Adrian Thatcher.

Adrian Thatcher: spirituality and the recovery of religious truth

In 'The Recovery of Christian Education' Thatcher argues that 'one of the most important tasks for the theologian is to draw attention to the climate of unbelief within which the religious educator operates' (Thatcher 1990: 274). This he links with the rise of emotivism, characterised by Alasdair MacIntyre as 'the doctrine that all evaluative judgements and more specifically all moral judgements are nothing but expressions of preference, expressions of attitude or feeling, insofar as they are moral or evaluative in character' (ibid.: 274). By drawing connections between unbelief and emotivism Thatcher arrives at the conclusion that, just as morally contemporary society needs to recover a sense of virtue, so theologically we need to recover a grasp of religious truth (ibid.: 275).

Thatcher then turns his attention to the viewpoint advocated by SCAA (1995a). He argues that SCAA's documentation is so vague that it simply states the obvious and offers no concrete guidance or direction. Further, SCAA fails to make any substantial connection between spiritual and a theological account of moral development. This, suggests Thatcher, is a result of SCAA's lack of any distinct faith stance within which to locate moral and spiritual development. For Thatcher, authentic spirituality must always be rooted in a specific world-view.

Dennis Starkings: the arts and aesthetic spirituality

Coming at the problem from a different perspective, Starkings argues the case for a broader definition of spirituality than Thatcher (Starkings 1993b). In considering his position you should ask yourself two questions: 'Does it overcome Thatcher's objections to SCAA?' and 'Does it offer a more workable approach?'

Starkings is concerned with the problematic divide between the religious and the secular as it affects our understanding of spirituality, and he sees the arts as a mediating instrument. He poses the problem of how to take an overall view of spirituality while maintaining the distinctiveness of (for example) Christian spirituality. He suggests that 'while the religious kinds of spirituality find their focus and authentication in the distinctive experience of worship, secular spirituality is authenticated in a progressive integration of life's experience' and yet that 'the religious and the secular are related to each other through the contemporary experience of living across essentially distinguishable frameworks of meaning' (ibid.: 9). Starkings's position is that

> [the] challenge for anyone who wishes to form a view of the nature of spirituality that is sufficient for the comprehensive purposes of a national education system is . . . to draw such a map of spirituality's overall landscape as may relate spirituality's distinctively religious forms to its broader and secular manifestations.
>
> (ibid.: 10)

He charts the steps towards this relationship by identifying Christian faith as the experience of moving towards God through the disclosures of revelation. Revelation is to be grappled with in the movement from unknowing to knowing. This he understands as worship, in its broadest sense. Starkings wishes to retain the distinctiveness of the religious path but assert the authenticity of the secular with reference to the spiritual value of music, ballet, painting or drama. He suggests that through these and other human activities we reach out towards some wisdom, some humanity, some integration of our life's experience (ibid.: 14). Thus both the religious and the secular use of the term refer to moving beyond the purely material, and in neither case can spiritual development be gained solely on the basis of confessional attachment. The important issue is to sustain the dynamics of the religious and secular options while discarding neither.

Clive Erricker: spiritual relativity

A fifth perspective, advanced by Clive Erricker (the author of this chapter), is that a relativist position is the most appropriate and workable approach to adopt (Erricker 1998: 51–64). He criticises Thatcher on the basis that a Christian theological perspective is inappropriate, given that both society and state schooling lack commitment to Christian belief and an education grounded in Christian nurture. The fear of secularity and relativism, he argues, is unfounded. Relativism is not to be equated with the idea that 'anything goes', but is a recognised philosophical standpoint that affirms divergence of view and on this basis calls for a consensus of values while accepting the distinctiveness of different epistemological and faith stances.

Erricker's argument is that spiritual development is concerned with helping pupils to reflect upon their own experiences and those of others in order to investigate the process of spiritual development itself. This position therefore opposes the idea of attempting to arrive at a shared definition or common theological basis upon which provision for spiritual development can proceed. Erricker reasons that to do the latter would result in precisely the opposite of what we are attempting to achieve educationally as well as bringing about the disaffection of pupils.

Andrew Wright: embodied spirituality

Wright situates himself between the positions of Thatcher and Erricker. In *Embodied Spirituality: The Place of Culture and Tradition in Contemporary Educational Discourse on Spirituality* (Wright 1997a) he draws on the work of Alasdair MacIntyre and Paul Ricoeur. Wright points out that it is necessary to understand spirituality in terms of communal identity, which must begin with 'recognising and nurturing children into the specific spiritual tradition they bring with them to the classroom' (ibid.: 16). He suggests that a 'spiritual education that seeks to dislocate itself from any specific tradition' ends up 'indoctrinating children into the spiritual tradition of romanticism' (ibid.: 17), which he identifies with the teachings of Rousseau and those of progressive child-centred educators. For Wright, it is also important that spiritual development is an enquiry into truth and truth claims, a position he describes as 'critical realist'. Here there is an obvious tension with Erricker's relativist position, stated above.

Task 10.2 Approaches to spiritual education

Consider two of the approaches outlined in the main text and construct a classroom activity for each that conveys the spirit of the approach in terms of its educational aims. Teach a lesson containing the activity and evaluate the response of your pupils. Share your findings with your tutor – or class teacher – identifying the implications for future planning and teaching

Here are some suggestions to help in your planning:

Jack Priestley. You might use a poem that would connect with the children's experience and imagination.

David Hay. You might introduce a contemplative or meditative activity.

Adrian Thatcher. You might identify how a parable can advance children's understanding of spiritual insight.

Dennis Starkings. You might identify how the performing arts and artistic expression might result in spiritual reflection.

Clive Erricker. You might interview children on the question of what really matters to them in their life.

Andrew Wright. You might wish to ask children to explain with which religious tradition they identify and how that contributes to their lifestyle or world-view.

UNDERSTANDING CHILDREN'S SPIRITUALITY

This section presents different approaches to researching spirituality in children's development and therefore different approaches to its inclusion in the curriculum. It considers the work of Robert Coles, David Hay and Rebecca Nye, and of the Children and Worldviews Project. All three approaches are empirically grounded in fieldwork that provides the basis of their understanding of children's spirituality. You should consider how their research can relate to your practice in the classroom as a teacher who is also engaged with discovering and reporting on the spirituality of your pupils.

Robert Coles

In Robert Coles's book *The Spiritual Life of Children* (1990), he explains how he began carrying out research into children's lives after witnessing the effect of race riots on children in New Orleans in 1960. At that point he turned from his training as a psychoanalyst to become a field worker, talking to children going about their everyday lives 'amid substantial social and emotional stress' (ibid.: xi). His work, specifically concerned with children's spirituality, took the form of a research project begun in 1985 spanning the Americas, Europe, the Middle East and Africa, and covering conversations with children of various faith backgrounds and others belonging to no faith community. His approach was based on the view that the construction of religious ideas was a valuable aspect of people's identity and that children themselves already evidenced this original and creative activity rather than simply being the receptors of adult ideas. Coles was influenced by the writings of Dr Ana-Maria Rizzuto and her view that 'it is in the nature of human beings, from early childhood until the last breath, to sift and sort and to play, first with toys and games and teddy bears and animals, then with ideas and words and images and sounds and notions' (ibid.: 6). He understood this activity as deriving from 'our predicament as human beings, young or old – and the way our minds deal with that predicament, from the earliest years to the final breath' (ibid.: 7).

Coles' approach can be characterised by the three distinct features.

1   *Qualitative.* Conducted through semi-structured interviews with individuals and groups.
2   *Anti-reductionist.* Not imposing a pre-established theoretical framework on the interpretation of findings.
3   *Non-judgemental.* Not subjecting respondent's views to a rational or systematic scrutiny.

Coles reports his conversations with children in detail in his book. A brief example is given in Figure 10.2. He does not seek to place the children's comments and observations within any predetermined theoretical framework, or to draw from them any general conclusions about the nature of children's spirituality:

> I have no doubt that psychiatric interpretations of much that children say about religious and spiritual matters can, in a sensitive doctor's hands, be of great interest; and I have no doubt that a cognitively based analysis of the manner in which the moral and religious and spiritual thinking of children changes over time can also be of great interest. Do I risk pomposity when I describe this work as phenomenological and existential rather than geared towards psychopathology, or towards the abstractions that go with 'stage theory', with 'levels' of 'development'?
>
> (ibid.: 39ff.)

The following extract is from an interview Coles carried out with a Hopi Indian girl (Coles 1990: 25). The girl is reporting a conversation she has had with her teacher.

Child. The sky watches us and listens to us. It talks to us and listens to us. It talks to us and hopes we are ready to talk back. The sky is where the God of the Anglos [white Americans] live, a teacher told us. She asked where our God lives. I said, 'I don't know.' I was telling the truth! Our God is the sky, and lives wherever the sky is. Our God is the sun and the moon, too; and our God is our [the Hopi] people, if we remember to stay here [on the consecrated land]. This is where we're supposed to be, and if we leave, we lose God.

Coles asks if she explained this to the teacher.

Child. No.
Coles. Why?
Child. Because she thinks that God is a person. If I'd told her, she'd give us that smile.
Coles. What smile?
Child. The smile that says to us, 'You kids are cute, but you're dumb. You're different – and you're all wrong!'

Figure 10.2 An example of Coles's research into the spirituality of childhood

David Hay and Rebecca Nye

Below is an extract from Hay and Nye's work, carried out at the University of Nottingham, illustrating its purpose and method:

> We have been working with children aged six and ten years in Nottingham and Birmingham and have had to consider how spirituality might be given expression at the fringes of its traditional vehicle in European culture, the language of Christian theology . . . Where the language and institutions of formal religion are absent or unconvincing for many people, we had to try to identify the areas of children's language and behaviour where the 'sparks of spirituality' may be found.
>
> For this purpose we needed to create a hypothetical map as a kind of template to guide our conversations with children. We examined the converging evidence of writers on spirituality and on child psychology, as well as our own experience of talking with children in the pilot stage of the project. As a result we proposed a set of three interrelated themes or categories of spiritual sensitivity which were basic enough to allow expression within or outside the familiar (usually religious) languages of spirituality. The intention is to make possible the identification of spirituality in a wider and more abstract context than has been achieved elsewhere. We thus are able to move beyond an understanding of children's spirituality based on 'knowledge' towards a more general psychological domain of spirituality as a basic form of knowing, available to us all as part of our biological inheritance.
>
> (Hay and Nye 1996: 9ff.)

Hay and Nye constructed a table of categories of spiritual sensitivity, referred to as 'a geography of the spirit', which is set out in Figure 10.3. Hay and Nye's approach can be characterised as follows:

- *Awareness sensing*. Being aware of oneself in the present moment. This can be understood in religious terms in the practice of meditation and contemplative prayer.
- *Mystery sensing*. Awareness of our experiences of realities that are in principle incomprehensible. They include experiences of fascination, awe and wonder.
- *Value sensing*. This concerns feelings of what really matters to us. Here strong feelings are a measure of matters of importance.
- *Relationship*. This refers to an awareness of our relationship with ourselves, with others and the world around us in a holistic sense.
- *Meaning*. This concerns questions of existential importance. Typically these may be 'Who am I?', 'Where do I belong?', 'What is my purpose?'

Source: Hay and Nye (1998: 57)

Figure 10.3 Hay and Nye's categories of spiritual sensitivity

- It seeks to uncover children's spirituality in a social context identified as secular.
- It affirms a belief in the innate spirituality of children.

Hay and Nye seek to relate children's spiritual experience to that traditionally expressed in religion.

The Children and Worldviews Project

This approach stems from the belief that the way in which children learn cannot be separated from who they are and the experiences that have shaped their identity. Children's experiences, and their interpretations of those experiences, form the vehicle by which all subsequent experiences (including formal learning experiences) are moulded and readjusted in order that the child can make sense of them. This selective patterning of experiences and reflections forms the child's world-view, the window through which he or she looks out on the world and which protects his or her sense of identity. This understanding of spiritual and moral development can be placed within a 'process approach' to education.

The personal construct theory of learning suggested by Kelly holds that an individual invariably approaches any situation in life with a personal theory of explanation (Kelly 1986). If these ideas, either explicitly taught or implicitly assimilated by the child, are ones which deal with existential issues, then we may be said to be considering children's spirituality. After looking at the information provided by conversations with children, the project developed the idea that the way to access children's understanding is to look at the metaphors that they use when talking about important issues. Affirming Cooper's suggestion that 'Metaphor's essential role is a cognitive one, sustained by our need to explain and understand through comparison' (Cooper 1986: 18), the project sought to engage with matters of importance to children and facilitate their accounts and explanations of their experiences. From these they identified children's use of metaphor as the key to unpacking their spiritual understanding.

The Children and Worldviews Project's approach can be characterised by the following features:

- It adopts an open-ended and process approach to enquiry into the development of children's spirituality.
- It identifies metaphorical language as a key to the expression of children's spirituality.
- It does not equate spirituality with overtly religious concepts and thinking.

These three approaches each have distinctive perspectives but also provide overlapping concerns and methods. They make it clear that spiritual education has to be pursued in a way that is often very different from the usual delivery of a curriculum subject, and offers models on which classroom practice can be based.

Using this chapter as an initial guide and means of orientation, consult:

- Robert Coles's (1990) *The Spiritual Life of Children*;
- David Hay and Rebecca Nye's (1998) *The Spirit of the Child*;
- The Children and Worldviews Project's *The Education of the Whole Child*.

Discuss and write down what you think are the essential principles to employ in the classroom on the basis of one of the approaches. Now construct a classroom activity that reflects one of the approaches in practice and plan and teach a lesson containing it. Record your findings, in preparation for a discussion with your tutor or class teacher.

APPROACHES TO SPIRITUAL EDUCATION IN RE

This section and the one that follows are essentially practical in nature. The issue addressed is how we can translate the approaches and theoretical stances presented above into the classroom context.

Broadly speaking, commentators are divided into those who believe that spiritual education must be addressed by first giving pupils a religious framework within which to investigate spirituality and those who believe that spirituality is present in the experiences and reflections of children as a matter of course, or even innate. The *Non-Statutory National Framework for RE* (QCA 2004) proceeds according to the first perspective by constructing two attainment targets: learning *about* and learning *from* religion. Within this model 'learning about religion' (the understanding of accurate information concerning religious teachings and practice), should proceed to 'learning from religion' (reflection on the spiritual, or faith awareness). The following classroom suggestion, based on this religion-centred model, uses an example drawn from the Buddhist tradition.

The Buddhist journey and children's journeys

The theme of journeys is often used in religious education. In the Buddhist tradition and in the Buddha's teachings it acts as a metaphor for life. We journey in Samsara (our worldly existence) as we pass from one life to the next. The Buddha's teachings are presented as the Noble Eightfold Path, which provides direction and leads us out of Samsara towards Nirvana (Enlightenment). This is illustrated in the 'wheel of becoming' (Figure 10.4), which depicts Buddhist teachings in a visual way.

In Figure 10.4 the wheel is divided by six spokes which connect to its hub. Around the circumference of the wheel is its rim. Within this structure the Buddhist world-view is illustrated. The hub shows three animals clinging on to one another: a pig, a cockerel and a snake. They represent the three forces that create our worldly existence: ignorance, desire or greed and aversion or hatred. They are the basis of

Figure 10.4 The wheel of becoming
Source: © Dharmachari Āloka – Friends of the Western Buddhist Order

Dukkha, unsatisfactoriness or dis-ease, which the Buddha called the first noble truth. These give rise to the six realms of existence that are depicted between the spokes of the wheel. At the top is the realm of the gods, which is a place of pleasure and happiness but prone to the influence of pride and delusion, which are the forces that produce its nemesis. Below and to its right is the realm of the asuras, or jealous gods. They are afflicted with envy, which produces enmity and conflict characteristic of their world. Working clockwise, the next realm is that of animals, ruled by ignorance and instinctive desire. At the bottom is the realm of hell, full of pain and fear. Moving upwards, we reach the realm of the hungry ghosts who are ruled by unquenchable desire. They can never be satisfied. This is illustrated by their huge stomachs and thin throats. They can never eat or drink enough to end their craving. The last realm is that of human beings. Here we find scenes of birth, work, enjoyment, conflict and death, as well as figures in meditation, reflecting on these experiences. The scenes relate to the four sights Siddhartha experienced when he travelled beyond the palace walls before seeking the end of suffering, which can also be found in the pictures on the rim of the wheel. This is the realm in which the possibility of enlightenment presents itself. It is why a human birth is so precious. We travel through these realms in our different rebirths according to the law of karma.

We can also understand this whole picture psychologically. During our lives we experience these different states of mind, associated with the different realms, and by identifying them we can deal with them appropriately, rather than becoming caught up in the emotions they invoke. In this way we learn how to make the best use of our lives and progress toward enlightenment. Pleasure, anger and jealousy, instinctive desires, fear and pain, craving, all these no longer control us. We recognise them for what they are: passing states. We do not cling to them or reject them. In this way we practise 'letting go', the basic Buddhist attitude.

Task 10.4 suggests an activity through which you can experiment with enabling children to bring their own experiences, imagination, thoughts and feelings to the picture.

Task 10.4 The wheel of becoming: classroom activity

Use the following at an appropriate stage in a lesson within a relevant Scheme of Work.

Get your pupils to think of the wheel as a big picture story, like a cartoon. The idea is to enter the picture imaginatively themselves. Talk through what is happening in the different realms and what it would be like to be there.

- How would you feel?
- What would you like to be doing there?
- Where would you most like to be?
- Where would you least like to be?
- Who would be there with you?
- What would you want to happen?
- What would you not want to happen?
- What would you be thinking and doing?

If your pupils are confident enough, you can introduce the connections between passing from one realm to another, i.e. moving from one state of mind to another. Sometimes we feel happy and sometimes sad. Why does this happen? Sometimes we feel safe and sometimes scared. Why does this happen? According to what the pupils say, you can ask them to think about that, how they deal with it, and the results can be shared in the class or a group. If they get this far they offer many suggestions which you can use to introduce further activities. You now have an opportunity to explain further the Buddhist ideas in the picture, to which they can respond.

You may use the activity given or a different stimulus. Report back to your tutor an evaluation of your session(s): it is important to bear in mind that you are reporting on the value of what you did for the development of your pupils' spirituality. You need to consider how you were able to assess this. Pay particular attention to what you think worked and what you could have done more effectively.

SPIRITUAL EDUCATION ACROSS THE CURRICULUM: STORY AND SPIRITUALITY

Working with children's experience or innate spirituality can be undertaken by assuming their capacity to relate implicitly to spiritual ideas, rationally, emotionally and imaginatively. The approach outlined here accords with this understanding. Story is used as the vehicle to address spirituality and adopts the procedure of telling a story which is passed on to the pupils as potential storytellers in their own right. What is important is not their literal understanding or factual recall of the story but their capacity to pass it on as a matter of importance to the community of listeners. The story of the temple bells, as set out in Figure 10.5, has an implicit relationship with religion, but that need not be the case with other stories that could be chosen. When telling the story in the classroom you can introduce moments at which everyone stops and listens and sees images in the story with closed eyes – in other words, use the story as a form of meditation. The purpose of the ritual and sharing, at the end, is to transfer the story to the listeners and encourage them to link it with their own experiences and reflections. This can lead into further expressive and creative activities.

(Reproduced with amendment from *The Song of the Bird* by Anthony de Mello. © 1982 by Anthony de Mello, S.J. Used by permission of Doubleday, a division of Random House, Inc.)

When he was young a boy used to have a story read to him in bed about a temple and, because it was his favourite story, his parents read it to him again and again. The story told of a temple in a far-off land that had a thousand bells. When the bells rang they made the most beautiful sound in the whole world, and people came from all over the world to hear them. As the boy grew older the story stayed with him. But in the story there was a moment when the temple was destroyed by a huge wave and the ruins were carried to the bottom of the sea. Yet, so it was said, it was still possible to hear the bells if you sat on the shore and listened patiently and silently enough. When he grew up the boy set out to go and hear the bells. He travelled a long distance to the island, where he sat quietly on the beach to hear this most beautiful of sounds. For a whole year he sat there every day, but all he heard was the sound of the gulls in the air, the wind in the trees and the waves on the shore. After a year he decided to go home, disappointed. But before he did he went to the beach to sit for one last time and listen to the sounds which had become so familiar and which he had come to love: the gulls, the wind and the waves. As he did so, sitting silently and still, he heard, at first, one faint bell, then another, and another, until he could hear the sound of the whole thousand bells. It was the most beautiful sound he had ever heard.

Figure 10.5 The story of the temple bells

At the end of the story and the activity that follows it you may wish to distribute a shell to each of the listeners and say that they can now tell the story to someone else by using the shell. Thus the story can start from the object that has become a symbol or image by virtue of embodying a story. One variation is not to tell the ending but to ask the listeners to imagine their own ending. Did the boy hear the bells? In time and with many tellings the story has come to incorporate embellishments – for example, a café/inn where the boy stayed when he first arrived on the island, people in the café whom the boy asked about the bells, etc. This involves listeners in the role of playing these people. Responses then become incorporated in the next telling of the story, and so on.

> **Task 10.5 Story and spirituality in the curriculum**
>
> After telling the story of the temple bells in Figure 10.5 you might ask your pupils to do the following:
>
> - Close their eyes and go back through the story in their minds.
> - Choose their favourite moment.
> - Put their hands out with their palms up next to one another.
> - Transfer their favourite moment from your mind into their hands and close them together.
> - Turn to the person next to them and tell them what they have in their hands and why.
> - Discuss their conversations with the whole class.
>
> Carry out the above activity or adapt the process to a different story at an appropriate time/stage in a relevant lesson within a Scheme of Work. Record key features of the experience, and questions arising from the activity, and report back to your fellow student teachers how it worked in the classroom and what you think was achieved.
>   The important thing is, of course, not the particular story nor the specific activities but the process employed, especially adapting the content and the process to the age of the group and the curriculum. It is important to be aware how the process depends on the involvement of the listeners.

SUMMARY AND KEY POINTS

Understanding the place of spiritual education in the classroom depends on your recognition of the approaches that are available, the processes of application that you can employ, the aims you wish to pursue beyond subject knowledge and the relationship you have with your pupils. Most importantly, you must identify spiritual development not as something that arises from curriculum knowledge alone, but as something you facilitate on the basis of specific aims, objectives and strategies you employ directed toward that end and consonant with both pupils' development and subject understanding. It is important to realise that in religious education the process of addressing spiritual development is important and ongoing.

FURTHER READING

Barnes, L. P. and Kay, W. K. (2002) *Religious Education in England and Wales: Innovations and Reflections*, Leicester: Religious and Theological Studies Fellowship. Chapter 4 provides an overview of developments and discusses a range of interpretations of spiritual development.

Best, R. (ed.) (1996) *Education, Spirituality and the Whole Child*, London: Cassell. Contains a range of articles devoted to different approaches and strategies that can be employed in addressing spiritual education and its associated areas of values and moral education. It is a stimulus to furthering development in social, moral, spiritual and cultural education.

Erricker, C. and Erricker, J. (2000) *Reconstructing Religious, Spiritual and Moral Education*, London: RoutledgeFalmer. This is both a theoretical and practical volume that sets out the case for a relativist and postmodern approach to RE encompassing spiritual education.

Hampshire County Council (2004) *Living Difference: The Agreed Syllabus for Religious Education in Hampshire, Portsmouth and Southampton*, Winchester: Hampshire County Council. This Agreed Syllabus is based upon a methodology for teaching and learning that addresses conceptual enquiry and promotes pupils' spiritual development by focusing on pupils communicating their own beliefs and values.

Ofsted (2003) *Promoting and Evaluating Pupils' Spiritual, Moral, Social and Cultural Development: Guidance for Schools*, London: Office for Standards in Education. This is Ofsted's latest guidance. It provides examples of what schools should be doing to encourage spiritual development and ways in which pupils may be understood to be developing spiritually.

11 Collective worship

Derek Webster

INTRODUCTION

Collective worship has been a feature of school life in Great Britain for centuries. Yet it was not until the 1944 Education Act that it became a legal requirement. This requirement has been reaffirmed by more recent legislation. School worship offers teachers an opportunity to raise important questions of meaning and value for their pupils. These questions arise from teachers' specialist subject areas, e.g. science, geography, information technology as well as their own experiences. Such questions are significant for pupils in secondary schools because they offer a means of thinking about themselves, of forming their values, developing their attitudes and coming to terms with their own feelings. Indeed, at its best, collective worship contributes to the understanding of how to live in the global society of the new millennium. Seen in this light, it is an asset available to all teachers. Instead of being a tiresome daily ritual, an irritant to the senior management team or the RE department, it can be an exciting instrument to be used by schools as they work to achieve their educational ends.

Historically religious education has been very closely related to collective worship in schools; it is only in the past few decades that a clear distinction has been drawn between the two. In many schools, the RE department is expected to contribute to collective worship, and student teachers within such a school may well be invited to assist with preparation and planning. The purpose of this chapter is to acquaint you with an understanding of the nature of collective worship in different types of schools and the legal framework within which collective worship occurs; it should also hopefully reveal something of the potential that collective worship holds for realising educational objectives.

OBJECTIVES

By the end of this chapter you should be able to:

- be aware of the legislation governing collective worship in schools;
- understand the reasons for its controversial nature;
- know the aims collective worship seeks to achieve;
- perceive the educational possibilities it enshrines.

THE LEGAL FRAMEWORK OF COLLECTIVE WORSHIP

There is a flexibility in modern collective worship which commends itself to teachers. They have control over its timing and the approach they wish to take as well as significant freedom in devising appropriate content. They do, however, work within the broad pattern set down by the 1988 Education Reform Act, the Education Act of 1993 and more recent legislation (see below). Guidance in relation to collective worship was given in Circular 3/89 (DES 1989) and in Circular 1/94 (DfE 1994a). Key features in the legal framework affect the responsibility for collective worship in each school; its location, timing and character; the attendance and right of withdrawal of pupils and staff; and the circumstances under which the requirement of Christian worship can be waived.

Responsibility and nature of collective worship

All maintained schools must provide daily collective worship for all registered pupils (apart from those who have been withdrawn from this by their parents). The precise nature of the collective worship at a foundation or voluntary school will depend on the religious character of the school. Whether a foundation or voluntary school has a religious character and the particular religion or religious denomination concerned is set out in The Designation of Schools Having a Religious Character (England) Order 1999 (SI 1999 No. 2432).

Collective worship may be provided within daily assembly but legally it need not; it can take place at any time in the school day and the whole school does not need to get together at the same time. Governing bodies may even arrange for worship to be conducted outside school. This allows schools with religious affiliations to observe holy seasons and festivals in an appropriate setting. When this is done, however, there is still a requirement to hold a statutory act of collective worship in school (HMSO 1988, Section 6: 4–6). This seems an odd and unreasonable requirement to many.

Daily collective worship must be wholly or mainly of a broadly Christian character. The precise nature will depend on the family background, ages and abilities of the pupils. It is acceptable for schools to split the collective worship sessions over the school year to be 51 per cent Christian and 49 per cent other faiths or interests. Most schools should be able to include all pupils in their act of collective worship. There may be exceptional cases, however, where, in view of the family background of some or all pupils, the head teacher and governing body feel that a broadly Christian act of worship is not suitable. In these cases a determination (as described below) may be sought.

Collective worship can be organised into form groups or year groups or whatever is appropriate for the school. It cannot be organised in faith groups unless an exception has been sought and granted by the local Standing Advisory Council on Religions Education (SACRE). Such an exemption is called a 'determination' and can be granted for no more than a five-year period (HMSO 1988, Section 12.5b). Such an arrangement allows schools to respond sensitively to situations where they have large groups of pupils of particular faiths. Schools can then seek to offer worship according to these pupils' own traditions. Collective worship in foundation schools with a religious character and voluntary schools is in accordance with the school's trust deed (i.e., the deed that designates the religious affiliation of the school). Where provision is not made by a trust deed, the worship should be in accordance with the beliefs of the religion or denomination specified for the school.

The head teacher is responsible for arranging the daily collective worship after consulting with the governing body. This does not mean that it is the Head who always and necessarily conducts collective worship, rather, it is a statement of accountability. The Head simply ensures that worship occurs and is suitably organised. Indeed, it is common practice for Heads to handle the responsibility by sharing it with others in school, including pupils, as well as people in the local community.

Attendance and the right of withdrawal from collective worship

Collective worship is compulsory for all pupils in maintained schools unless parents exercise their right of withdrawal. Where a parent wishes to invoke the right of withdrawal, the school is bound to accede, though without having the responsibility to provide any alternative worship. A non-denominational school may, however, offer alternative worship if provision does not involve it in additional expense (HMSO 1988, Sections 9.1, 9.3). Although attendance at assembly is incorporated into all teachers' contracts, it remains subject to their right not to take part in collective worship. They too have a right of withdrawal and may not be discriminated against in any way for exercising it. This provision also includes head teachers.

Distinctions and meanings

It is clear that this legislation draws an important distinction between an assembly and an act of collective worship. Although worship always involves a school, or groups within a school, assembling together, not every assembly is an occasion for worship. An assembly has many purposes. They can range from discussing arrangements for the school skiing holiday to stressing the importance of using the litter bins in the playground. It is, however, quite possible for it to become an act of collective worship when it aims to offer an opportunity for pupils to worship.

A further crucial distinction is that between collective worship and corporate worship (HMSO 1988, Section 6.1). The spectrum of beliefs among young people in a school is very wide. Collective worship acknowledges this by presupposing no unanimity of view on religious matters and making no assumptions about the commitment of pupils, religious or secular. It is accommodating and flexible and can countenance diversity of perspective and individuality of approach. This is in contrast to corporate worship, which implies a body of people united by a common belief system and a shared practice of faith.

Task 11.1 Experiences of worship

Reflect on your own experience of acts of worship while a pupil at secondary school.

- What is your overall impression of them?
- What would have improved them?
- Are there any that stick in your mind? What was memorable about them?

Share your experience with other student teachers. Compile a list of the features that contribute to a successful act of collective worship in schools.

Criticisms of the legislation on collective worship

The legislation providing for school worship has proved to be controversial and divisive within both the teaching profession and religious communities. Each part of the legislation creates anxiety for some group or party. First, there are those who feel that worship should be a voluntary activity, one into which pupils should opt rather than be compulsorily driven. Compulsion in the difficult area of personal beliefs seems out of place in a modern educational philosophy and runs counter to the values of freedom and respect which schools seek to encourage. Second, others maintain that if worship is really educational the retention of a legal right of withdrawal from it is unnecessary. To retain it throws the shadows of indoctrination and faith nurture over it, linking it with a confessionalism that is wholly inappropriate in a modern education.

Third, there are many who think that Circular 1/94, in explaining that an act of collective worship which is broadly Christian 'must contain some elements which relate specifically to the traditions of Christian belief and which accord a special status to Jesus Christ' (DFE 1994: 21) overemphasises and misleads. It jeopardises the educational nature of worship and creates the fear that schools become extensions of the church, become communities of worshipping Christians. Furthermore, it is insensitive and possibly offensive to members of some Muslim, Sikh and Jewish traditions. The common view is that Circular 1/94 no longer enjoys political support.

Fourth, there are those who believe that the legislation takes the matter of content and approach out of the hands of the teachers who best know their own schools and local communities. This can create situations in schools where pupils (and staff) are asked to engage in the hypocrisy of a public proclamation of belief where none exists. Fifth, there is a widespread and deep dissatisfaction with the prescription that collective worship has to be a daily activity. There is important support for an arrangement which would allow fewer but better-quality acts of worship. Sixth, there is a view in some quarters that the legislation should be tougher and go further. It is concerned at the unconscious espousal of secular humanism by the young people of today and urges that worship should be a bulwark against the rising tide of relativism in global society. As a school cannot be neutral in its values, so it cannot be uncommitted in faith. If it does not actively promote one faith (usually Christianity), others promote differing faiths or liberal agnosticism.

It is quite obvious that behind each criticism of the legislation dealing with collective worship lies assumptions about its nature and purpose that emerge from positions affirming particular values which are often well hidden. Collective worship is a contentious activity and a contestable concept. Ofsted inspections consistently show a large minority of secondary schools failing to comply with the legal requirements for collective worship and the compulsory nature of collective worship is a perennial item on the agenda of governors' meetings and teachers' conferences; it has been an issue of lively debate in schools since the 1988 Education Reform Act and shows little sign of abating.

Task 11.2 Observing collective worship

Attend collective worship in your school and obtain the guidelines which it follows. Read and think about them then ask yourself:

- Do the guidelines fit within the prescribed legal framework for worship?
- Do the acts of collective worship in school you have seen fit within the legal framework?

Compare and discuss your observation with another student teacher.

AIMS AND NATURE OF COLLECTIVE WORSHIP

The act of collective worship in school is seen by many to have six key aims. The first is a moral one. Collective worship analyses contemporary issues affecting young people and presents varying responses to them. Most common are matters dealing with the Third World, the environment, drug abuse and the innate dignity of all people. The second is to help pupils identify and think about the spiritual dimension of living. It reminds them of what is inexplicable about themselves, of the mysterious universe in which their lives are set and of the absolute strangeness of the common things which they take for granted. The third aim concentrates on helping young people to develop their own values further. Worship enables them to consider the boundaries of their friendships, their responsibilities to employers and the duties they have as citizens. The fourth aim emphasises and celebrates shared values, especially as they are evident in the life of each school community. Typical topics include discussion of the ways in which it is proper to share and to love, ways in which respect and responsibility can be shown in school, home and society. The fifth aim is set to encourage a community spirit, 'togetherness' with others and a sense of obligation to them as human beings. It focuses on the common bonds that unite men and women of all races and religions. The final aim has to do with reflection on that which is beyond the physical world – that which is sometimes called God and sometimes the Absolute, the Real or the Utterly Mysterious. This something can be pondered through silence, self-reflection, music, artistic creation, scripture, prayer, poetry and hymnody.

Circular 1/94, *Religious Education and Collective Worship*, expresses the aims of collective worship in this way:

> Collective worship in schools should aim to provide the opportunity for pupils to worship God, to consider spiritual and moral issues and to explore their own beliefs; to encourage participation and response, whether through active involvement in the presentation of worship or through listening to and joining in the worship offered; and to develop community spirit, promote a common ethos and shared values, and reinforce positive attitudes.
>
> (DFE 1994: 20)

This quotation provides a helpful summary of the previous six aims and brings neatly together the key purposes of school worship and unwittingly illustrates their weaknesses. What is striking about the aims is the diversity of elements it contains. 'To encourage participation and response' is less an aim than a methodological principle. To envisage pupils 'listening to and joining in the worship offered' is not an aim but a desirable effect. Aims such as 'to develop community spirit, promote a common ethos and shared values' are very broad and occur across the whole curriculum as well as the life of the school. It is therefore better to see them as secondary consequences of worship rather than primary aims. An aim such as 'to reinforce positive attitudes' seems very laudable. But unless there is some explanation of the kind of reinforcement foreseen and the sorts of attitudes wanted, it is pointless. The questions tumble on amid this curious mixture of ideas. For instance, is any one of these aims more important than any other? Are they in a sequence? Clearly the problem is one of values. Schools are asked to encourage young people to walk a particular path but that path is paved with judgements about what is worthwhile, some of which are not clear and some of which are contestable.

Is it bound to be like this with worship or could it be different? The criticisms just made might all be met. Words could be changed or omitted, ideas tidied up and values explained. Yet there remains one aim in Circular 1/94 which it is difficult to avoid and which somehow seems to be at the heart of worship. Schools are required 'to provide the opportunity for pupils to worship God'. While some teachers rejoice at this aim and some find it an impossibility, the majority view it with a mixture of embarrassment and puzzlement. The reason is simply that worshipping God is an activity which is contestable. There is disagreement over its importance, over the kinds of assumptions it makes, the sort of knowledge it seeks to foster, the type of behaviour it proposes to promote and the range of ideals it desires to approve. The best way to make progress in what can easily become an impasse is to decide what is going to count as worship in the context of schools.

The *Shorter Oxford English Dictionary* (2007) gives the main definition of worship as 'To honour or revere as a supernatural being or power'. This accords with the practice of religious people and can be observed in temples, churches, mosques and synagogues. It resonates with the view expressed in Circular 1/94, which states that although the word 'worship' is not defined in the legislation of 1988 and 1993,

> [it] should be taken to have its natural and ordinary meaning. That is, it must in some sense reflect something special or separate from ordinary school activities and should be concerned with reverence or veneration paid to a divine being or power.
>
> (DFE 1994: 21)

This view, which does not have the force of law, is a disputed interpretation. Some see behind it the influence of 'right-wing' Christians in politics and education determined to impose a particular understanding of worship on the nation's schools. Others feel that it offers schools an opportunity to deliver what their young people have a right to receive. This definition could be called a strong one. It has historical roots but is felt by many schools, particularly those with no denominational allegiance or affiliation, to be inflexible. It assumes the existence of a supernatural being and suggests that the appropriate response to such a being is one of adoration. A more accommodating view is suggested by Brian Gates in his 1989 Hockerill Lecture, *The National Curriculum and Values in Education*. He sees worship as 'a generic activity of ascribing worth and value, identifying targets and ideals from and for life and work' (Gates 1989: 13).

This fits well with the further view of worship in *The Shorter Oxford English Dictionary* as: 'to regard with extreme respect or devotion . . . to honour, to salute'. This definition of worship may be called a weak one. Yet it expresses a view which is common in some of the guidance given to their schools by Local Education Authorities.

A middle way is difficult to find and probably unnecessary, for informed opinion is coming round to the view that the legislation permits worship according to each definition. The second weak one is certainly the one that has the widest support among teachers and governors in non-denominational schools faced with organising worship. It enables them to frame aims for collective worship that take into account, in a very precise way, the social composition of their schools, the ethnic origins of their young people and the gifts and abilities of individual pupils. These aims give them the opportunity to deploy staff in ways that recognise their strengths and interests. Finally, they permit schools to acknowledge the community and environment in which they are set. It is immediately obvious from this that the justification of worship in schools and the criteria of its success are educational. In the more usual corporate worship of Sikhs and Hindus, Christians or Jews within their own communities, the justification and criteria are, of course, theological. The weak definition, then, seems to give schools aims for collective worship which have the greatest flexibility.

COLLECTIVE WORSHIP IN COMMUNITY AND SCHOOLS WITH A RELIGIOUS CHARACTER

Community schools

A single and clear definition of worship with which everyone agrees does not, then, exist. Given that it is a contestable concept with deep historical roots, seen by some as a socially or culturally conditioned idea at whose centre is an unverifiable experience, perhaps that is inevitable. Yet while there are those who regard it as wholly reducible and explicable in behavioural terms, there are others who understand it as the response of love to a Divine Person. Between these two ends of the spectrum almost every position imaginable can be found. The problem this gives community (state-controlled) schools is easily put though difficult to solve. How can teachers, some of whom are non-believing, devise models of worship which allow them to retain their own integrity and which also suit the needs of agnostic pupils from a mainly non-religious background? The model which emerges from a majority of secondary schools, seriously attempting to keep within the law and to use worship as an educational instrument, is one which takes as its starting point something akin to the weak definition of worship.

It is a model deriving from a very loose positivist theoretical foundation. It places greater emphasis on the human than on the divine and is sympathetic to those approaches to worship which focus on the richness of human possibility. It sees society and the physical world in terms of what they are themselves rather than in terms of a theologically based grand design. So nature is not an epiphany of God but an instrument which, through technology, can be bent to serve human purposes. Society is not a divinely sanctioned structure of preordained groups but is pluralist, owing to the effects of immigration, urbanisation and class differentiation. The model takes religions not as an overarching frame of reference but as one thread among others set equally within human affairs. So religions have no authority outside their own sphere and may not judge what lies beyond them. Finally, the model sets reason, seen at its best in scientific thinking, as sovereign in understanding society.

Despite many local variations, this model provides a common content for most state schools. It covers three areas: socio-political matters of contemporary significance; personal and moral themes relevant to young people; and school and local community issues. The first of these typically includes gender stereotyping, racial prejudice, homelessness, unemployment, pollution and refugees. The second usually covers rules of family and community living, responsibility in relationships, friends and enemies, duties to others in society, especially those in the Third World, charitable giving and issues of public concern such as HIV/AIDS. The final one deals with the local environment, including that of the school, personal achievements, the value of people, disabled men and women, strangers in the community and service to others.

This, then, is a model which looks for what redeems others from misery and injustice; it celebrates human victories over suffering and hardship. It enables many agnostic teachers to share in collective worship without compromising their personal honesty. However, there are those who criticise the model, pointing out that its emphasis on human matters diminishes the Divine Being, its concern with social and political matters encourages controversy, and its simplistic presentation of complex issues can amount to indoctrination. They fear that its elevation of reason is at the expense of the affective and unconscious in human affairs; that in allowing religion to be a private matter it betrays the spiritual basis of the human person. Those who defend the model reply that worship which arises out of human living is bound to witness to the concerns of that living; that these issues, because they are important, have a political dimension; that reason is a safeguard against indoctrination and sloppy emotional thinking. They assert, finally, that the concept of worship is so broad that it can accommodate a model with a human emphasis as well as one which takes a divine perspective.

Faith community schools

The model of worship which emerges from the practice of faith community schools, the greatest number of which are Anglican and Roman Catholic, is a more theologically based one. The nature of these schools and the historic context of their religious foundation mean that generally they see it as their role to nurture pupils into a particular faith. Sometimes, although not necessarily, this can also mean the assertion of traditional personal, social and political values. Schools of a faith community often have a philosophy which takes a hierarchical view of the structure of reality and presents spiritual values as paramount. It sees the world as a theatre for the activity of God and an expression of his creative power. Human beings are made in God's image and their society is an instrument of his will. These ideas do not go unchallenged, for some believers feel that there is an otherworldliness about this philosophy which fails to acknowledge the pluralist nature of society and is meaningless to pupils. They think that it imposes on young people controversial beliefs, and fosters an obsolete world-view without intellectual credibility. More traditional believers reply, however, that traditional beliefs and values witness to the eternal truths which stand above the fashions and contemporary fads of teenagers.

The content of acts of worship can be very traditional in a small minority of denominational schools. They may be led only by a senior member of staff or an authorised member of the religious community to which the school is attached. They can include the lections for the week, set prayers for the season and hymns which mark the religious pattern of the year. Worship in this mode can quickly subordinate educational common sense to theological rigorism. Less traditional worship employs a more modern idiom. Its prayer is informal, its Scripture is updated, its music has the rhythms and beats of the pop scene, and it uses material which moves easily from drama, film and mime to dance, drawing and poetry.

There are, however, some schools which eschew both these emphases, the traditional and the modern, in the Christian model. They look for a more exploratory approach to worship that affirms the place of questioning and seeking, investigating and challenging in religions. Taking seriously the view that all dogmas are only partial and all doctrines provisional, they prize the quest for truth and the energetic intellectual effort that goes with it. They are hospitable to new insights, acknowledge the ambiguities and sharpness of existence and know that the language of faith is only proximate and corrigible. This emphasis in the denominational model of collective worship is positive about the dialogue of the great religions of the world with one another. It allows that religions do not have all the answers and invites pupils to begin a quest. It is, however, an emphasis or a model which has drawn criticism upon itself. It appears to some to have a theological base which is too fluid; it can appear ambivalent in its witness to a particular faith, even partial; it may be suitable only to older, brighter pupils; and it tends to subordinate theology to education. Those who defend it stress its value in taking pupils to the point where they ponder mystery and build bridges between faiths.

For a very few schools such bridges would include the possibility of inter-faith worship. The essential feature of the inter-faith model of worship is a pattern of ideas which help world faiths to meet each other with sympathy so that a genuine attempt can be made to understand their different thinking and practice. In such a meeting they reflect on what they share, on the ideas they have in common and on the values which unite them. It is, however, a model viewed with deep suspicion, even hostility, and remains controversial to many traditional religious believers. Believers worship in the context of a particular religion, not of no faith, or an amalgam of religions. So some would argue that there cannot be worship unless it is set in the context of a particular religion. To mix the faiths is to deny the distinctiveness of each and to concoct a syncretistic mishmash of ideas confusing to pupils. Those wishing to experiment with the inter-faith model ask each of the religious traditions how far they can walk with other traditions, share the richness of their teaching with them and listen to them.

Task 11.3 Assessing collective worship

Attend acts of collective worship over a few days and write down the extent to which they involve:

- different members of staff or visitors;
- pupils of varying ages;

and the extent to which they:

- have an imaginative content;
- use a variety of media.

Note down your overall impression of their:

- strengths;
- weaknesses.

What would you change if you were the member of staff responsible for collective worship? Why?

Within your tutor group compare the acts of collective worship reported by other student teachers. Do they have any common features? Write a short summary of this meeting, identifying implications for your current school experience and when applying for a first teaching post.

EDUCATION, WORSHIP AND RE

Worship has a close relationship with other areas of the curriculum. It ponders the universe, wondering with the sciences how things come to be and what their purposes are. Probing the mysteries of time and place, it looks in awe at the ever-changing patterns of human history and geography and seeks their meaning. It stands in astonishment at human achievement in the arts: at poetry, whose words capture essences; at drama, which is revelatory of the human spirit; at music, which carries men and women to the threshold of mystery; at art, which becomes a theophany. Worship reflects on the values embedded in human ideals and aspirations as they occur in literature and philosophy. It sees what is noble and worthy as well as what is hideous and evil in the thinking and action of men and women. Of course, it sees with a particular slant and in a certain context. Worship is akin to wearing dark glasses which exclude some items in order to see other items better. So it looks for what integrates and is holistic, for what draws things together. It also sees with a prophetic eye and raises difficult value questions. Those who support it most ardently say that worship seeks the truth: those who deny its place in schools say it is a lie that distorts understanding.

RE in the secondary school curriculum aims to help pupils understand religions and offers a context in which they can reflect on their own beliefs and values. Worship should echo this. Both RE and the act of worship at their best raise questions whose answers are never finally given. What is my origin and end? What is my duty to my neighbour? How may people find justice? What are truth, freedom and beauty? Can my guilt be cleansed? Both engage in a style of thinking which is compassionate, responsible and thankful, which sifts evidence and which does not claim to know all the answers. Both press to the limit and seek the boundaries of knowledge. Both have practical consequences in the lives of pupils. For they affect the attitudes they develop, their understanding of people and the responsibility they feel they have to themselves and others. Religious education and worship can differ sharply in content, in perspective, in the level of empathetic response they demand and in the instruments by which they are assessed. But what draws them most closely together is the foundation on which each stands, the warrant of the place each has in schools, for these are wholly educational.

The act of collective worship and RE share with the rest of the school curriculum the tasks of helping pupils to enlarge their horizons. They work towards that end by affirming the questioning and exploratory nature of the educational venture. They prize a quest for truth which stresses vigorous intellectual effort and honest reporting, for integrity does not take short cuts or trade in deceit. They acknowledge the uncertainties, the ambiguities and pain of existence, looking directly at human evil which many would prefer to veil. They testify to the paradoxes and illogicalities that hold sway among human beings, knowing that every system is imperfect and each life is unfinished. They espouse that critical openness which protests at victimisation, exclusion and destruction among human beings. And finally they refuse to regard as absolute the thinking of the past or overestimate that of the present in challenging current moral reflection.

Task 11.4 Organising collective worship

If you have the opportunity, get involved with a class teacher who is preparing a group to lead or be involved in collective worship. What are the challenges? How can you contribute?

SUMMARY AND KEY POINTS

As the legislation sees it, collective worship (at its best) is a key element in helping pupils to achieve a deeper realisation of their own gifts and responsibilities. It allows the depths within young people to resonate with what they take to be ultimate in their world; it correlates symbols and images with a mystery that seems to inhabit every human being; it speaks of the freedom in involvement and the fulfilment in self-emptying. Although the legislation is imperfect and its aims are inadequately worked out, it steers in broadly the right direction. The practical problems it poses for schools can be worked through, given good will and a clearer understanding of the educational justification and developmental possibilities of worship.

Collective worship is, then, a treasure house and a superb opportunity for teachers of all subject areas. It is at its best when many and diverse enthusiasms are brought to it. It interrogates values and ideals, encourages creative growth and human achievement, recognises the principles beneath human actions and transmits new knowledge. Seen properly, it stands at the centre of the educational venture. It does not indoctrinate; rather the reverse, it challenges the prevailing secular humanism found in state schools and calls for consideration of competing world-views. In doing so, it deepens the humanity of pupils.

FURTHER READING

Copley, T. (2000) *Spiritual Development in the State School: Worship and Spirituality in the Education System of England and Wales*, Exeter: University of Exeter Press. Discusses school worship within the wider area of spiritual development.

Department for Education (1994) *Religious Education and Collective Worship*, Circular 1/94, London: DFE. This is essential reading for those who need to be aware of the legal situation regarding collective worship. It is an interpretation by the DFE of the implications of the legislation of 1989 and 1993 for schools. Effectively it represents the intentions of the government of the time. It has, however, never been tested in the courts.

Webster, D. (1995) *Collective Worship in Schools: Contemporary Approaches*, Cleethorpes: Kenelm Press. This book is one of the few in this area to take seriously the possibility of inter-faith collective worship. It also emphasises the educational nature of collective worship in schools as opposed to the theological nature of corporate worship in faith communities. Relating worship to the spiritual dimension of education, it offers an educational justification of collective worship.

Web resources

www.reweb.org.uk/collective_worship_resources.shtml Provides links to a number of useful and relevant WWW sites.

12 Religious Education and moral education

L. Philip Barnes

INTRODUCTION

Religious Education has traditionally been regarded by educationalists, politicians and parents alike as a major vehicle for moral education. As recently as 1990 the National Curriculum Council commented that the contribution of religious education to an understanding of values was 'too obvious' to warrant discussion (*National Curriculum Council* 1990: 2). But what exactly is the relationship of religious education to moral education? In what ways does religious education serve as a vehicle of moral education in schools and in what ways can it serve? In order to begin to answer these questions it is helpful to develop a genealogical-historical account of the educational role of religious education in relation to morality and moral education. Our concerns are not purely historical but interpretive and critical. We can only appreciate the potential of religious education as a vehicle of moral education if we understand the history of the relationship between the two; that is, if we are familiar with the historical debates and considerations that have contributed to current interpretations, demarcations and practices. What society expects of religious education in relation to morality is historically conditioned; it is also of course politically and legislatively conditioned. Following our historical overview, attention is given to the current legislative framework and some of the non-statutory documents that set out the aims and expectations of schools in relation to moral education and moral development, particularly those aims and expectations that have an application to religious education. This requires some discussion and unpacking of the relationship between moral education and other aspects of the curriculum, particularly spiritual development and education for citizenship (though given that separate chapters are devoted to spirituality and citizenship in this volume, discussion of these themes is brief). Following this, a closer focus on the contribution religious education can make to moral education in the secondary school is pursued along with a brief discussion of the issue of the moral development of pupils in religious schools. Some final comments are added on indoctrination and on the role of the teacher as model and example of moral development.

OBJECTIVES

By the end of this chapter you should be able to:

- describe aspects of the historical relationship between moral education and religious education;
- appreciate the intellectual, social and political influences and debates that have shaped current interpretations of and current practice in moral education;
- identify appropriate religious material and sources that contribute to the moral development of pupils and their communities;
- begin to develop a professional understanding of and attitude to teaching and learning within the context of religious education as a vehicle for moral development.

A GENEALOGICAL ACCOUNT OF MORAL EDUCATION IN RELIGIOUS EDUCATION

There are four basic models of the relationship of religious education and moral education that can be distinguished in the history of modern religious education in Britain. Each represents a different conception of morality and of the needs of society in relation to moral education in schools. The Christian–cultural model interprets Christianity as a source both of moral guidance and of national identity and cohesion. This model predominated in British education up to the 1960s. The multicultural model, which succeeded it, admits of greater internal diversity than the Christian-cultural model but broadly views acquaintance with the diversity of religions as a means to develop tolerance, understanding and mutual respect among Britain's increasingly diverse cultural and religious population. This view dominated up to the late 1980s. The third model is the spirituality model. This model picks up identified associations between spirituality and the cultivation of certain attitudes and dispositions that are regarded as conducive to positive and mindful conduct. The fourth and final model to be identified is offered more tentatively, as it is in the process of developing and consolidating its relationship to religious education. This may be referred to it as the civic model, as the motivation behind it is the concern to produce good citizens. On this interpretation the study of religion provides the context for the cultivation of civic virtue and participation in democratic society. The origins of this model can be traced to the late 1990s and political support for citizenship education by successive Labour Governments.

The Christian-cultural model

Until the 1960s, religious education was synonymous with moral education, in the sense that religious education subsumed moral education: compulsory religious education was necessarily compulsory moral education. It is often noted by social commentators, and occasionally with a hint of incredulity and disapproval, that the 1944 Education Act legislated for 'religious instruction' and religious observance in the form of 'collective worship' (in all grant aided schools) but not for any other subject or activity. One explanation for this is that religion was considerably more significant to people and to society then than now, and this certainly is true, but equally importantly (though often overlooked) and implicit in this explanation is the notion that religion is essential to morality: religion provides the necessary foundation for moral beliefs and behaviour. To the minds of the supporters of the 1944 Education Act, to legislate for religious education was simultaneously to legislate for moral education. Support for religion in education was as much prompted by concern for the cultivation of moral virtue as it was by concern for the cultivation of formal religious observance. Religion in the form of Christianity provided a foundation for personal behaviour, which in turn ensured high moral standards in public life. In addition, there was an influential body of opinion during the Second World War and in the immediate post-war period that identified Christianity with the historical emergence of democracy and regarded it as providing both a justification for democracy and a bulwark against totalitarian in either of its fascist or communist forms. The Earl of Shelbourne, on moving the passage of the Education Bill in the Lords, which later became the 1944 Education Act, stated that the legislation was the beginning of a process that would lead to 'an England which avows as never before the principles of liberty, justice, toleration and discipline on which this realm depends and which themselves are founded on the teaching of the Church of Christ' (Parliamentary Debates (Lords), Vol. 132, cols 970–971). Confidence in the truth of Christianity and its positive effect on morality is revealed in the Agreed Syllabuses, whose production was required by the Act. The Surrey Syllabus of 1947 stated in its preamble that its general aim was to give children 'knowledge of the common Christian faith held by their fathers for 2000 years' and to help them 'seek for themselves in Christianity principles which would give purpose to life and a guide to all its problems'. In a similar vein, the Birmingham Syllabus of the same year stated that 'Pupils should be made to realise that no other standards . . . can give so satisfactory and complete a solution to their problems as those based on the mission and message of Jesus.' Many more statements of a similar vein could be added. The syllabuses reflected the thinking of the time which was that Britain was a Christian country and that schools had an important role to play in the promotion and continuation of Christian culture and Christian society. By teaching a broad non-denominational version of Christianity in a nurturing environment, it was hoped to inculcate Christian beliefs and values in the young and thus lay down a firm moral foundation for post-war recovery. Such a form of religious education, it was presumed, would command broad public support and could be deemed appropriate to both the educational and religious needs of pupils.

The period between 1944 and the early 1960s was one of relative stability in religious education, as it was in the country generally, politically, economically and socially. Religious education was perceived as performing the religious function of nurturing and commending Christian faith and as substantially contributing to education's civic function of producing good citizens. In a sense, religious education, the school and wider society spoke with one voice and endorsed the transmission of Christian beliefs and values through public institutions. Yet, when one looks at the Agreed Syllabuses of the period there is no sustained emphasis upon explicit moral instruction within religious education. The inculcation of Christian morality in schools and in religious education was as much implicit as explicit. Certainly, moral instruction was a constant theme in school assemblies in the context of collective worship but such instruction elsewhere was often casual and oblique. Religious instruction (as it was then called) was largely biblical in content, with certain amounts of Church history and doctrine. Instruction in religion was regarded as the authoritarian imparting of facts that the teacher knew and the pupils respectfully accepted. In other words, a traditional knowledge-centred view of education was taken for granted, as it was taken for granted in other subjects. The focus was on the content to be transmitted rather than the educational or psychological needs of the pupils. The content of Christian morality was presented as fixed and unchanging, and for the most part assumed, though no doubt reinforced on occasions through word and deed.

From a liberal perspective, one could characterise this association of moral education with traditional Christian beliefs and values as oppressive and indoctrinatory. One is tempted to cite John Stuart Mill's remark about 'the tyranny of the majority', in that Christianity so determined morality that any public departure from it or public questioning of its truth was often interpreted as a rejection of all norms of civilised behaviour. Christian morality was imposed rather than freely chosen and affirmed; and alongside the imposition of Christian morality there was a considerable measure of hypocrisy, gender and religious discrimination and racism. Yet we must not be oblivious to the positive effects of the attempt to create (perpetuate even) a Christian society through education: criminal and anti-social behaviour was negligible; truancy from school and absenteeism from work were rare, as was divorce, and political participation was high. Levels of what we now call social capital, were also high: individuals were typically members of a close-knit communities, surrounded by networks of social support and encouragement. If imposed morality was oppressive for some, it also yielded positive effects for others.

The multicultural model

It is widely recognised that during the decade of the 1960s important and enduring changes occurred in British society. Economic, social and intellectual influences all contributed to create a new cultural situation. Some historians speak of a transition from a traditional conservative society to that of a secular society. Such a manner of speaking, however, does not capture the complex nature of the religious and moral shifts within society. Certainly there was diminishing numerical support for institutional religion and widespread questioning of traditional Christian beliefs and values (questioning initiated in part by Christian theologians themselves), but there was also, chiefly as a result of post-war immigration from former colonies, a growing awareness of the multi-faith nature of modern Britain. Many of the immigrants brought with them their own traditional but non-Christian forms of religion and worship. Religious diversity became a characteristic feature of much urban life, and often religious diversity was compounded by racial and ethnic diversity. Islamic mosques, Hindu temples and Sikh gurdwaras became as common as Christian churches in some areas, particularly in the large urban cities of the North-East and the Midlands. The influx of non-Christian pupils into the state school system naturally challenged Christianity's moral and religious hegemony over education. This hegemony was challenged from other sources as well. It was proving increasingly difficult to sustain Christian confessional religious education in the face of pupil disinterest and public questioning of fundamental Christian beliefs and moral values. In addition, although less conspicuous than religious pluralism, moral pluralism was becoming a feature of British society: the post-war consensus that Christian doctrine and Christian morality provided a foundation for public and private standards of practice, which were assumed by and instilled in the public institutions of society, was breaking down. The growth of religious and moral pluralism had the effect of relativising religion while tacitly strengthening the position of secular neutrality.

Moral and religious education become problematic in a pluralist society, chiefly because any endorsement of morality or religion that goes beyond basic consensus is controversial. Yet the fragmented nature of society militates against moral consensus. Fear of conflict between rival groups and communities and a growing recognition of racism, both individual and communal, lie behind much educational policy and practice in Britain from the late 1960s until the present. Likewise consciousness of moral and religious pluralism has dominated thinking about religious education over this same period. Rather than instil Christian standards, religious education has come to see its moral purpose as that of preparing pupils to live in a multicultural society, where difference and diversity obtain, and the chief task of education is to develop tolerance, understanding and mutual respect among the increasingly diverse cultural and religious population.

The publication of the document *Religious Education in Secondary Schools* in 1971, written under the direction of Professor Ninian Smart of Lancaster University, set the agenda and determined the form of subsequent religious education (Schools Council 1971). It gave support to a multi-faith or phenomenological approach to religious education, where the focus fell on the study of explicitly religious material drawn from a range of religions. Although Smart recognised that morality was a component of religion, his suggested emphasis for education was elsewhere. The heart of religious education should be a dispassionate study of religious phenomena. Like most philosophers of the time he regarded the realm of morality as distinct from the realm of religion (by the way, the reasons then proffered for a sharp distinction between religion and morality now seem much less convincing) – the moral realm was autonomous. Such a view naturally gave support to independent programmes of moral education unconnected with religion and religious education. Religious education pursued a moral purpose, not in the sense of providing explicit moral teaching, but in the sense of serving to develop the procedural moral values of tolerance and respect for difference. In this way, religious education saw itself as making a valuable contribution to both moral education and anti-racist education. The outworking of this interpretation of the relationship of religious education to the moral purposes of schooling has not been entirely successful. First, the assumption of phenomenological religious education that tolerance would develop in line with religious understanding revealed itself to be misplaced: there is little evidence that non-dogmatic religious education in itself does anything to develop a positive attitude towards those of different ethnic, racial or religious identity, despite such a connection being much trumpeted by some religious educators. Second, the neutral approach to religious beliefs and practices often associated with multi-faith or phenomenological religious education is alleged by critics to encourage religious and moral relativism. Finally, the focus on explicitly religious material, to the virtual exclusion of the moral content of religion and reference to the moral demands of religion, has, according to some educators, resulted in pupil indifference, in that religion is not viewed as relevant to the moral and religious issues with which pupils have to grapple.

By the 1980s criticisms of multi-faith, phenomenological religious education were accumulating within the profession, against the background of a perception among the wider educational community that secular or liberal forms of moral education were also failing. In response, some religious educators sought to revise multi-faith religious education and make it more relevant to the religious and moral needs of pupils; others sought to integrate the theme of spiritual development into religious education. (I acknowledge that the two responses should not be sharply distinguished from each other, in that moves to revise multi-faith religious education, although wider than initiatives to develop spirituality, often also included a reassertion of the importance of spiritual development within religious education.)

The spirituality model

Although the themes of spirituality and spiritual development are not new in British education (see Copley 2000), they have certainly come to prominence in the last few decades (as is reflected in the inclusion of a separate chapter on 'spirituality' in this volume). One can see the obvious relevance of spirituality to religious education, but how does spirituality relate to moral development within religious education? And why has there been political support, particularly from the 1980s onward, for spiritual development conjoined with moral development in schools? Certainly a renewed focus on spiritual development is probably in part designed to assuage the voice of those critics who allege that religion is increasingly marginalised in British institutional life, particularly within the domain of education. More important still, however, in accounting for political endorsements of spiritual and moral development (and the connection between them) is the accumulating evidence of the positive effects of religion and spirituality both for individuals and for society in general. At a personal level, there is a close relationship between spiritual maturity and perceptions of personal well-being, expressed in terms of mental health, self-fulfilment, perceived contentment and happiness. At a social level, the spiritually mature are more likely to make a positive contribution to the community and less likely to engage in anti-social and criminal activities.

In a multicultural society, for reasons we have already reviewed, it becomes problematic to endorse any one religion in public institutions over any other, or even religion over non-religion (fear of this exerts an equally strong influence over legislation and political initiatives). Yet there is accumulating evidence that the effects of ('intrinsic' rather than 'extrinsic') religion for individuals and for society are chiefly positive. Religious individuals are more likely to sustain stable faithful family units, less likely to smoke and consume alcohol in excess, if at all, more likely to support the community through social and charitable enterprises, more likely to keep the law, and so on. Governments and legislators, however, often feel that they cannot endorse individual religions or religion *per se* (though this does not mean that they preserve moral neutrality about their own chosen 'moral' causes). It is at this point that the notions of 'spirituality' and 'spiritual development' become relevant, for they can be used to provide support for moral development while preserving the neutrality that many believe is required of a liberal democratic state. The advantage of the language of spirituality over traditional religious language is precisely that the former admits a degree of ambiguity of usage and application that is denied to the former; it is also a means of connecting moral development to those who are not religious. One further advantage of the spirituality model of the relationship of moral education to religious education is that it furthers moral development by seeking to enhance the dispositions of love, sympathy and responsibility that are believed to provide the mainspring for moral action, while simultaneously refusing to elevate any particular morality or any particular moral stance over others. According to this view, by fostering spiritual development, religious education contributes to the moral development of the individual and of society.

The civic model

The fourth and final model of the relationship of moral education to religious education, which we have identified as the civic model, is offered more tentatively, as it is in the process of developing and consolidating its position within religious education (see the chapter on 'Citizenship' in this volume). As moral pluralism has made it increasingly difficult for schools to prescribe a personal morality (for liberal freedom requires that individuals can do what they choose within the limits of the law), so there has been a shift in moral education away from the personal aspects of morality (or what some disparagingly refer to as *private* morality) to the notion of social responsibility. Public education should be concerned with the creation of good citizens and not with the private lives and behaviour of individuals. Interest in the subject of citizenship within British education had been growing for some time, and after a decade of deliberation it was introduced, through the instrument of the Citizenship Order 2000, as a statutory element within the National Curriculum of England (HMSO 2000). This represents a new departure for formal education in Britain, where traditionally the cultivation of civic virtue and support for a democratic system of government were regarded as implicit elements within the curriculum, to be achieved by the conscious pursuit of excellence across a range of liberal arts subjects. The question naturally arises whether explicit teaching on good citizenship is the best way, or even a good way, to develop civic virtue and to encourage participation in the democratic institutions of the state. If one of the purposes of education is the creation of good citizens, is this best achieved through a course of study devoted to citizenship or is it best achieved by a broad liberal education that inculcates and models good behaviour? Presumably the two approaches need not be set in opposition to each other.

In any case, the theme of citizenship suggests new possibilities and curriculum initiatives for religious education, though religious educators need to be aware of the ideological potential that education for citizenship can hold if it were to be used to pursue narrowly political purposes that are designed to erode personal freedoms or to advance economic policies that are inattentive to moral and religious considerations.

Task 12.1 Assessing models of moral education in RE

Consider the four different models we have identified of the relationship of moral education to religious education: the Christian-cultural model; the multicultural model; the spirituality model; and the civic model:

●   What are the strengths and weakness of each?
●   What type of society is assumed by each and what understanding of the aims of state-funded education is presupposed by each?

In the light of your reflections, write a summary of what you think it is appropriate to teach pupils in: (1) a community school; (2) a Christian faith school; and (3) a Muslim school.

THE LEGISLATIVE FRAMEWORK AND NON-STATUTORY DOCUMENTATION FOR MORAL EDUCATION

The moral purpose of education is a common and constant theme in modern British educational legislation. Section 7 of the 1944 Education Act required Local Education Authority schools 'to contribute towards the spiritual, moral, mental and physical development of the community' (HMSO 1944); and Section 1(2) of the Education Reform Act, 1988 (HMSO 1988) requires the curriculum in a maintained school to be 'balanced and broadly-based' and to promote 'the spiritual, moral, cultural, mental and physical development of pupils at the school and of the society'. The similarity of wording is striking, and we may conclude that the 1988 Education Reform Act deliberately intended to reiterate earlier legislative commitments to the moral aims of education and to the moral development of pupils.

In order to clarify the ways in which schools could meet the requirement of promoting the spiritual and moral development of pupils through the newly introduced National Curriculum (one of the central 'reforms' of the 1988 Education Reform Act), the School Curriculum and Assessment Authority (now the Qualifications and Curriculum Authority) republished the National Curriculum Council's 1993 discussion paper, *Spiritual and Moral Development* in 1995 (SCAA 1995) and used it as a basis for a major conference entitled 'Education for Adult Life: Spiritual and moral aspects of the curriculum' on 15 January 1996. The paper is attentive to the complexity of morality and moral behaviour when it admits that the notion of moral development cannot be defined by a 'simple statement'. Moral development is described as involving different elements: acting on principle, knowledge of conventional and legally required codes of conduct, an understanding of the nature of moral criteria and the ability to apply them to life, a knowledge of right and wrong, and finally an appreciation and a commitment to doing what is right and the promotion of goodness. One outcome of the conference was a further discussion paper entitled, *Education for Adult Life: The Spiritual and Moral Development of Young People* (SCAA 1996a) that summarised its deliberations. In this paper, while talk of right and wrong is retained, the language of values comes to predominate as the form of language best suited to the promotion of moral development in schools. Another outcome of the conference was the establishment of the National Forum for Values in Education and the Community. This brought together prominent educationalists, politicians, community leaders, and representatives from the different religions. A consultation exercise was undertaken in order to take account of public opinion on the role of schools in the promotion of spiritual and moral values. The remit of the Forum was to decide whether there are any values that are commonly agreed upon across society, not whether there are any values that should be agreed upon across society. The members of the Forum reported their findings in December 1996 (Figure 12.1). Its positive conclusion was that there was considerable consensus in society on certain fundamental values and that schools and teachers 'can therefore expect the support and encouragement of society if they base their teaching and the school ethos on these values'. The consensus identified is considerable, though it must be borne in mind that its expression as shared *values* (for values are broad and general expressions of moral commitment) can disguise fundamental differences at the level of application to human action and activity.

The statement of values by the Forum for Values in Education and the Community (December 1996).

Society

We value truth, freedom, justice, human rights, the rule of law and collective effort for the common good. In particular, we value families as sources of love and support for all their members, and as the basis of a society in which people care for others.
  On the basis of these values, we should:

- understand and carry out our responsibilities as citizens
- refuse to support values or actions that may be harmful to individuals or communities
- support families in raising children and caring for dependants
- support the institution of marriage
- recognise that the love and commitment required for a secure and happy childhood can also be found in families of different kinds

(Continued)

- help people to know about the law and legal processes
- respect the rule of law and encourage others to do so
- respect religious and cultural diversity
- promote opportunities for all
- support those who cannot, by themselves, sustain a dignified life-style
- promote participation in the democratic process by all sectors of the community
- contribute to, as well as benefit fairly from, economic and cultural resources
- make truth, integrity, honesty and goodwill priorities in public and private life.

Relationships

We value others for themselves, not only for what they have or what they can do for us. We value relationships as fundamental to the development and fulfilment of ourselves and others, and to the good of the community.

On the basis of these values, we should:

- respect others, including children
- care for others and exercise good in our dealings with them
- show others they are valued
- earn loyalty, trust and confidence
- work cooperatively with others
- respect the privacy and property of others
- resolve disputes peacefully.

The self

We value ourselves as unique human beings capable of spiritual, moral, intellectual and physical growth and development.

On the basis of these values, we should:

- develop an understanding of our own characters, strengths and weaknesses
- develop self-respect and self-discipline
- clarify the meaning and purpose in our lives and decide, on the basis of this, how we believe that our lives should be lived
- make responsible use of our talents, rights and opportunities
- strive, throughout life, for knowledge, wisdom and understanding
- take responsibility, within our capabilities, for our own lives.

The environment

We value the environment, both natural and shaped by humanity, as the basis of life and a source of wonder and inspiration.

On the basis of these values, we should:

- accept our responsibility to maintain a sustainable environment for future generations
- understand the place of human beings within nature
- understand our responsibilities for other species
- ensure that development can be justified
- preserve balance and diversity in nature wherever possible
- preserve areas of beauty and interest for future generations
- repair, wherever possible, habitats damaged by human development and other means.

Figure 12.1 Shared values in society

Task 12.2 Choosing religious content for moral development

- Work through the statement produced by the Forum for Values in Education and the Community and identify content from the main religions that could be used to illustrate and exemplify one of the outcomes listed under each of the four sets of values identified by the Forum as agreed upon within society. For each outcome you should include material drawn from Christianity and from one other religion.
- Produce lesson notes for two different lessons, one illustrating the use of Christianity and the other the use of a different religion, to show how religious content can be used to convey the agreed moral values of society.

'Raising standards in education' has been a constant refrain of politicians since the 1980s, endorsed by successive Conservative and Labour Governments, along with the conviction that a rigorous regimen of testing both for pupils and schools is one of the best ways of raising both educational and 'moral' standards. Schools rightly complain that if they are to be tested and held accountable for the quality of the education they provide, then it is only fair that there is a clear statement of what is expected of them and the criteria by which they are to be judged. This has led in turn to the production of a series of documents by the Office for Standards in Education (Ofsted) that clarifies the inspection process and provides guidelines for promoting and evaluating different areas of the curriculum. In March 2004, Ofsted produced a guide to the assessment of the spiritual, moral, social and cultural aspects of the curriculum: *Promoting and Evaluating Pupils' Spiritual, Moral, Social and Cultural Development* (available at www.ofsted.gov.uk) (Figure 12.2). This is an important document for it provides a clear statement of the content and skills that schools and teachers are expected to deliver in pursuit of the moral development of pupils. It begins with a somewhat less than robust definition of moral development and then more helpfully lists the characteristics that morally aware pupils should be developing and those that schools which are encouraging pupils' moral development should be exhibiting.

Moral development is about the building, by pupils, of a framework of moral values which regulates their personal behaviour. It is also about the development of pupils' understanding of society's shared and agreed values. It is about understanding that there are issues where there is disagreement and it is also about understanding that society's values change. Moral development is about gaining an understanding of the range of views and the reasons for the range. It is also about developing an opinion about the different views.

Pupils who are becoming morally aware are likely to be developing some or all of the following characteristics:

- an ability to distinguish right from wrong, based on a knowledge of the moral codes of their own and other cultures
- a confidence to act consistently in accordance with their own principles

(Continued)

- an ability to think through the consequences of their own and others' actions
- a willingness to express their views on ethical issues and personal values
- an ability to make responsible and reasoned judgements on moral dilemmas
- a commitment to personal values in areas which are considered right by some and wrong by others
- a considerate style of life
- a respect for others' needs, interests and feelings, as well as their own
- a desire to explore their own and others' views
- an understanding of the need to review and reassess their values, codes and principles in the light of experience.

Schools that are encouraging pupils' moral development are, therefore, likely to be:

- providing a clear moral code as a basis for behaviour which is promoted consistently through all aspects of the school
- promoting measures to prevent discrimination on the basis of race, religion, gender, sexual orientation, age and other criteria
- giving pupils opportunities across the curriculum to explore and develop moral concepts and values – for example, personal rights and responsibilities, truth, justice, equality of opportunity, right and wrong
- developing an open and safe learning environment in which pupils can express their views and practise moral decision-making
- rewarding expressions of moral insights and good behaviour
- making an issue of breaches of agreed moral codes where they arise – for example, in the press, on television and the internet as well as in school
- modelling, through the quality of relationships and interactions, the principles which they wish to promote – for example, fairness, integrity, respect for people, pupils' welfare, respect for minority interests, resolution of conflict, keeping promises and contracts
- recognising and respecting the codes and morals of the different cultures represented in the school and wider community
- encouraging pupils to take responsibility for their actions; for example, respect for property, care of the environment, and developing codes of behaviour
- providing models of moral virtue through literature, humanities, sciences, arts, assemblies and acts of worship
- reinforcing the school's values through images, posters, classroom displays, screensavers, exhibitions
- monitoring, in simple, pragmatic ways, the success of what is provided.

Source: Ofsted (2004: 15–18)

It is important to remember that the above statements on moral development are applicable to whole-school policies and practices, and not just religious education.

Figure 12.2 Ofsted guidance on the assessment of moral development

Task 12.3 Assessing Ofsted guidance on moral development

- Do you think that the Ofsted definition of moral development is satisfactory? What other elements could have been included? (You might want to look at some of the accounts of moral development developed by psychologists and educationalists: the work of the American, Lawrence Kohlberg has been particularly influential in education; it is briefly summarised in Table 12.1).
- Consider the list of characteristics that Ofsted believes morally aware pupils should be developing and the further list of characteristics that morally facilitating schools should be exhibiting. What contribution can religious education make to the attainment of both sets of characteristics and by what means?

In preparation for a discussion within your tutor group about official policy on moral development, write paragraph responses to the above questions.

MORAL DEVELOPMENT IN CHURCH SCHOOLS

The task of contributing through religious education to the moral development of pupils in Church schools (or indeed non-Christian schools of a religious foundation) should be somewhat easier than the same task in non-religious community schools. This is because Church schools (Anglican or Catholic) by their nature profess a set of common values and embrace a shared vision of the good life. The great religions, although subsuming morality under religion, all affirm the importance of moral behaviour. Moreover, there are those who argue that religion is more successful in inspiring moral behaviour and eliciting moral responses than secular non-religious versions of morality. Of course we might also want to speak about the power of religion to inspire less worthy attitudes and behaviour. In the wake of the 9/11 terrorist attacks on the United States, some social commentators have drawn attention to the destructive nature of religion. Doubtless there is much to be said on this issue, but for the most part religious morality is beneficial to the individual and to society. Religious individuals are committed to the preservation of the family unit and less likely to divorce; the children of religious parents are less likely to be sexually promiscuous, take illegal drugs, smoke, engage in anti-social or criminal behaviour, and so on (see Francis 2001). Religious morality is broad and deep, by which I mean that it contains prescriptions and rules that apply to most human situations and its teaching embraces motivation, concepts of reward and punishment, and notions of personal loyalty and faithfulness. Religious morality typically involves a commitment both to the development of character and to the development of community; and in turn religious individuals can expect the support of the community in the achievement of religious and moral goals. The claimed absoluteness and universalism of religious prescriptions and ends are regarded by some as contrasting with the implicit relativism of much modern morality, with its debilitating influence over commitment and behaviour.

There are a number of respects in which Church schools and religious education in Church schools can extend and reconceptualise the role of religious morality, and in this way contribute to the moral development of pupils. First, religious schools can place the theme of moral development in a wider religious context that gives meaning and purpose to human existence and behaviour. Faithfulness to moral injunctions takes on a deeper meaning when the injunctions are believed to be of divine origin and when obedience brings divine rewards. Second, moral injunctions and behaviour are reinforced by the distinctive ethos of Church schools, which is in part created by the school community's commitment to shared values and beliefs. Such shared beliefs and values go beyond the 'thin' concept of shared morality that often obtains in non-religious schools. Indeed, moral development in Church schools may well be assisted by its reinforcement through regular worship and open confession of beliefs that are believed by the faithful to carry moral implications. Moral education in Church schools may be more involving than non-religious schools, in that it is not merely intellectual and rational. The worshipping community engages the emotions and stimulates the will to moral behaviour. Finally, the distinctive nature and content of religious ethics can contribute to the pursuit of morality by providing both intellectual resources for moral commitments and practical resources for moral living. For example, the belief that humanity is created in the 'likeness and image of God' has given to Christians a firm belief in the value and importance of human life, and in this way provides a firm foundation for assertions of human rights and human dignity. Equally the same doctrine can contribute to one's self-acceptance and self-esteem; both notions that contribute to a robust sense of self-identity, which in turn contribute to a strong sense of moral identity. At a practical level, Christianity's emphasis upon divine grace and forgiveness holds up the possibility of a new beginning and provides an opportunity for moral regeneration.

Lawrence Kohlberg (1927–1987) was, for many years, a professor at Harvard University, who became influential through his theory of moral development, which he popularised through research studies conducted at Harvard's Centre for Moral Education. Kohlberg was originally a cognitive psychologist and his account of moral development owes much to the research of the Swiss psychologist Jean Piaget who believed that cognitive thinking developed in progressive stages. Kohlberg believed, on the basis of his empirical studies and philosophical commitments, that people progressed in their moral reasoning through a series of stages. He believed that there were six identifiable stages which could be more generally classified into three levels (Table 12.1).

The details of Kohlberg's stage account theory of moral development can be found in *The Philosophy of Moral Development* (1981). One of the most influential critiques of his position is Carol Gilligan's *In a Different Voice* (1982). Gilligan argues that Kohlberg's rule-oriented conception of morality has an orientation toward justice, which she associates with male thinking, whereas women and girls are perhaps more likely to approach moral dilemmas with a 'care' orientation: Gillingham's insights have been extended and applied to education by Nel Nodding in *Caring: A Feminine Approach to Ethics and Moral Education* (2003).

Level	Stage	Social orientation
Pre-conventional	1	Obedience and punishment
	2	Individualism, instrumentalism and exchange
Conventional	3	Conformity, 'Good boy/girl'
	4	Law and order orientation
Post-conventional	5	Social contract/legal point of view
	6	Universal ethical principle orientation

Figure 12.3 A summary of Lawrence Kohlberg's stages of moral development

INDOCTRINATION AND EXAMPLE IN EDUCATING FOR MORAL DEVELOPMENT

Despite what has been said above, it would be wise not to exaggerate the contribution church schools can make to the moral development of pupils. It may be that the parents of pupils and the pupils themselves are less committed to the professed religious and moral values of the school than they should be. In other words, moral pluralism may be as deeply represented in Church schools as in other types of school. As a result the sense of community and that of striving in pursuit of a common religious and moral purpose are weakened. There is also the issue of diversity within the different religions. Can we still speak of a common Christian ethic, or of a distinctively Catholic ethic, and if we can speak of a common Catholic ethic is it one that is shared by all Catholics, or is it a backward-looking ethic that seeks to identify authentic morality with the pronouncements of the official teaching office of the church – pronouncements to which uncritical obedience is expected?

To mention the notion of uncritical obedience to religious and moral teaching naturally raises the issue of indoctrination. Is moral education pursued in a confessional religious context *necessarily* indoctrinatory? And what about the danger of liberal secular indoctrination: do non-religious schools indoctrinate pupils into secular forms of morality? One cannot hope to provide adequate and convincing answers to such questions in this context. Let us briefly focus our discussion, given the subject of this chapter, on the issue of religious and moral indoctrination in religious institutions; though it should also be noted that there is a corresponding danger of indoctrination into secular forms of morality in some schools.

Are all forms of confessional religious education or moral education indoctrinatory? To answer this we need a clearer understanding of what constitutes (illegitimate) indoctrination in an educational context. Intuitively, we tend to think of the term properly applying to situations where pupils are not encouraged to think for themselves or to question the beliefs and values of the world-view into which they are being inducted. Institutions indoctrinate when they forbid and censure criticism, and when individuals are treated differentially on the basis of their commitment to the beliefs and values of the institution, and so on. More philosophically, indoctrination is often interpreted as any attempt to frustrate the growth of pupils towards normal and realistic rational autonomy. Do confessional religious education and confessional moral education (or religious schools for that matter) frustrate the growth of pupils towards (normal and realistic) rational autonomy? They may do. Confessional education may use unworthy and uneducational means of eliciting and maintaining distinctively religious and moral commitments, and in the process frustrate and arrest the development of normal rational autonomy. But there is no reason why confessional education or religious schools must of necessity indoctrinate. In fact, there are positive reasons why confessional education should ensure that it does not indoctrinate. The first is that religions in general and Christianity in particular acknowledge that religious belief and conviction (with their associated moral corollaries) must be freely chosen to be religiously valuable. One may compel belief by social pressure or psychological technique but genuine conviction and belief cannot be compelled in this way; and presumably God has the requisite perfections to know whether an individual's faith and behaviour are genuine and authentic or not. Second, in liberal Western societies, where individuals are invariably exposed to different belief and value systems – let us call this value pluralism – there is some evidence to suggest that attempts to establish and inculcate religious beliefs in schools by unworthy and exclusively non-rational means is ultimately self-defeating, in that the convictions are renounced upon leaving the indoctrinatory educational context. In other words, religious indoctrination does not work in a liberal democratic context of value pluralism. Finally, religious adherents typically claim that religious belief and practice can enhance rather than frustrate personal autonomy by providing individuals with a strong sense of self-identity and self-esteem, which facilitates responsible behaviour; commitment to religion can also free individuals from the desires, motivations, and behaviour that impede positive, self-directed decisions and actions. In the light of these considerations it is not at all obvious that confessional religious education or confessional moral education must be indoctrinatory, or that reflective and committed religious believers would wish them to be indoctrinatory. It is surely possible to nurture religious commitment and religious moral commitment in a context where pupils' autonomy and personal integrity are not compromised; that is, in a context where pupils are encouraged to think, reflect upon and even question religious values and where appeals are made to reason and to evidence when appropriate. It is not at all obvious that confessional education construed in this way is necessarily indoctrinatory.

Task 12.4 Using newspaper reports as a source for moral reflection

Create a portfolio containing newspaper reports that raise moral issues. Organise your collection into stories that are relevant and topical for different year groups. Devise a series of questions that will engage pupils in moral debate and reflection. (You should begin with factual questions and move on to evaluative questions.)

Task 12.5 Indoctrination and moral development

- Write definitions of the words 'indoctrination' and 'education'.
- Does indoctrination have any role in education?
- How would you respond to the suggestion that pupils in schools should be indoctrinated into good moral behaviour?

Write a one-page response to these questions in preparation for a group debate on the subject, 'Good moral education is successful indoctrination'.

Our focus in this chapter has been chiefly on the formal aspects of moral education in relation to religious education and on the moral development of pupils; little has been said about the role of the teacher as an exemplar and model of moral behaviour and development. Educators have long recognised the importance of historical and contemporary examples of moral behaviour as an aid to moral development. Clearly, many of the great religious figures of antiquity and some contemporary figures whose lives and moral commitments have been changed by religion serve as moral models. But equally teachers themselves serve as models and exemplars of moral behaviour and attitude. All teachers, whether of religious education or not, can make a contribution to the moral development of pupils – by acts of kindness, by modelling respect and tolerance, by being sensitive to pupils' needs, by showing justice and fairness in dealing with pupils, and so on. It is also important that teachers do not overlook bad behaviour. Teachers need to have the courage to confront disruptive pupils and challenge anti-social behaviour. In these ways support is given to positive values and behaviour and the moral integrity of the teacher is established. The notion of the teacher as role model has not been a theme in much contemporary educational literature but this does not reduce its importance.

SUMMARY AND KEY POINTS

The aim of this chapter has been to provide an orientation to the subject of moral education within religious education and to introduce the main issues and debates that pertain to the role of the religious educator as facilitating the moral development of pupils. We have identified and reviewed four different models of the relationship of religious education to moral education: the Christian-cultural model; the multi-cultural model; the spirituality model, and the civic model. We have also provided a sketch both of the legislative position and of official documentation with regard to moral development; integrated into this has been a number of tasks and short discussions that aim to illustrate the relevance of religious content to the aims of moral education. We concluded with some brief remarks on indoctrination and on the role of the teacher as moral exemplar. The comments on indoctrination were for the most part intended to show that religious contributions to moral development need not be regarded as particularly controversial, and certainly they need not be any more controversial than secular contributions to moral development. The comments on the role of the teacher as moral exemplar remind us of the challenging nature of teaching, for teachers are required not just to teach about morality but to practise morality in the classroom.

FURTHER READING

Barnes, L.P. and Kay, W.K. (2002) *Religious Education in England and Wales: Innovations and Reflections*, Leicester: Religious and Theological Studies Fellowship. A review of developments in religious education with a clear focus on critical analysis and discussion. The chapter devoted to Spiritual Development also considers the themes of moral education and moral development within religious education.

Copley, T. (2008) *Teaching Religion: Religious Education in England and Wales 1944 to 2007*, Exeter: University of Exeter Press. Although not focused on moral education, it provides good background material on the shifting moral landscape and context within which religious education is practised, and on occasions refers explicitly to the relationship of religious education to moral education.

Francis, L.J. (2001) *The Values Debate: A Voice from the Pupils*, London: RoutledgeFalmer. Presents findings from a survey conducted among 30,000 13–15-year-olds throughout England and Wales, giving particular attention to social, personal and moral issues.

Haydon, G. (1997) *Teaching About Values: A New Approach*, London: Cassell. Clear, informed and wide-ranging discussion of values and their place in education.

Thiesen, E.J. (1993) *Teaching for Commitment: Liberal Education, Indoctrination and Christian Nurture*, Leominster: Gracewing. Philosophically sophisticated and extended discussion of the concepts of indoctrination and rational autonomy, within the context of a defence of religious nurture in education.

Wright, A. (1993) *Religious Education in the Secondary School: Prospects for Religious Literacy*, London: David Fulton Publishers. Chapter 6, entitled 'Religion for Citizenship', contains some perceptive remarks on moral education and its role within religious education.

13 Religious Education and citizenship: A human rights approach

Liam Gearon

Introduction

The rise in interest in religion in global politics parallels the international development of interest in civic education. World events have heightened the need for increased attention to religion in education, either within citizenship or religious education. Our understanding of religion in education needs to take a wide historical and political, as well as a philosophical perspective. So we need to recognise the macro-socio-political context on which new forms of citizenship have arisen. This chapter presents a possible bridge between the two subjects through a human rights approach: through a survey of critical theoretical (philosophical, political, historical) contexts, and then through an outline set of practical strategies for implementation.

OBJECTIVES

By the end of this chapter you should be able to:

- understand how issues of critical, global political import have an effect upon education;
- understand some of these debates surround RE and Citizenship;
- have the basic tools to construct lessons and schemes of work in RE and Citizenship in the light of some of these issues and debates.

RELIGION, EDUCATION AND CITIZENSHIP: FOUR CRITICAL CONTEXTS

Critical context 1: religion and global governance

> Thesis 1 The role of religion in public and political life has been overplayed.

The post-Enlightenment secularisation thesis common among classical social and political theorists (Durkheim, Weber, Marx) presents us with the expectation of the decline in the public role of religion and at the very least its marginalisation in the private sphere. The implication of this is that former elevations of the social significance of religion have been exaggerated.

> Anti-thesis 1 There is increasing evidence of the importance of religion in post-Cold War public and political life, often but not exclusively centring on issues of human rights, including freedom of religion or belief.

There are a number of indicators at the level of global governance that highlight the importance of freedom of religion or belief, where religion and rights are seen as a barometer of wider democratic freedoms. The United States of America provides a clear example. The 1998 International Religious Freedom Act made it a requirement for the US Secretary of State to publish an Annual Report on religious freedom worldwide. Published each September, the Annual Report on International Religious Freedom is submitted to the Committee on International Relations at the US House of Representatives and the Committee on Foreign Relations of the US Senate by the Department of State. The report is extensive and provides country-by-country accounts of religious freedoms, the infringements of and improvements in relation to such rights to belief. It is available at www.house.gov/international_relations/. Essentially, the US Department of State clearly links freedom of religion and the likelihood that countries that preserve this will respect other fundamental rights.

Critical context 2: religion and the UN

> Thesis 2 The United Nations (UN) has incorporated and defined freedom of religion or belief since the 1948 Universal Declaration of Human Rights, but the early history of the United Nations tended to downplay religious and ideological diversity.

The Universal Declaration of Human Rights includes a number of articles of relevance to freedom of religion and belief. These include Article 2 (forbidding prejudicial distinctions of any kind, including those related to religion), Article 26 (on the right to a particular religious education) and Article 29 (on responsibilities and proscription against limitations of proclaimed rights). The foundation stone of freedom of religion and belief, though, is to be found in Article 18 of the Universal Declaration of Human Rights. This states:

Everyone has the right to freedom of: thought, conscience and religion; this right includes freedom to change his religion or belief, and freedom, either alone or in community with others and in public or private, to manifest his religion or belief in teaching, practice, worship and observance.

Anti-thesis 2 After a long neglect (or low level treatment) of religion explicitly, the UN from the late 1970s began to recognise the international significance of religion for a stable world order.

Thus, during the 1990s, religion emerges explicitly in numerous international statements, gaining a new and unprecedented prominence. For instance, there was the Cairo Declaration on Human Rights in Islam (1990), the Fundamental Agreement between the Holy See and the State of Israel (1993). The Vienna Declaration and Plan of Action (1993) also gave some prominence to religion, which culminated in the Oslo Declaration on Freedom of Religion and Belief (1998). This Declaration extended the notion of freedom of religion to include freedom of *belief* and thus allowing for a wider interpretation (Figure 13.1). This in turn has had the effect of linking rights of freedom of thought, conscience and religion to later generation rights of human solidarity. Most notable is the linking of religious intolerance to the ending of racism, xenophobia and discrimination more broadly.

- Declaration on the Elimination of All Forms of Intolerance and of Discrimination based on Religion or Belief (25 November 1981)
- Declaration on the Rights of Persons Belonging to National or Ethnic, Religious and Linguistic Minorities (18 December 1992)
- Oslo Declaration on Freedom of Religion and Belief (1998)
- World Conference against Racism, Xenophobia and Related Forms of Discrimination (September, 2002)

For a full text of the document, follow links at www.ohchr.org

---

Figure 13.1 International legal standards: defending freedom of religion and belief

The post–September 11 context has further highlighted the issue of potential violent conflict between world-views. This fissure between universal rights and particular cultural, especially religious, traditions has, however, been a live one for many years.

Religion tended to have been underplayed in the UN system for the same reasons as the historical and political aspects of religion have been excluded from school curricula: post-confessional RE in Britain has tended to focus on the commonalities among religion and overlook those aspects of religion that might provoke disagreement. Historical and political circumstances – especially the continued trend of human beings to mass slaughter and genocidal killing over issues of nationhood, culture, ethnicity and religion – have forced the UN to take religion more seriously.

Critical context 3: religion in citizenship/human rights education

Thesis 3 The role of religion in civic education, citizenship, human rights education has been overplayed.

Curricula devised by non-governmental organisations (NGOs) (Amnesty International, Human Rights Watch), material presented by national governments in response to the International Decade of Human Rights Education, as well as a range of citizenship curricula in the UK and internationally have tended to marginalise the place of religion in citizenship.

Anti-thesis 3 Reflecting broader global trends there is increasing recognition of the importance of religion in citizenship and human rights education, although the recognition of the importance of teaching about religion remains arguably less strong in civic or citizenship education than in religious education.

There is increased evidence of the importance of freedom of religion or belief, both within mainstream and specialist NGOs. The US-based NGO called Freedom House provides a good example of this. A major achievement of Freedom House has been the publication of its highly accessible report, *Religious Freedom in the World* (Marshall 2000). Interestingly, one of the comments made is that there is much less criticism by the US Department of State of those countries that support the government's 'War on Terror' than those that do not: Human Rights Watch has made a similar claim.

The Freedom House global survey reviewed the state of religious freedom in the majority of the world's countries, providing useful snapshot insights into the political context of religious life in each. The survey criteria were developed from the UN Declaration on the Elimination of All Forms of Intolerance and of Discrimination Based on Religion or Belief, and related UN instruments. Even so, its assessment of the level of religious freedom may seem a little crude (there is a 1–7 scale, with 7 being the least intolerant and the US gaining an unambiguous 1). The Report also makes a link between freedom of religion and freedom of expression generally, for the simple reason that religious freedom cuts across a wide range of human rights.

Task 13.1 Promoting freedom of religion

Visit the website of Freedom House, a US-based NGO dealing with issues of freedom of expression, www.freedomhouse.org. Discuss some of the country case studies in small groups and devise a series of activities that could incorporate freedom of religion or belief within religious education.

Critical context 4: Citizenship/human rights education in Religious Education

Thesis 4 The political dimension (for example, citizenship/human rights) has been underplayed in religious education, and contentious historical contexts sidestepped.

With its emphasis on dialogue, understanding and tolerance, many theorists of religious education have focused upon the phenomenological and the psychological often to the detriment of the historical and the political aspects of religious education (see Grimmitt 2000). This is for the obvious reason that it is the historical and political aspects of religious education that are most often the cause of tensions and conflict

Anti-thesis 4 The exponential growth of civic or citizenship education around the world has forced religious education to consider the political and historical, a growth itself forced upon education by manifold changes in the world in which we live.

The shift in this tendency towards an increasing awareness of the importance of religion in education has been pursued by a number of theorists, e.g. Jackson (2003), who, for the most part, are responding to world events and to the increasing salience of religion in politics and religiously inspired conflict.

RELIGIOUS EDUCATION AND CITIZENSHIP: A HUMAN RIGHTS APPROACH

If we are to have a critical consciousness in religious education, it must be both historical and political, for religions influence history and politics. We cannot always try to seek unblemished religions or pure traditions. Indeed, good phenomenology (Smart 1989) attempts to place religious culture in its social and political context. So often, though, in religious education, the seemingly dysfunctional, impure mani-festations of a religion are ignored or proclaimed as simply aberrations, a false political representation, an impure form of this religion or a cultural construction. As religion manifests itself in the socio-political realm, so this is inevitably at least a part of what the tradition is as a whole. We may extend this analysis by suggesting that while religion does have a positive political role in the promotion of human rights and indeed suffers because of this involvement, religions continue to suffer immense persecution, for instance, religious traditions have also actually been a culpable force in the international denial of human rights, especially in the repression of women and indigenous peoples. Arguably, it is precisely because religions themselves are some of the worst offenders in denying human rights – historically through imperialism and today through fundamentalism – that religious educators need to take seriously the violent or potentially violent global realities of which religions, often through ethnic and cultural identity, are a root cause. It is precisely these sorts of realities that religious education often fails to acknowledge.

The best models for emulation for such a political religious education are those that look at the place of religion in the context of an international values consensus that, however short of perfection, has been agreed by democratic process and it is for this reason that a human rights approach might be tentatively welcomed. But it should be emphasised that human rights are themselves hugely contested and manipulated and have been since the inception of the Universal Declaration of Human Rights in 1948. Some in the developing world still view human rights as a further expression of Western imperialism, as (cultural and religious) indigenous practices are challenged by the 'superior' values of the West.

Figure 13.2 takes some of the elements of the Citizenship Order (HMSO 2000) and plots some possible religious education links. The teacher may add more, taking the list as a baseline for ideas and curriculum development. What is attempted here is an opening gambit trying to suggest links between broad, macro-level considerations with the day-to-day curriculum.

Teaching should ensure that knowledge and understanding about becoming informed citizens are acquired and applied when developing skills of enquiry and communication, and participation and responsible action.

1. Knowledge of and understanding about becoming informed citizens
Pupils should be taught about:

- the legal and human rights and responsibilities underpinning society and how they relate to citizens, including the role and operation of the criminal and civil justice systems

Possible RE links: religion and human rights – asylum, death penalty, freedom of religion, belief and expression, genocide, the rights of women, children and indigenous peoples; punishments for infringements of human rights, including the international criminal court, and the role of religious persons – victims and perpetrators – in atrocities, conflicts between civil-state law and religious law.

- the origins and implications of the diverse national, regional, religious and ethnic identities in the United Kingdom and the need for mutual respect and understanding

Possible RE links: the range of religious belief and practice of Christianity and the other principal religions in Great Britain, traditions beyond the six major world religious traditions, including, internationally, indigenous and tribal peoples; how powerful and numerically superior religious traditions have infringed the rights of religious and other minorities.

- the work of parliament, the government and the courts in making and shaping the law

(Continued)

Possible RE links: religion and the state, historically and today; in Britain the monarch as 'Defender of the Faith' and the challenges of a religiously diverse society; monarch as 'Defender of all Faiths'?

• the importance of playing an active part in democratic and electoral processes

Possible RE links: religion and democracy, authority structures within religious traditions as modelled on democratic or authoritarian/autocratic structures, relationship of religious traditions with the state, including official or state religions.

• how the economy functions, including the role of business and financial services

Possible RE links: the relationship of Protestantism to capitalism, the notion of the Protestant work ethic, religious attitudes to work and labour, and the lending of money for interest.

• the opportunities for individuals and voluntary groups to bring about social change locally, nationally, in Europe and internationally

Possible RE links: development education through religious and other aid/development agencies such as CAFOD, Christian Aid, OXFAM, especially initiatives such as Fair Trade; social teaching of religious traditions.

• the importance of a free press, and the media's role in society, including the internet, in providing information and affecting opinion

Possible RE links: freedom of expression, religion and the media, religious repression and censorship of artists and writers – historically and today.

• rights and responsibilities of consumers, employers and employees

Possible RE links: development education through religious and other aid/development agencies such as CAFOD, Christian Aid, OXFAM, especially initiatives such as Fair Trade.

• the United Kingdom's relations in Europe, including the European Union, and relations with the Commonwealth and the United Nations

Possible RE links: immigration and minorities, the UN Special Rapporteur on Religion and Belief, religious diversity in the Commonwealth, religion and the history of Empire and colonialism, international issues of religious freedom.

• the wider issues and challenges of global interdependence and responsibility, including sustainable development and Local Agenda 21.

Possible RE links: religion and the environment, stewardship and dominion, development education through religious and other aid/development agencies such as CAFOD, Christian Aid, OXFAM and environmental organisations such as Friends of the Earth, Green Peace and WWF.

(Continued)

2. Developing skills of enquiry and communication

Pupils should be taught to:

- research a topical political, spiritual, moral, social or cultural issue, problem or event by analysing information from different sources, including ICT-based sources, showing an awareness of the use and abuse of statistics;
- express, justify and defend orally and in writing a personal opinion about such issues, problems or events;
- contribute to group and exploratory class discussions, and take part in formal debates.

Possible RE links: Explore the range of internet sources for any or all of the issues in the last section, project work, surveys. Class debates, written assignment, issue-based focus on secular state and religious perspectives on the issues listed in the second half of this chapter.

3. Developing skills of participation and responsible action

Pupils should be taught to:

- use their imagination to consider other people's experiences and be able to think about, express, explain and critically evaluate views that are not their own;
- negotiate, decide and take part responsibly in school and community-based activities;
- reflect on the process of participating.

Possible RE links: critically explore the dissonance between universal human rights of the UN and possible clashes with particular cultural and especially religious world-views and ethical systems; explore possibilities for placements with or visits to leading religious/secular NGOs, local charities or religious community, exploring convergence of rights thinking between the religious and the secular; evaluation of work-based placement, for example, in a leading NGO, local charity or religious community, exploring further, on the basis of experience, the convergence of rights thinking between the religious and the secular.

Figure 13.2 Citizenship at Key Stage 3

On an even more fundamental level, having a grasp of the official documentation is an essential start for any planning. Figures 13.3 and 13.4 provide a checklist for both citizenship and religious education.

Your school experience involves you in planning teaching and learning activities for the short- and medium-term. The proforma in Figure 13.4 provides guidance for short-term planning in religious education and citizenship activity – within and beyond the classroom.

This is obviously not an exhaustive list of possibilities and a fuller consideration of citizenship and religious education can be found elsewhere (Gearon 2004).

DEPARTMENT FOR EDUCATION AND SKILLS (www.dfes.gov.uk)

- *Health and Safety of Pupils on Educational Visits (HASPEV)* (London: DfES)
- *The National Curriculum Handbook* (London: DfES)
- *The Report of the Post-16 Citizenship Advisory Group* (London: DfES)

OFFICE FOR STANDARDS IN EDUCATION (Ofsted) (www.ofsted.gov.uk)

- *Ofsted Handbook for the Inspection of Secondary Schools* (London: HMSO)

QUALIFICATIONS AND CURRICULUM AUTHORITY (www.qca.org.uk)

- *Citizenship at Key Stages 3 and 4: Initial Guidance*
- *Citizenship: A Scheme of Work for Key Stage 3: Teachers Guide*
- *Citizenship: A Scheme of Work for Key Stage 4: Teachers Guide*
- *Citizenship: A Scheme of Work for Key Stage 3*
- *Citizenship: A Scheme of Work for Key Stage 4*
- *Getting Involved: Extending Opportunities for Pupil Participation (KS3)*
- *Staying Involved: Extending Opportunities for Pupil Participation (KS4)*
- *Citizenship: A Guide for Senior Managers and Governors*

REPORTS (Available at www.citfou.org.uk)

- Crick, B. (1998) *Education for Citizenship and the Teaching of Democracy in Schools: Final Report of the Advisory Group on Citizenship* (London: QCA) [The Crick Report]
- Further Education Funding Council *Citizenship in Further Education* (London: DfEE/FEFC)

Figure 13.3 Key Citizenship guidance: an online checklist

Long-term planning: Scheme of work/Short-term planning: Lesson plan

- Key Stage
- Theme
- Link to Programme of Study
- Date
- Class

Religious Education learning outcomes (Attainment Targets 1 and 2)

- **AT 1**
- **AT 2**

Citizenship learning outcomes (using appropriate assessment criteria in relation to):

- Knowledge and understanding about becoming informed citizens

(Continued)

- Developing skills of enquiry and communication
- Developing skills of participation and responsible action

Key skills checklist

- Communication
- Application of number
- ICT
- Working with others
- Improving own learning and performance
- Problem-solving

Citizenship through Religious Education lesson/activity

- Introduction
- Activity 1
- Activity 2
- Activity 3
- Conclusion

Differentiation

SEN (confidential – liaison with SEN co-ordinator)

Assessment opportunities

- Informal (written formative, peer/self-assessment, oral question and answer)
- Formal (diagnostic, summative, coursework/examination preparation)
- Appropriate assessment criteria: Yes/No
- Recorded: Yes/No
- Feedback to pupils: Yes/No
- Reported externally (for example, parents): Yes/No

Resources

- ICT
- TV/ video/camcorder/projector
- Visitor/guest speaker
- Visit
- Other

Teaching methods checklist

- Art
- Discussion
- Drama
- Experiential
- Formal assessment
- Group work
- Pair work
- Question and answer

(Continued)

- Research
- Test
- Visit
- Visitor
- Written work
- Other

Use these checklists to enhance RE by integrating themes and resources from citizenship.

Figure 13.4 Planning for citizenship education in RE

Task 13.2 The contribution of RE to the pursuit of tolerance

Look up the study prepared under the guidance of Prof. Abdelfattah Amor, 'The Role of Religious Education in the Pursuit of Tolerance and Non-Discrimination', http://www.unhchr.ch/html/menu2/7/b/cfedu-basicdoc.htm.
   In small groups, consider how your teaching might contribute to this mission.

SUMMARY AND KEY POINTS

On the basis of this chapter we can make two rather expansive, summary observations from the world of education and the world of global politics: first, evidence shows an increased emphasis upon religion in school education; second, evidence shows an increased emphasis upon religion and culture in international politics. These trends reveal that we live in a world that reflects tensions between world-views. There are endemic tensions between religions and wider political life, and sometimes clashes over universal rights and religious traditions that need to be resolved in educational contexts. Historical evidence points out that these tensions are of at least four kinds and each on its own is a reminder of why a carefully worked out strategy linking religious education and citizenship is so important.

First, there are tensions between particular cultural and especially religious systems and the notion of universal human rights. Examples here are the right to freedom of expression that might give offence to religious sensibility or the tension between democratic political systems and religiously inspired systems of governance or, and perhaps especially, issues of universal rights between men and women, obvious within a secular system of rights but far less obvious within particular religious traditions.

Second, there are tensions between religious traditions or different cultural world-views. Religious, cultural and ethnic difference remains the major source of conflict in a post-Cold War world. In a world weary of wars and with a clear awareness of the systematic Nazi and related practices of mass death, the 1948 Genocide Convention was born out of a 'never again' mentality and yet since then genocide, defined here as the systematic and deliberate targeting for extinction of particular sections of a population, has happened again and again. Third, there are tensions within and between human rights themselves, for example, between freedom of religion or belief and freedom of expression. Here the tensions between religious traditions and universal human rights contribute to these tensions within human rights law between rights that seem to compete rather than be complementary. Fourth, however, there is a wider tension: the tension between a stated universality of rights and the factual inequality. Thus, the 1993 World Conference on Human Rights resulted in the Vienna Plan of Action. Priorities for the global implementation of human rights were listed and, as with the majority of recent UN world conferences, a five-year review was planned. The United Nations Commissioner for Human Rights concludes the Vienna +5 review in a final paragraph as follows:

> The international community must conclude that five years after Vienna, a wide gap continues to exist between the promise of human rights and their reality in the lives of people throughout the world. At the beginning of the twenty-first century, making all human rights a reality for all remains not only our fundamental challenge but our solemn responsibility.
>
> (UN 1998)

For all this, human rights in the UN system thus imply universality. Yet human values are by their nature contested and history reveals a tragically imperfect world where inequalities abound and justice is too often absent. It is this most fundamental sense of inequality that arguably presents the greatest cause of conflict the world over.

The task for religious educators is twofold: first, to continue the development of a theoretical context for the complex relationship – religious, political, philosophical, historical – between religious education and citizenship; and, second, to advance practical strategies whereby this can be worked into classroom practice.

FURTHER READING

Arthur, J. and Wright, D. (2001) *Teaching Citizenship in the Secondary School*, London: David Fulton Publishers. Excellent source of information and strategy.

Gearon, L. (2003) *Learning to Teach Citizenship in the Secondary School*. London: Routledge. Provides an overview of critical issues in teaching citizenship.

Gearon, L. (2004) *Citizenship through Secondary Religious Education*. London: Routledge. A critical account of the possibilities for teaching and learning in citizenship and religious education, research-based but with practical suggestions.

Gearon, L. (ed.) (2007) *Teaching Citizenship in the Secondary School: A Practical Guide* London: Routledge. An edited collection from leading teacher educators on how to teach citizenship, practical but research-informed.

Jackson, R. (ed.) (2003) *International Perspectives on Citizenship, Education and Religious Diversity*. London: Routledge. An authoritative and scholarly account of the interplay of citizenship and religion from an international educational perspective.

Part V

Supporting professional development

14 Information and communications technology

Andrew Clutterbuck

INTRODUCTION

There is a whole range of information and communications technology (ICT). You are likely to be familiar with the more traditional ones (e.g. radio, television, video), and have probably experienced them as part of your own education. This chapter is concerned solely with computer-related ICT. The computer, by virtue of its multi-functional capacities, stands apart from these others. It can be used for writing, reading, viewing, listening, drawing, speaking, thinking, searching and modelling. It is both an educational resource: a provider of information and understanding, and a tool for education: supporting the learning process by promoting thinking, reflection and the organisation of information. Its usefulness in the school curriculum extends to all subjects, including RE, and to all teachers.

The potential of the computer in education is not, however, a quality of the machine per se; it is dependent on the presence and skills of the teacher to manage the learning situation, the processes involved and the learning resulting from its use. Where pupils are left on their own with ICT, their learning potential drops away steeply. This chapter provides practical guidance to support your use of ICT in RE both in the classroom and in your other professional activities.

OBJECTIVES

By the end of this chapter you should be able to:

- access the standards expected of newly qualified teachers (NQTs) in ICT;

- understand the potential of ICT in education and RE;
- have a working knowledge of the ICT available to the RE teacher and the language used to articulate ICT issues;
- begin to understand how current and future ICT can be integrated effectively into your teaching and other professional activities;
- start integrating ICT effectively into your teaching and other professional activities and be open to future developments in ICT;
- identify opportunities to develop your understanding of ICT and of how ICT can contribute to your professional development in both ICT and RE.

ICT AND EDUCATION

The world in which we live, teach and learn

There is now little resistance to ICT in education; the benefits it brings to teaching and learning and to the other professional activities of teachers are widely appreciated. Equally pupils are also familiar with the uses of ICT and the ways in which it can be used to support their everyday activities, including learning. As skills develop and disperse throughout the pupil population it is likely that demands will be made in the school context for these different ways of teaching and learning to be acknowledged. Pupils regularly bring into the RE classroom information on religion they have retrieved from the World Wide Web and almost all formal assignments are word-processed. They may also begin actively to question whether there are alternative, better, ways of researching, producing and presenting their learning than through the traditional methods of teacher talk, textbook and exercise book. The responsibility of the RE teacher in this situation is twofold. First, to educate pupils in the use of ICT to maximise their learning potential and, second, to integrate ICT effectively in the teaching and learning of RE. Competence in ICT becomes increasingly necessary as a prerequisite of employment and access to continuing education. Pupils need to be prepared for the world outside school, and in this, RE, like every other subject on the school curriculum, has a responsibility for developing pupils' skills and abilities.

Task 14.1 The generic benefits of ICT

Many benefits are listed for computer-related ICT. Discuss what may be meant by the following benefits. Consider the legitimacy of the claims and their value to the RE teacher.

ICT is of value in the RE classroom because it:

- is interesting and enjoyable for pupils;
- improves pupils' motivation and the desire to learn;

- is patient and responsive;
- raises the status of the subject;
- is pupil-centred;
- supports open, independent and flexible learning;
- supports discussion, collaboration and sharing;
- is emotionally neutral, blind to gender, race, age and disability;
- promotes deeper understanding;
- improves pupils' presentation and pride in their work;
- improves pupils' creativity;
- encourages pupils to experiment and try things out.

Share your responses with other student teachers.

Your teacher education, ICT and you

The Training and Development Agency (TDA) for Schools makes clear the importance it attaches to ICT in education when it lists professional skills in ICT as part of the 'Professional Knowledge and Understanding' that is necessary for the attainment of Qualified Teacher Status (TDA 2007: 9). Teachers are expected to 'use ICT effectively, both to teach their subject and to support their wider professional role' (TDA 2006: 10); a Skills Test in ICT (as in numeracy and literacy) must be successfully completed. The Training and Development Agency for Schools currently funds a range of projects that are intended to encourage the use of ICT in schools and to illustrate its contribution to effective teaching and learning. Courses in Initial Teacher Education audit student knowledge, understanding and skills in ICT and, where gaps are identified, make arrangements to ensure that the relevant experience is gained during the course. Formal requirements for competence in ICT may appear to be an added burden if you perceive your essential concern as getting to grips with the practicalities of curriculum design, new subject content and classroom management. But the message is that ICT is not an 'added extra'; rather, ICT should be an integral consideration for you in all aspects of teaching, learning and management.

The scope for ICT in RE

We turn now to the extent to which RE is expected to integrate ICT and the scope for such integration. With the exception of physical education, all National Curriculum subject orders have a generic sentence stating that 'Pupils should be given the opportunities, where appropriate, to develop and apply their IT capability in their study of x'. The RE curriculum, by contrast, is formulated under locally Agreed Syllabuses and, although some may mention ICT, or refer simply to information technology (IT), there is clearly no national or uniform requirement. The non-statutory Model Syllabuses for RE often limit their mention of IT to those situations in which pupils have special needs of a particular sort (e.g. aural, visual, motor skills, etc.). This lack of an explicit requirement in RE-centred legislation and guidance regarding ICT should, however, be seen in the context both of the ICT requirements stipulated for the education of all teachers; and of course Ofsted inspectors are concerned with IT as a Key Skill throughout the curriculum.

Evidence suggests that initially the use of ICT in RE was limited but that the situation is rapidly changing. While there may have been a variety of reasons for a certain reluctance among religious educators to use ICT, there is nothing inherent in it that constitutes a fundamental obstacle to its educational use in RE. Neither information nor communication are newcomers to RE: both have an essential presence in every good teaching and learning situation. Information of some sort or other is a necessary basis for understanding, evaluating or criticising the world, including the religious world, in which we find ourselves. Communication, again in various forms, describes the process of dialogue between teacher, pupils and sometimes a wider audience, for the purposes of sharing, enhancing and expressing understanding. It is the technology component that is comparatively new, yet this, it must be stressed, is not an end in itself but a means by which support is provided for the 'information' and 'communication' aspects of learning and teaching. While there are certainly moral, ethical and social issues concerning ICT which need to be discussed, there is no reason why RE alone should be concerned with these aspects of ICT.

Task 14.2 Prospects for ICT's impact on RE

Access your Local Agreed Syllabuses on RE (most are available online) and note any references to the role of ICT in RE. How detailed and useful is this source for classroom planning and pedagogy? If there is a list of ICT resources, how useful is it? Create a database for this information for later access and to add to.

Given the lack of detail in some Agreed Syllabuses on how, when and where ICT may be integrated into RE, and the ongoing development of ICT provision in schools, effective integration is to some extent down to your imagination and willingness to engage in (calculated) risk. The rest of this chapter is an invitation to consider ICT's practical potential for your professional activities.

PRACTICAL CONSIDERATIONS

Experience, policy and access

Your school should have an ICT policy in force and it is worthwhile asking your school-based tutor what its implications are for RE and for your teaching. The school's policy may, for example, plan for pupils' ICT skills to be developed or consolidated in other areas of the curriculum, including, possibly, RE. There may be schemes of work relating to ICT and to its assessment in RE, and these are relevant to and useful for your planning and preparation.

You should also ascertain the way in which the school's ICT policy has affected the location of computers: a dedicated suite (the 'computer room'), dispersal throughout the school's classrooms, or a mixed mode, with a dedicated suite and some dispersal. Each has advantages and disadvantages for you and your pupils. The first, for example, means that, although an entire class can be accommodated, it is necessary to book the room at a time convenient for your teaching. The second allows more immediate access but is likely to allow only a small number of pupils to work at any one time. Whatever the case, you need to be sure that you are aware of how and when access is available to you.

Meeting the school's ICT co-ordinator is also a good idea, and the ICT technician. These people, along with your school-based tutor, not only can help you in your planning and preparation, and possibly support your use of ICT, but they can advise you on the software available, the access pupils have to computers (e.g. scheduled lessons, open access, after school, lunchtimes, homework clubs, libraries, cyber cafés, home provision) and the pupils' levels of use, confidence and competence with ICT. It goes without saying that using ICT resources with which pupils are already familiar is easier than having to teach new applications and packages in addition to RE.

Task 14.3 Carrying out an ICT audit

Using this section and the ones following, construct audit forms which you can use to audit ICT in your IHE and in your school experience placements (see Leask and Pachler 2005; 149–64, for helpful suggestions and advice). These audits should enable you to identify opportunities to gain and consolidate your experience and progressively fill any gaps identified in your personal audit carried out by your IHE. Keep these records in your professional development portfolio.

Planning and monitoring the use of ICT

As a student teacher of RE your primary concern is with the teaching of RE. The teaching and learning outcomes for RE are your primary planning considerations. However, an integral part of the next stage of this planning process should also be an assessment of whether ICT is capable of effectively enhancing the quality of teaching and learning. Unless it fulfils this criterion it should not be used. This assessment demands of you an awareness of what ICT is able to offer and of the ICT that is available to you and your pupils. Including ICT at any cost, either as the primary basis of your planning, or as a final consideration in the planning cycle, has two possible outcomes: the 'bolt-on' ICT experience or the distortion of RE to suit the capacity of ICT.

Where ICT is considered to be capable of enhancing the quality of teaching and learning, its proper integration into RE is well under way: it is there because it has a worthwhile contribution to make. Your next steps are in the active management and mediation of the role of ICT in the classroom context. Using whiteboard, television, video and overhead projector is reasonably straightforward because we have probably seen them used in our own education and because pupils are familiar with their use in the classroom. ICT presents new challenges. There are, however, constructive steps you can take in order to maximise success: Figure 14.1 gives details.

In the context of your pupils' use of ICT there are a number of things you can consider monitoring. Several writers point to ICT bringing about a transformation in the teacher's role, in the relationship between teacher and pupil and in the learning process. It would be worthwhile considering the nature and extent of any changes which occur during your pupils' use of ICT in RE. For example, is there more or less communication and interaction between pupils when ICT is used? Has the learning experience been enhanced? You should monitor uptake and use to ensure that one gender group is not at a disadvantage and that ICT-competent pupils, whatever their gender, do not exclude others. These are real issues which need action on your part in order to ensure equality of access and opportunity.

You should ensure that you:

- are familiar with the ICT resource that your pupils are using;
- have, if possible, given consideration to the positioning of ICT devices (is there enough room for pupils to take notes, does the layout promote pupil discussion and collaboration?);
- have written down, for pupil use, clear instructions on the operation of the ICT resource;
- have provided pupils with clear details on what the purposes and processes of the ICT activity are and that these are achievable within the time available;
- have an alternative plan should the ICT resource fail or the activity not meet its objectives;
- feel confident, competent and comfortable using ICT with a particular group of pupils.

You might consider:

- working with a smaller group of pupils (you could negotiate this with your school-based tutor);
- asking another teacher, possibly the ICT co-ordinator or an RE teacher, to be present to assist you;
- preparing the ground for ICT in your lessons by asking pupils to complete some ICT-related work outside class time (resources permitting);
- observing teachers, even from other subject areas, in their use of ICT in the classroom;
- awaiting an opportunity to introduce ICT as an incidental part of a lesson for a small group of pupils;
- arranging pupil groups in such a way as to maintain on-task activity (e.g. mix boys with girls, ICT/RE ability levels, friendship groups);
- using ICT with which pupils are very familiar or which is simple and efficient in its operation.

Figure 14.1 Some suggestions for the successful use of ICT

Content-free (generic) applications

Content-free applications provide a framework to support an activity but are dependent upon you to supply the information essential to their working. As they are 'content-free', their uses are not restricted to any area of the curriculum, although some may prove more useful in one area than another. They include the following:

- word-processing packages;
- graphics and drawing packages;
- spreadsheet packages;
- database packages;
- PowerPoint.

Typically these applications are integrated with each other. However they are organised, their utility both to you and to your pupils should not be underestimated. Such packages alone provide a successful basis on which to begin to integrate ICT into RE.

Generic applications possess the general capacity to save on time by cutting out repetitive or difficult labour and by enhancing presentation. The corollary of this labour-saving is that they should allow attention and time to be directed to the more intrinsically valuable learning activities of reflection, experimentation, creativity and analysis. Too often, however, content-free applications are used only for their presentational capacity: the labour is conducted elsewhere in the traditional fashion. For example, asking a pupil to word-process a completed piece of work is using the word-processor as a typewriter, and although that may sometimes be justifiable, it is not exploiting the full potential of the application.

To consider their utility in the RE classroom, we need to understand the type of data generic applications require (see Figure 14.2). From this it is clear that some have a more immediate use in the RE classroom than others. The word-processor and graphics/drawing packages, for example, support two types of information commonly used in RE and within religions. Although we shall spend time considering these two packages, it may be useful to consider the occasions when a database or a spreadsheet can be used effectively in RE.

The word-processor can be viewed as supporting the three aspects of the writing process shown in Figure 14.3. Ordinarily, in asking pupils to produce written work,

Application	Type of information required
Word-processor	Words, text
Graphics/drawing	Pictures, diagrams, images
Spreadsheet	Numerical values
Database	Words or numerical values relevant to a group of similarly structured entities

Figure 14.2 Content-free applications and their information requirements

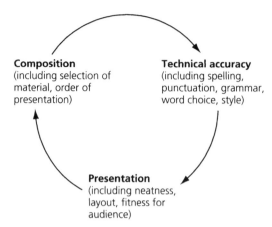

Composition
(including selection of
material, order of
presentation)

Technical accuracy
(including spelling,
punctuation, grammar,
word choice, style)

Presentation
(including neatness,
layout, fitness for
audience)

Figure 14.3 Aspects of the writing process

we ask them to handle all three aspects together. And, unless we allow for the labour-intensive task of redrafting, we often expect the first piece of work to be the final piece of work. Word-processors allow this process to be broken down and the various aspects of writing to be effectively supported. Research points to the word-processor's capacity to facilitate writing and thinking as being beneficial to all pupils, and especially so to those with special educational needs (SEN), for whom writing can often be one of the most demanding of activities. In RE pupils are asked to articulate complex, subtle ideas, often expressed through new vocabularies, and this demand can be problematic in the traditional writing process. The word-processor is able to support pupils in their expression by removing some of the labour, allowing the process to be broken down, facilitating revision and creativity.

You should consider which aspect(s) of the writing process you wish to support. For example, pupils could use the word-processor to 'brainstorm' their ideas and then experiment with placing them in some kind of order to be written up elsewhere. Alternatively, first drafts may be completed on paper and then progressively revised and checked on the word-processor until a final version is produced. Presentation may be usefully exploited if pupils are asked to produce material for a specific purpose (e.g. a leaflet, newspaper article or review, poster, letter) and/or when an audience is specified (e.g. faith community, parents, other pupils). Here pupils need to consider layout, size and format, fonts and style of language: the fact that they are engaged in effective communication for an audience necessitates understanding of the material.

The technical accuracy of writing can be assisted not just by detaching it from other aspects of writing but by the use of checkers for spelling, grammar and style. A thesaurus can be useful in helping pupils to develop and extend their vocabulary and consider their audience and purpose.

The word-processor is not only useful for pupils to use on an individual basis: it is an excellent means by which to produce collaborative work, provided, as for all group work, the activity is sufficiently complex to engender discussion. The word-processor can become the 'mediator' between pupils as they discuss and record their understandings, with ideas easily deleted, added or amended in the course of the work.

From this it should be clear that even the use of the word-processor requires you to think carefully about why, when, how and which pupils are going to use it. The focus should be on the composition and structuring of ideas. Establishing a clear purpose encourages your pupils to maximise what the word-processor has to offer, thereby enhancing their learning experience.

Pictures, graphics and drawings can be used by most word-processors, and these add an extra dimension to the pupils' work. There is a variety of ways of getting artwork into documents: clip art is often available as part of a word-processor or drawing package (but it can tend towards the stereotypical) and scanners can be used (copyright permitting).

Finally, content-free applications are very useful for you in your teaching and administration. They can, for example, be used to do the following:

- produce professional print materials that are, clear, attractive, adaptable and reusable, using graphics and pictures to help break up and provide visual cues to the text;
- keep up-to-date records on pupils (marks, assessments, progress, observations) which are easily sorted and calculated. (Note, however, that confidentiality needs to be assured.)

Content-based packages

Content-based packages are available as CD-ROMs. They are essentially databases containing either general information (as in an encyclopaedia-type package) or information specific to RE. Figure 14.4 shows how it is possible to locate what these packages offer along two continua. The first deals with their mode(s) of communication. Truly multimedia packages offer more than a textbook could provide, although this does not mean that their information content is any better. Such packages are

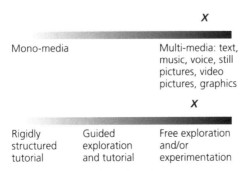

Figure 14.4 The dimensions of content-based packages

seeking to utilise other media through which learning may take place. Where only text or text and still pictures are used, they are replicating the form of their conceptual forebear: the book. The second continuum shows that such packages can also be understood in terms of the learning processes they offer to pupils. At one end there is the rigidly structured package where 'pages' are turned in strict sequence or a page is selected for the pupil on the basis of the pupil's response to an activity. At the other end are those which permit pupils to explore and/or experiment by inputting information of their own.

There is no 'better' position for any package to be on these continua, but you need to know that they offer and require different things of pupils and therefore your role in using them in the classroom is different. A rigidly structured package is going to be restricted in its use in the RE curriculum. It is likely to have a highly specific content and to present it in a particular way. A free-exploration package, on the other hand, could be specific or general in content but demands more of pupils in terms of knowing the purpose of their enquiry and how to locate the necessary information. Multimedia packages tend to be very attractive, but you should be able to justify the inclusion of so many media in terms of the content – sometimes the media are just gimmicks. Mono-media packages, such as 'picture galleries', can be very useful and can, for example, allow two or more pictures to be placed side by side for comparative analysis, or for close-ups to be viewed – things a book would not permit with such ease. It is also possible for groups of pupils to work together – again something which wouldn't be so easy with one textbook.

As well as being aware of the purposes of a content-based package you need to ensure that your pupils are aware of why and how they should be using them. Give pupils guidance on how to access the main features of the package and ensure they have enough time to experiment with the way things work. You can minimise your technical input by inducting a small group of pupils into the use of the package and then getting individuals from this group to induct others. Rigidly structured packages tend to be more straightforward: process and content are already determined. By contrast, exploration-type packages demand different, query-based, skills. These skills are akin to those needed for use of the World Wide Web and are dealt with in that section.

THE INTERNET

The internet offers access to information via the World Wide Web (WWW) and the capacity to communicate with others via email. The striking things about this access are that it is both cheap and unrestricted by geographical distance. It is possible to look at the treasures of the Vatican or those at the Victoria and Albert Museum, and to communicate with pupils and teachers in India or in a nearby school. Access to such information and the capacity for communication make the internet a highly valuable resource for RE: from the classroom the religious world outside becomes accessible and, if you so wish, you become accessible to the outside world. The internet is especially valuable to RE, given RE's broad nature, its need for resources and its emphasis on communication.

The World Wide Web

The WWW is a vast, expanding, changing and interlinked collection of resources which can draw upon a range of media. There are resources on the WWW which are capable of contributing to all areas of the RE curriculum. When using the WWW (as with using free-exploration content-based packages) you need to be aware of the processes involved in resource-based learning. Figure 14.5 gives a representation of the process.

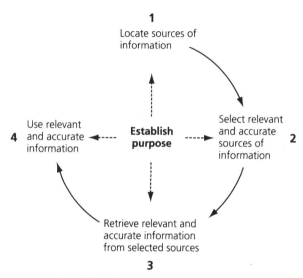

Figure 14.5 The resource-based learning process

At the centre of all resource-based learning is the need to establish a purpose. This should be expressed in terms of what is to be researched and how the findings are to be communicated. The 'what' may be thought of in terms of an area, focus, topic or question(s) and the 'how' as, among others, a written assignment, presentation, discussion, report, synopsis, etc. With the purpose established, it is possible for you to access the process at points 1, 2, 3 or 4. By preparing a hand-out for your pupils, for example, you are asking them to work from point 3: you have already undertaken the location and selection of resources. Alternatively, you might present your pupils with a number of resources (books, video, etc.) and then ask them to select those which they use. In this case you are asking them to work from point 2. As a resource the WWW differs from other resources in the skills it requires in two important respects:

- It is vast in size: there are problems in locating relevant resources.
- It is unregulated: there are problems in selecting relevant and accurate resources.

What this means is that you and your pupils need to have developed the skills associated with points 1, 2 and 3 of Figure 14.5 in a way which is appropriate to the WWW. Your pupils' skills should be developed over time, and initially it would be appropriate for you to locate and specify those resources which are relevant and useful for them to work with, so entering the process at point 3 in Figure 14.5. As their skills improve, you can increase the range of WWW resources available to them, and educate them in criteria for selection of resources, until they are able to conduct full searches on their own.

At the outset, however, you are likely to be the one locating the resources, and this can be tackled in two ways. The first is to use the capacity of the WWW itself, which supports a number of 'search engines'. These respond to your query by scanning the WWW and listing sites of possible interest. Using a search engine needs practice, as entering a query such as 'Islam' yields thousands of sites, many of which are of no use to you or your pupils. Alternatively, you could go direct to a site which provides links with areas likely to satisfy your query. The WWW sites listed in Task 14.4 have links with resources on most religions, information on social, moral and ethical issues, newspaper items of interest for RE, and discussion groups. If pupils have completed an activity which has involved searching on the WWW you should ask them to evaluate their search strategy, and to share with others any good resources they have located.

Task 14.4 Exploring RE and religion on the World Wide Web

Access the WWW sites below and bookmark each to ensure ease of return on future occasions. Explore their opening menu options and note what facilities they offer to users. Some are subscription-based services, but these usually provide a free area so that you may see what is available.

Choose one religious tradition and one Key Stage and, using the WWW sites listed below, compile a list of WWW resources on a topic such as places of worship, pilgrimage, practices, festivals, writings, beliefs, ethics, rites of passage (you may wish to focus on particular aspects of these suggestions). You could explore the menus they offer or, if available, use their search facilities. Working with your intended learning outcomes, select the resources most appropriate to your purposes and construct a lesson and activity outline which show how you propose to use the WWW resources.

Using the WWW sites below, locate a school RE WWW site. Consider what purposes the site serves and in what ways it enhances pupils' experience of RE and their religious understanding.

- www.reonline.org.uk/
  An RE site providing access to a family of RE WWW sites.
- www.theresite.co.uk/
  An RE site providing access to a family of RE WWW sites.
- www.interfaithstudies.org/
  A site dedicated to inter-faith studies.
- www.re-net.ac.uk
  TDA-funded website designed to present the evidence base for RE in IHEs.

The selection of resources is more difficult. It is important to be aware that the WWW is capable of offering access to the world of living religion: people's feelings, evaluations and personal reflections. WWW resources may not always present religions as the neatly 'packaged' phenomena we have grown accustomed to in print and video media developed for the classroom: they present both the core and the edges of religions, the controversial and the problematic. This access to the 'unmediated' in religions offers opportunities for pupils to experience the religious world first-hand, to begin to question the 'world religions' construct and to develop a language with which to participate in the ideas religious people articulate. There is also the potential for pupils to experience the need for methodology in their study, and to critically experiment with a variety of methodologies. In short, your selection should, where appropriate, allow your pupils to come into contact with this 'real' religious world.

When considering the use of relevant and accurate information (point 4 in Figure 14.5), make sure your pupils are engaged in an activity requiring them to use the material they have researched. There is sometimes a great temptation to simply copy what they have found. This stems from the assumptions that the location, selection and retrieval of material constitute the totality of the activity, and that copyright and plagiarism are issues they need not consider. By carefully specifying the purpose of their work and how their findings are to be communicated you can challenge your pupils in a variety of ways to use, evaluate and respond to the material. With experience it is also possible to give your pupils' work a wider audience by publishing it on the WWW, on the school's website, for example.

Finally, given the concern about pupils gaining access to undesirable WWW sites, you should take the practical step of locating the computer screen so that it is clearly visible to you and other pupils. You might also consider using the cache facility to store on disk the sites you have selected for your pupils: this enables them to simulate use of the WWW but prevents them accessing anything beyond those sites. In addition, many schools have implemented other measures to limit WWW access and/ or to screen out undesirable sites.

Email and discussion groups

With electronic mail (email), pupils and teachers are able to communicate with others, both individuals and organisations, anywhere in the world via the internet. The strengths of this form of communication are that it overcomes the time and labour costs of letter writing and the intrusion and expense of telephone communication. An email can be despatched immediately, delivered soon after, but read and responded to at the convenience of the recipient.

Of the various email projects involving pupils communicating with other pupils, many comment on its capacity to enhance multicultural awareness, facilitate religious and cultural exchange, and to overcome prejudice (Ipgrave 2003). These projects clearly show the potential value of email to RE: not only is the content of the email exchanges relevant, but the process of two-way communication supports dialogue, negotiation and evaluation, all of which are vitally important to the subject. Through email pupils become real and significant people in the world outside the classroom: they become seekers of understanding and potential resources in enhancing the understanding of others. Implicit in this is an understanding of such communication tending to be more individual and perhaps more personal, and this requires you as the teacher to move into a more supportive role, allowing your pupils scope to explore their ideas and to assimilate those of others.

As with all teaching and learning activities, you need to be clear about your aims, objectives and intended outcomes in establishing email communication. It may, for example, be to clarify the content of a WWW site, to seek an answer to a specific question concerning a religion, to ask for help in identifying resources, or to present current understanding in order to receive constructive feedback. Establishing a purpose helps to clarify the other elements you need to consider in email communication:

- the email initiator (individual pupil, group of pupils, whole class);
- the email recipient (pupil(s), organisation, individual 'expert', discussion group, bulletin board);
- the time frame (one-off email or extended exchange).

A group of pupils working together increases communication by providing opportunities for the group to discuss both outgoing and incoming emails. Where WWW authors give an email address it is reasonable for them to expect to receive email from pupils who have questions to ask. With other email contacts you may need to consider sending an email to check whether they are able to help your pupils. Discussion groups and bulletin boards support exchange between people with shared interests. Questions or contributions to an ongoing discussion can be left on a 'notice board' which others can read and to which they are free to respond. The task here, for you or your pupils, would be to locate appropriate discussion groups with which they could make contact.

Task 14.5 Communications and projects on the World Wide Web

Explore the WWW sites below. You should be able to find, among other things, examples and details of how to set up collaborative projects with other schools in the UK and abroad, how to locate email contacts for yourself and your pupils, helpful advice on publishing on the WWW, and how you might best develop your pupils' use of the internet. File this information for future reference with other website data.

- http://www.eun.org/portal/index.htm
  European Schoolnet
- http://www.gsh.org/
  The Global School net

YOUR PROFESSIONAL DEVELOPMENT NOW AND IN THE FUTURE USING ICT

Developing your professional skills as an RE teacher

ICT is a rich environment which can readily facilitate your professional development in RE. The World Wide Web provides access to innumerable resources that are useful to your planning and preparation, such as:

- information from and about religions and social, philosophical and ethical issues;
- RE schemes of work, lesson plans and creative ideas, including those using ICT, shared by RE teachers;
- opportunities to look at the RE work of other schools;
- details about and reviews of books, resources, content-based packages/CD-ROMs and WWW sites, written by RE teachers;
- access to the world's libraries, newspapers and databases;
- details of programmes relevant to RE on all the major television channels;
- book samples and facilities for ordering inspection copies;
- access to free software (shareware) and to samples of software.

The internet can also serve to keep you informed about courses, conferences, developments in RE, government legislation and non-statutory guidance, allowing you either immediate access to documents and publications or the facility to request them. Email enables you to communicate with other teachers of RE and to comment upon and share materials and ideas with them. Most important, ICT offers the opportunity to reflect upon and consider the RE curriculum, how you teach and how pupils learn. In this chapter the criterion proposed for using ICT is that it should 'effectively enhance the quality of teaching and learning'. Enhancement in this context suggests enhancement of what already is, but ICT may also offer the potential to transform aspects of content and method in teaching and learning.

Task 14.6 Development through the World Wide Web

For information on developments and initiatives in education relevant to your teacher education and your future professional development the sites below provide access to official documents and reports:

- www.dfes.gov.uk
  The Department for Schools, Skills and Families
- www.becta.org.uk/
  The British Educational Communications and Technology Service

Developing your competence in ICT

Teachers are expected to continue to improve their teaching skills and keep up to date with ICT and its application to subject pedagogy. Some of this development is accomplished by working towards effective integration of ICT into your teaching, learning and administration. This necessarily implies that such integration should be critical and reflective. You may subscribe to publications which keep you informed about developments in ICT and ICT in RE, request software catalogues and regularly visit WWW sites of relevance. Ideas for developing ICT in RE can also be picked up and adapted from those developed in other subjects and for other age groups. By maintaining contact with your RE Curriculum Adviser, reading, being aware of courses available to you, and ensuring that your ICT needs figure in your appraisal, you should be equipped to access opportunities to develop your skills.

SUMMARY AND KEY POINTS

There is clearly an important role for ICT in RE: ICT offers support for fundamental skills in RE. RE has justifiably supported the need for communication, encouraging pupils to explore their religious environments, bringing artefacts and guest speakers into the classroom: ICT offers, through the internet, the possibility of bringing the religious world outside the classroom within ready and immediate reach of every pupil. This is an opportunity not to be missed. Crucial to this, however, are your skills as a teacher, your development of the necessary competences in ICT to manage the learning situation such that your pupils' learning experience in RE is effectively enhanced. ICT is no replacement for a good teacher.

FURTHER READING

Abbott, C. (2000) *ICT: Changing Education*, London, RoutledgeFalmer. Useful and accessible guide to the uses and history of ICT in British education.

Ferrigan, C. (2005) *Passing the ICT Skills Test (Achieving QTS)*, Exeter: Learning Matters Ltd. A guide, as the title indicates, to passing the ICT Skills Test.

Kennewell, S. (2006) *A Practical Guide to Teaching ICT in the Secondary School*, London, Routledge. This book provides useful supportive reading for those seeking to enhance their skills in the successful development of ICT in secondary schools and in developing their pupils' skills.

Leask, M. and Pachler, N. (eds) (2005) *Learning to Teach Using ICT in the Secondary School*, 2nd edn, London: Routledge. Informative, helpful and wide-ranging.

QCA National Curriculum in Action: www.ncaction.org.uk/subjects/re/ict-lrn.htm. National Curriculum site that provides information and links to other websites on ICT and RE.

Web resources

ICT in RE: //re-xs.ucsm.ac.uk/cupboard/ict/index2.html. Excellent list of resources, reports and software.

Better RE for teachers, advisers and RE professionals: http://betterre.reonline.org.uk/ using_ict/ Useful information and resources.

15 Professional development

Joy Schmack

INTRODUCTION

> When I started teaching, my short and long-term aims were simply to survive! I felt I never had time to plan my development, never had time to go on courses, and never had time to read more about my subject. For three years I drifted from term to term, responding to whatever the latest initiatives were but without any sense of ownership of my own growth. When the time came to apply for Head of Department posts I realised I had little more to offer than when I started teaching. True to say I learnt the hard way, 'If you don't know where you're going, you'll never get there.'
>
> (RE teacher)

This chapter charts the various stages in personal and professional development you are likely to be challenged by during your first teaching post. lt aims to highlight the many opportunities which exist within the school, the local community and the broader national framework and infrastructure that support the subject, and seek to raise your awareness of the range of individuals and organisations available to support you. It reflects upon the importance of the Training and Development Agency (TDA) for School's Career Entry and Development Profile (CEDP) and the proposed TDA Standards for Subject Leaders in Religious Education as tools of reflective practice. Throughout the chapter there is an emphasis on the necessity of taking ownership of your own development and planning both in the short and long term.

OBJECTIVES

By the end of this chapter you should be able to:

*   understand the variety of roles you need to develop as a teacher of RE;
*   reflect on the range of opportunities that exist for your own professional and personal development;
*   develop strategies for keeping yourself up to date in your subject.

OBTAINING YOUR FIRST TEACHING JOB

> I was so proud when I got the first post I applied for, I didn't consider the limited range of opportunities I would be given. The structure of the school meant it was very difficult to get a wider range of experience for me to move on in later years.
>
> (RE teacher)

It is a sobering thought that your first teaching post has a huge effect on the whole of your teaching career. You may find yourself faced with a wide range of decisions when choosing your first school: Specialist academy? Selective grammar school? Faith community school? Single sex? Co-educational? Community school? It is in this post that you can learn more about your subject and explore different styles of pedagogy and management. You need to be a fast learner, as many teachers of RE take up a head of department role as early as their third year of teaching. It is vital to find the right type of school for you and your expertise. It may not seem so when you are applying for posts but RE specialists are in demand and it is important to make an informed choice. It is naturally tempting to jump at the first job offered to you, but it is probably best to observe a little caution and be reflective in any decision you make. You need to do your homework and find out information that then needs to be considered in the light of your own educational and philosophical viewpoint. It is very difficult to work to the best of your ability in a system to which you are opposed philosophically and educationally.

Consider the following advertisement:

Green Road School. Required for September, a highly qualified NQT to teach RE and PSE throughout the school. Green Road is a highly successful school with a strong record of academic and extra-curricular achievement. The school is situated in pleasant countryside within easy reach of London and adjacent to woodland and a golf course.

Sounds like an ideal place to spend a holiday but what does the advertisement really tell you about the state of RE at Green Road? The reality may be that the school achieves excellent academic GCSE results in many areas of the curriculum but no status is accorded to RE. The school may be breaking statutory requirements at Key Stages 3 and 4 and, with an Ofsted inspection looming, decides to appoint a newly qualified teacher (NQT) to act as head of department in an attempt to appease the inspectors. It is, then, vitally important to find out all you can about a school before you get too involved in the application process.

Finding out about schools prior to application

The nature of the school

You need to find out basic information about the school. Information supplied to potential applicants is a good place to start in your search for information. You ought also to look at Ofsted reports and the school's public examination profile. Remember if you are applying to a Faith Character School the RE report is not with the whole-school Ofsted report (but it can be requested from the school). If you have the opportunity, listen to what local people have to say about any school you intend to apply to and, if possible, visit the school at the end of the day to get some idea of interaction between pupils and pupils and between pupils and staff. Some schools welcome informal discussions and visits prior to the formal interviewing procedure. Information you should acquire for might include, for example:

- What category of school is it?
- Is it a single-sex school and is it planning to remain so?
- Is there a sixth form and is it considered viable?
- Is there a selection criterion for entry into the school, and if so, what is it?
- Is the teaching contract temporary or permanent?
- What are the terms and conditions attached to the post?
- What is its policy regarding RE and collective worship?
- Is the school ethos likely to fit in with your character, personality and teaching style?

The status of RE

In addition, you need to find out about the nature and status of RE in the school. It is vital to understand the structure of the RE department. Many RE departments are located within Humanities departments, where they may be regarded as Cinderella not only in terms of status but also in terms of budget and resourcing allocations. You should make sure that you are aware of any other responsibilities the department may have, e.g. significant contributions to spiritual, moral, social and cultural development (SMSC), charity fund-raising, citizenship education. Departments have a wide range of practices regarding lunchtime devotional clubs (e.g. the Christian Union) and collective worship. For some it is an integral part of the role of the department, whereas for others it is something they take no part in. Questions you ought to be asking of the department at this preliminary stage include:

- What is the school's policy regarding RE and collective worship?
- What are the timetabling arrangements?
- How does the school ensure it is compliant at Key Stage 4?
- What is the take-up of the subject at GCSE and GCE A Level? What does the public examination profile of the RE department look like?
- What is the budget allocation for RE? How does it compare with other Humanities subjects?
- Which Agreed Syllabus is taught?
- What is the philosophical stance behind the Agreed Syllabus?
- How many religions are required at each Key Stage and what are they?

Induction support

Finally, you need to find out what induction and in-service training support you are likely to receive.

- What form does the institution's and the Local Authority's or Diocesan induction programme take?
- Is there an RE specialist who takes responsibility for mentoring you during your induction into the profession? If so, how experienced is this person? Is this the kind of person with whom you are likely to work well?
- What support is there from the Local Authority in terms of a teachers' centre, resource centre or advisory service?
- Is there an RE or Humanities adviser available for you to consult?

Ofsted reports

It would be a grave error to automatically disregard schools that Ofsted has deemed to 'have serious weaknesses' or to be 'in need of special measures'. Some of the most stimulating and rigorous RE departments are in schools which have been 'named and shamed'. When you have decided to apply for a school you need to obtain a copy of the previous Ofsted report. (All reports are easily available on the internet.) Look carefully at the whole report and consider the implications of the following for RE.

- What are the key points for action?
- What comments are made about the spiritual, moral, social and cultural development of pupils?
- What points are made about the leadership and management of the school?
- How do Key Stage 4 examination results reflect the national picture?
- How do GCSE RE entry numbers and results compare with other subjects in the school?
- What is the ethnic diversity within the school community?
- What issues are raised in the parents' questionnaire response?

When deciding on your first job you need to think about where you want to be in five years' time and ensure the post you are applying for gives you a relevant range of opportunities and experiences. It can be a difficult leap, for example, from a single-sex church school to a multi-faith, inner city community school without the appropriate groundwork. Consequently, at this initial stage in your career it is important to look out for a post which has the widest range of career opportunities and experiences to draw upon in later years. This lays the foundation of the rest of your professional and personal development.

> **Task 15.1 Gathering school information before applying for a job**
>
> The sections above contain a number of lists of questions to which you should gain answers before applying for an RE job in a school. When contemplating whether you should apply for a particular job or not, seek out the appropriate information and note down answers to these questions. This should clarify the issue of whether you should proceed with a formal application.

The application process

Start looking early. Many schools plan their budget a year in advance and start to advertise in January or February for a post to be taken up in the following September. However, do not panic if no suitable job is advertised immediately. Remember you should complete your skills tests as soon as possible. You cannot start your QTS year until you have met all the standards and that includes the three skills tests! Although jobs appear from the start of the year, the vast majority of posts for NQTs are not advertised until after Easter, and many not until the second half of the summer term. The most obvious places to look are the *Times Educational Supplement*, and the *Guardian Education Supplement*. Each offers services where they text or email suitable vacancies to you. Many LAs and Dioceses run teaching pools to which you can apply. Take time to consider the advertisement and consider the skills required. If a job looks as if it may suit you, don't hesitate to ring or write for further information. Most schools now require a stamped addressed envelope: be sure to ask how much postage is required. If you decide to apply you should be willing to take time and care over your application.

It is obviously a compliment when student teachers are offered a post in the school in which they have done their teaching practice. This can have many positive factors as you begin your job in September, such as knowing the department and school structure, and knowing many of the pupils. You must, however, establish that a wider range of opportunities will be offered to you than when you were on teaching practice. It would be helpful if you could be offered interview experience so that you have had that experience when you apply for your next post.

It is important to attend any interview with a clear and objective view as to the experiences you are hoping for in your first post. Interviews differ between schools and it is easy to get caught up in the momentum of the day and allow the process to become simply a competition among the various candidates. Delighted as you may feel if selected, always beware that 'morning after' feeling when you wake to realise that perhaps it isn't the school for you.

As part of the interview procedure many schools now offer a chance for you to teach a lesson. This is an excellent opportunity for you to assess the attitudes of the pupils to the subject and for you also to evaluate the resources available. You need to follow the good practice you have learnt through your teacher education course. Request some information about the class and their prior knowledge if this is not given to you. Ensure you have a copy of the lesson plan and resources available for the observer. Look at the quality and quantity of wall displays and the range of books in the library concerned with RE. If possible, look at the staff room notice boards to see if there is a range of career development opportunities displayed.

Have a talk with the head of department to try to establish where the department is going and what your role in the department could be. Of particular interest may be the department's approach to Key Stage 4 RE. Is it compliant with the agreed syllabus? Do all pupils follow short or long course GCSE? Is RE part of a non-exam carousel with an option group for GCSE? The answers have a direct impact upon your timetable in your NQT year.

Unlike many other subjects you may find that the head of department is your only other subject colleague, so it is important that you share a similar philosophy or at least can ensure that your differences won't be to the detriment of the department. Of particular interest is the department's attitude to having students teachers of RE. An opinion I heard expressed recently was that 'They're more trouble than they're worth'. Such a response could certainly be grounds to doubt the level of support a teacher would get in the first year. In my experience, no two RE departments are the same. Each has its own ethos and philosophy, its own role in the school, its own links with the community and its own roles in contributing to the personal, spiritual, moral, social and cultural dimensions of the school.

Now for the $64,000 question. What happens if by July you have not found a suitable position? The answer is simple: don't panic! An initial step is to keep looking in the press, particularly, at this time, the local press. Sign on with a teacher employment agency. Doing supply work gives you the opportunity to gain more experience in a variety of schools. It also gives you time to reflect on why you have not gained a position. Are your CV and references effective in revealing your abilities? Have you always directed your application to the job specification? How professional is your self-presentation, both on paper and in face-to-face situations? Has all your teaching experience been in a limited environment, e.g. all girls' schools? What have you learnt from the interview feedback that you have been given from earlier interviews? Further help and advice on getting your first post is given in Capel *et al.* (2005), Unit 8.1.

Task 15.2 Preparing to apply for your first teaching post

It is important to consider your own philosophical and educational rationale. First, consider the following types of schools and write down some brief notes reflecting your reasons for wanting/not wanting to teach in each type.

- academy;
- community school;
- independent school;
- single-sex school;
- denominational school.

Now look below at the list of interview questions and consider what your response may be to each. As you see, the types of questions give a clear indication of how the school management views RE. You need to consider how you would honestly reply to each.

- What was your best lesson and why? What was your worst lesson and why?
- What would you consider your particular strengths and weaknesses in terms of class management?
- Describe your own faith journey.
- How can RE support the delivery of Citizenship?
- What book has had the most influence on your life and why?
- Where do you see your career in three years?
- What is the difference between RE and catechesis?

File your notes for reference.

ESTABLISHING YOURSELF IN YOUR FIRST POST

> I went from day to day dealing with everything that I needed to. It wasn't until the end of the year that I realised I had done nothing for my own professional development. I made sure that changed the next year.
>
> (RE teacher)

Don't be surprised if by your first half-term you feel the only focus in your development plan is to get through the next half-term. Without doubt this is one of the busiest times of your life but it is essential that you are proactive in this year when your practical experiences are built more rapidly and critically than at any other time in your career as a teacher.

You will be assigned a mentor but there are many people within the school community who can also help your development. It is important to seek advice actively from the appropriate individuals, as there are many aspects of school life that may not have been covered on your course (advice on planning for a school trip, for example).

An important step during your first month in the school is to take on the responsibility and ownership of your career development. Remember your PGCE year was only the first year of your development. You need to plan your short-term and long-term programme for development and the routes you take to achieve it. It is important that this plan is shared and, if necessary, negotiated with your head of department and your mentor. This gives you a sense of direction and purpose. An obvious support in identifying your professional needs is your Career Entry and Development Profile (CEDP) mentioned earlier.

Your Career Entry and Development Profile

One of the most useful tools in establishing your priority needs is the CEDP. If you haven't already come across this document, you will do before the end of your PGCE programme. You are expected to fill in the profile before completing your PGCE and take it with you to your first teaching post. The CEDP offers structured guidance to you at three transition points in your professional development: towards the end of your initial teacher education programme and at the start and end of your induction programme. It also allows you to take responsibility from the earliest point in your career for your own professional development. The purposes of the Profile are to:

- help teachers to make constructive connections between initial teacher education, induction and the later stages of their development as a teacher;
- guide the processes of reflection and collaborative discussion;
- focus their reflections on their achievements and goals.

Creating a personal development plan

You should use your CEDP as the basis for negotiating a personal development plan with your mentor. Your development plan should consist of some small targets that are easily and rapidly achievable as well as the broader focuses of development. It should not be a case of merely making existing skills more explicit but should include needs identification and prioritisation. You need to look critically and objectively for the gap between your present and your anticipated performance. It is useful to consult the TDA online support tool 'Professional and Career Development' which helps teachers to map their chosen route through the profession (www.tda.gov.uk/teachers.aspx).

Once you have identified your needs, it is important to decide who supports you, how and when. You also need to agree when you are to review the success of the programme and the next steps forward. For example, an outline personal development plan might contain elements such as those outlined in Figure 15.1.

Target	Who involved	How	Start/review	Indicator of success
Knowledge of GCE A Level	Head of department	• Lesson observation • Team teaching • Read set texts • Attend relevant meetings • Moderate exam marking • Attend one-day in-service course	October–July	• Confidence with subject matter • Successful teaching • Contribution to curriculum development at GCE A Level

Figure 15.1 Sample personal development plan

The following list contains the most popular needs development areas:

- the development of ICT and RE;
- target setting in RE;
- differentiation and RE;
- implementing effective assessment;
- knowledge of world faiths;
- teaching and learning strategies to engage pupils;
- special educational needs and RE;
- making effective use of educational visits;
- effective use of resources;
- effective target setting.

In addition to subject-specific issues you also need to conduct a needs analysis of your skills and knowledge in generic issues such as pastoral care, pre-vocational training, health and safety requirements and raising standards of achievement.

All schools should have their own structured induction programme that is utilised for all NQTs. This programme should aim to help you build on the knowledge and skills you have acquired already and to support your individual professional development needs. To give you time to focus on your targets in your induction year, you should have a 90 per cent timetable compared to established classroom teachers.

At the end of each term, time must be planned to review your development as a whole and decide the priorities for next term. This record of termly achievements and experience acts as an excellent aide-mémoire when applying for your next position. When drawing up your action plan it is important to reflect upon the variety of strategies which helps your development and to take the opportunity to draw upon as wide a range of experience as possible. These are just a few suggestions:

- observation by or of other colleagues;
- visits to other schools;
- in-service training courses;
- material resources;
- support from professional advisers and consultants.

Establishing yourself in your school

Your first port of call within any school must be your own department. Tensions can, and often do, exist in hard-pressed departments and it is vital that there is a structured channel of communication and support. Frequently I hear departmental heads lamenting that their new teachers are not showing initiative. Simultaneously new teachers report their frustrations with departmental heads who don't delegate or hold proper meetings. Such simple misconceptions only need time for quality communication; but time is always at a premium in schools. Try to be as enthusiastic, committed and supportive of your head of department as possible, whatever the challenges facing you. Though it is easy simply to mutter and complain about things you are not happy with, the professional option is to communicate your views in a responsible way that conveys enthusiasm for the subject and support for the department.

It is important to negotiate the areas of departmental responsibility you are to develop each term and to discuss what are the indicators of success. It is also important to negotiate the areas that you 'shadow'. There should be a balance between departmental and personal needs. One word of warning: be aware of what you can confidently take on. It is by no means rare for NQTs in their first term to be given the 'challenge' of whole-school collective worship. Normally it is simply because nobody else wants to do it: beware of being taken advantage of because of your NQT status. The school views you as far more professional if you do a few jobs well rather than a range of responsibilities half well. By the completion of your second year of teaching you should have taken responsibility or shadowed all the activities necessary for running a department. In particular, try to gain experience of management issues such as budgeting, resourcing, stocktaking, timetabling, etc.

Since the introduction of the short course GCSE many more pupils are taking a final examination at the end of Key Stage 4. If you are not given an examination group during your first year, it is essential to shadow the whole process: planning the course content; ways of promoting the subject with pupils and with parents; strategies for the interpreting and application of an exam syllabus; effective use of resources; setting and moderation of coursework; setting and marking of exam papers; target setting; revision techniques. In doing so, you lay sound foundations for your future involvement in examination teaching.

During this first year it can be extremely rewarding to work on one joint project with colleagues from other departments. All too often RE is marginalised and it is important to look at strategies to highlight the ethos of the subject. Such small-scale projects are often of personal interest and allow you to mix with a wider range of staff than your own department. Recent projects I have observed have included RE and Art departments collaborating on a project concerning local places of worship; RE and Drama departments working on a project called 'Response to the Holocaust' and RE and Science departments holding a lunchtime debate on 'Are humans playing God?'.

Time should be available for you to observe the teaching of others and for them to observe you. Lesson observation both by and of the NQT is often the most highly rated induction activity. Daunting as this may seem, it is an essential step to be able to discuss with a colleague and reflect on practice. The majority of staff spend between 170 and 190 days on their own in the classroom in their first year. One NQT recently remarked about her first year:

> I felt so isolated in the classroom. Closing the door and just getting on with it. I desperately wanted to discuss with colleagues if I was doing things correctly but I was afraid to ask them to watch in case they thought I was having problems. I just wish that mutual classroom observation had been built into my induction programme.
>
> (RE teacher)

CONSOLIDATING YOUR PROFESSIONAL DEVELOPMENT

Utilising local support networks

> I needed to talk to other RE professionals. Each day was filled with thoughts about my own school and my own teaching. I needed to swap experiences with others.
>
> (RE teacher)

Every Local Authority's Agreed Syllabus must reflect the faith communities of the area. In turn, these local requirements are translated into your school's schemes of work. If you are new to the area you need to acquaint yourself quickly with the range of resources that are available. One of the greatest resources for RE teachers is their local faith community. Links with it not only enrich any scheme of work, showing the true integrity of the religion as practised locally, but also are a support in terms of resources. The most obvious way to find the variety of local faith communities within the area is by asking the pupils themselves. Failing that, relevant information can be found in Yellow Pages. For security reasons it is important to contact the faith community prior to your visit. This is also the time to clarify dress code and practices. It's worth asking whether you are allowed to take photographs during your visit. These can be an excellent classroom resource when taken with a digital camera. Many areas have an established Inter-Faith Group which can be accessed through the Interfaith Network Association. Your links with the local communities support many attributes of your personal and professional development:

- increasing your own knowledge of faith traditions and how they are practised within your locality;
- expanding your range of classroom resources;

- enabling you to invite visiting speakers in from the communities to talk to your classes;
- assisting you in making effective class visits to places of worship.

Another local feature of key importance to your professional development is the work of the LA and the Teachers' Development Centre. These usually run a range of in-service courses and professional meetings, as well as incorporating a variety of services such as reprographics and resources. Some include an RE resource centre which is invaluable for you. Different schools have different funding arrangements with the LA and it is important to be aware what the arrangements are and how best to use the service.

Most LAs provide a central programme to support school induction of NQTs. This can be very valuable to newly qualified RE teachers, who often come from small departments where there is no other NQT. Centrally run programmes enable cross-transfer of skills, initiatives and inspiration as well as enabling you to see practice in other schools.

It is common practice for NQTs to be allowed to go on a few courses during their first year. The courses need to be carefully selected, bearing in mind your career profile and targets. The average cost of a day course (including supply cover and travel expenses) is around £350, so the school has a right to see its money used effectively and making an impact on your practice.

Take care when reading course details and ensure the course fulfils your needs. Remember that any course run from outside the LA's area may well bear little resemblance to the Agreed Syllabus which your school is following. Certain questions should be reflected upon before you consult your head teacher or mentor:

- How does the course link with my agreed targets?
- What do I expect to gain from the day?
- How does it affect my classroom practice?
- How does the course contribute to department and school development plans?
- How do I disseminate what I have learned to the department and the school?

In addition to day courses many LAs run twilight courses for teachers. These usually run between 4.30 p.m. and 6.00 p.m. and do not require supply cover. They can be valuable in enabling RE teachers to meet and discuss matters of common interest, consider new initiatives and developments in the subject, and to work together to devise projects, such as baseline assessment for Year 7 entry or review new resources.

An important body to become involved with is your local Standing Advisory Council on Religious Education (SACRE), whose role it is to offer help, support and advice to the teaching of RE in the local schools. The membership of any SACRE normally consists of representatives of four bodies: local councillors, teachers and head teachers, the Church of England, and other faith traditions represented in the district. Usually a SACRE meets once a term to discuss events affecting RE within schools, including Ofsted reports and other related issues. When a new Agreed Syllabus for

RE is to be written many SACREs become transformed into Agreed Syllabus Conferences with the brief to undertake this role. One way of getting on to the SACRE is to contact your union representative and see if there is a vacancy on the teachers' group. If you belong to a faith group you can always contact it to offer your services. Being a member of the SACRE broadens your knowledge of all aspects of RE.

Utilising national networks

> After three years in teaching I began to feel jaded. Then someone told me they'd got a grant through the British Council for educational research. I sent in an application form and research submission and within four months, I was conducting research into Holocaust education in Israel. That experience recharged my batteries and gave me an enthusiasm I thought I had lost.
>
> (RE teacher)

There are many books and publications that are of interest and use during your early years of teaching. The most commonly read are *REtoday*, a high-quality glossy magazine devoted to topical and practical issues in the teaching of RE that includes national and international news concerning RE and forthcoming events, and *REsource*, a companion publication that contains short reflective articles on the theory and practice of RE (both are published by Christian Education Publications). The *British Journal of Religious Education* and the *Journal of Beliefs and Values* are the standard academic journals in the field. They include original research and articles on a wide range of religious education issues. If you are prepared to set some quality reading time aside, then these periodicals give you many ideas for classroom practice in addition to increasing your own subject development.

To understand the integrity of a religious tradition and its views on contemporary issues there is no better place to look than the range of newspapers reflecting multi-cultural Britain. Do refer to your SHAP calendars (www.shap.org/), listing all the major religious festivals each year, and make your purchases at relevant times, e.g. the *Jewish Chronicle* just before Pesach, or *Eastern Eye* just before Diwali that throws light on the integrity of the religion rather than the stereotypes and platitudes that abound in many textbooks. Similarly obtaining the *Church Times*, the *Tablet* and the *Methodist Recorder* all in the same week show the different viewpoints on topical issues across a range of Christian denominations.

You need to become aware of the range of organisations that can offer support, assistance and resources to RE teachers and of their differing rationale and strategies. Making an approach in order to obtain support from a relevant organisation should be a part of your development plan. Such contacts can open up 'golden' opportunities but should be made only when you are certain you are able to respond appropriately to the support offered. Once you have settled into your first school you need to think in terms of more formal ways of increasing your expertise and skills as an RE teacher: attendance at conferences, involvement and even secondment on research projects, further study, including possibly M A and M Phil/Ph D research. Most PGCE courses now have the potential to contribute 60 credit points towards a Master's course (normally requiring 180 credit points).

The St Gabriel's Trust has been a terrific support and revitaliser of RE in schools. It annually provides grants for teacher-led in-service training, realising the importance of network development to stop teachers from feeling professionally isolated. Past areas of study have included sixth-form RE; producing resource boxes for studying world faiths; photo-packs about local churches and short course GCSE. As one teacher involved said:

> When we were awarded a St Gabriel's grant we knew it might help with the instigation of the short course GCSE, but we had no idea of the other ramifications. Throughout the year I felt inspired about my teaching – the first time in many years. It was invigorating to sit and discuss with other colleagues, to share good practice and good resources. Even when the grant ended, our group decided to meet regularly and to take on new initiatives together.

In addition to awarding grants, St Gabriel's runs an annual RE Teachers' Weekend where 250 teachers from different types of schools meet to share ideas and attend seminars on over twenty topics. The two days provide free in-service training with all conference fees and accommodation paid for by the St Gabriel's Programme. For more information or to receive the regular newsletter, contact the Development Officer, Culham College Institute, The Malthouse, 60 East St Helen Street, Abingdon, Oxon. OX145EB, or you can visit the website: http://www.culham. ac.uk/sg.

Other supportive bodies for the developments of RE include the Farmington Institute. Although its aims are to support, encourage and improve Christian education, the institute takes a particular interest in developing good relations with world religions. Each year it awards a number of primary and secondary Farmington Fellowships that release teachers for a term to study an aspect of RE at a university or institution of higher education.

The Stapleford Centre is one of the leading lights in promoting the personal and professional development of teachers from a Christian perspective. In addition to providing a range of courses it regularly publishes Christian resources for the teaching of values across the curriculum.

There are numerous non-subject-specific agencies which may be able to support your development, e.g. the Churchill Trust or the British Council. Some agencies have a very definite focus for their support such as the Holocaust Education Trust, which subsidises in-service training on the teaching of the Holocaust. It is important to be proactive and realise the potential of some of the declared national/international years of special interest. An important motto to remember in the fight against fossilisation in RE is that 'If we don't move forward we'll find we're going backwards.'

There is no finer way to get to know a GCSE syllabus than to become an exam marker. It is true you won't get rich quickly (or even slowly) but you gain an excellent working knowledge of the syllabus content, marking scheme and standards in other schools. Advertisements for external examiners and coursework moderators are regularly featured in the *Times Educational Supplement*. Remember, though, that if you do apply and are accepted it is vital to realise the implications for your time schedule and to plan round a potentially very busy June.

British Education Leadership, Management and Administration Society: www.shu.ac.uk
British Educational Research Association: www.bera.ac.uk
Collaborative Action Research Network: www.did.stu.mmu.ac.uk/carn/
Culham College Institute: www.culham.ac.uk
Farmington Institute: http://farmington.virtualsite.co.uk
Holocaust Education Trust: www.het.org.uk
Key RE site: www.theredirectory.org.uk
Official Government site: www.teachernet.gov.uk
R.E. Today services: www.retoday.org.uk
Stapleford Centre: www.stapleford-centre.org

Figure 15.2 Useful websites

Further research and study

It is important that the daily grind and the surplus of paperwork don't let you forget the love of the subject that led you into teaching. It is easy to lose touch with the academic rigour and argument that are such a vital part of the subject. Thankfully, it has never been easier to further your development through studying for an MA. There are a wide range of courses available now following a variety of study systems and forms of organisation. It is true the majority of teachers have to fit any further study or qualifications into their working life; gone are the days when schools could offer secondments, although many still help towards the cost of the fees. Before embarking on an MA you must reflect upon your own personality and personal and professional commitments.

The teacher who has a lot of extracurricular activities may be tempted to apply for a distance learning MA, which does not necessitate attending regular weekly lectures. The disadvantage of this option is that it is easy to feel isolated and miss the valuable discourse resulting from seminars and workshops. Distance learning also necessitates a tremendous amount of self-discipline, as there is less supervision and personal contact. Again it is important right from the first year of teaching to consider when is the best time to embark on an MA. Many teachers have regretted not starting during their first two years of teaching, so seeing it as a natural development of their first degree. Some teachers have enjoyed a gap of five or six years, believing they had more to offer in their studies because of the accrued experience. It is important to select what is right for you and to include it in your development plan. Whatever MA you choose to do, whenever you choose to do it, you can be sure that the effort in terms of your own development is well worth while.

Further help on your professional development can be found in Unit 8.2 Developing further as a teacher (Capel *et al.* 2005) and for teachers in their first years of teaching *Starting to Teach in Secondary School: A Companion for the Newly Qualified Teacher* (Capel *et al.* 2004).

Task 15.3 Keeping up the momentum and focusing on further study

You want to teach RE because of your enthusiasm for the subject. It is important this zeal is never lost and that your teaching allows it to be enriched. Here are some suggestions for keeping up your momentum:

- Make a list of professional organisations you can affiliate with, and the magazines and journals you intend to subscribe to. Don't wait till next year to join up: do it now!
- Ensure you are on the alert system of organisations such as QCA and Ofsted to ensure that you receive information and research findings as soon as they are published.
- Set yourself targets for keeping your professional reading and study up to scratch – both in the field of RE itself and in the 'subject knowledge' areas of Religious Studies, Theology, Philosophy, Anthropology, etc.
- Set up a mutual support network among your fellow student teachers. Consider having regular email conversations during your first year of teaching, and regular reunions for social as well as professional purposes!
- Write out a medium-term plan for your professional development. Where do you want to be in ten years' time? What in-service courses and IHE study programmes do you need to take up to achieve it? Discuss the draft plan with your tutor.
- Have you reached the limit of your academic development yet? Have you considered the possibility of a part-time MA course in RE, or even of future doctoral research? Identify and record people and institutions to whom you can turn for advice.

SUMMARY AND KEY POINTS

We began the chapter by indicating how important it was to be thinking about your second post when you've only just started your first. Hopefully if you realised the details of your development plan you have

- increased and kept up to date with your subject knowledge;
- experienced or shadowed a range of responsibilities within your school;
- developed those areas that need addressing in your Career Entry and Development Profile;
- taken part in effective in-service training;
- initiated and organised cross-curricular projects;
- experienced a wide range of teaching strategies;
- obtained a further qualification.

FURTHER READING

Capel, S., Leask, M. and Turner, T. (2005) *Learning to Teach in the Secondary School: A Companion to School Experience*, London: RoutledgeFalmer.

Capel, S., Leask, M. and Turner, T. (2004) *Starting to Teach in the Secondary School*, London: RoutledgeFalmer.

Both standard texts and invaluable guides.

Appendix

Useful addresses and contacts

Alison Seaman and L. Philip Barnes

GOVERNMENT OFFICES

England

Department for Children, Schools and Families
Sanctuary Buildings
Great Smith Street
London
SW1P 3BT
Telephone: 0870 001 0336
Email: info@dcsf.gsi.gov.uk
Website: www.dfes.gov.uk/

Northern Ireland

Department for Education for Northern Ireland
Rathgael House
43 Balloo Road
Bangor
Co Down
BT19 7PR
Telephone: 028 9127 9279
Email: mail@deni.gov.uk
Website: www.deni.gov.uk

Scotland

Scottish Executive Education Department
Victoria Quay
Edinburgh
EH6 6QQ
Telephone: 0131 556 8400 or 08457 741741 (for local rate throughout UK)
Email: ceu@scotland.gov.uk
Website: www.scotland.gov.uk/Topics/Education

Wales

The Department for Children, Education, Lifelong Learning and Skills
Welsh Assembly Government
Cathays Park
Cardiff
CF10 3NQ
Telephone: 0845 010 3300 (English) or 0845 010 4400 (Welsh)
Email: through web link: http://wag-en.custhelp.com/cgi-bin/wag_
en.cfg/php/enduser/std_alp.php
Website: http://new.wales.gov.uk/about/departments/dcells/?lang=en

Official Bodies

Qualifications and Curriculum Authority
83 Piccadilly
London
W1J 8QA
Telephone: 020 7509 5555
Email: info@qca.org.uk
Website: www.qca.org.uk

Training and Development Agency for Schools
151 Buckingham Palace Road
London
SW1W 9SZ
Telephone: 020 7023 8000
Email: corporatecomms@tda.gov.uk
Website: www.tda.gov.uk

General Teaching Council for England
Victoria Square House
Victoria Square
Birmingham

B2 4AJ
Telephone: 0870 001 0308
Email: info@gtce.org.uk
Website: www.gtce.org.uk

General Teaching Council for Northern Ireland
4th Floor Albany House
73–75 Great Victoria Street
Belfast BT2 7AF
Telephone: 028 9033 3390
Email: info@gtcni.org.uk
Website: www.gtcni.org.uk/

General Teaching Council for Scotland
Clerwood House
96 Clermiston Road
Edinburgh
EH12 6UT
Telephone: 0131 314 6000
Email: gtcs@gtcs.org.uk
Website: http://www.gtcs.org.uk/Home/home.asp

General Teaching Council for Wales
4th Floor, Southgate House
Wood Street
Cardiff
CF10 1EW
Telephone: 029 2055 0350
Email: information@gtcw.org.uk
Website: www.gtcw.org.uk

NATIONAL AND REGIONAL RESOURCE CENTRES

Welsh National Centre for RE
University of Wales Bangor
Normal Site (Meirion)
Bangor
Gwynedd
Wales
LL57 2PZ
Telephone: 01248 382566
Email: practical_theology@bangor.ac.uk
Website: http://www.bangor.ac.uk/rs/pt/wncre/index.php.en

The David Hope RE Centre in York
York St John University
Lord Mayor's Walk
York
YO31 7EX
Tel: 01904 876605
Email: r.wolfe@yorksj.ac.uk
Website: http://www2.yorksj.ac.uk/default.asp?Page_ID=345&Parent_ID=341

FAITH COMMUNITY EDUCATION AND RESOURCE ORGANISATIONS

The following organisations provide educational support and resources related to specific religious traditions.

Buddhism

Buddhist Society
58 Eccleston Square
London
SW1V 1PH
Tel: 020 7834 5858
Email: info@thebuddhistsociety.org.uk
Website: www.thebuddhistsociety.org.uk

Christianity

The Church of England Board of Education / The National Society
Church House
Great Smith Street
London
SW1P 3NZ
Telephone: 020 7898 1518
Email: info@natsoc.c-of-e.org.uk
Website: www.natsoc.org.uk

Catholic Education Service for England and Wales
39 Eccleston Square
London
SW1V 1BX
Telephone: 020 7901 4880
Email: general@cesew.org.uk
Website: www.cesew.org.uk

Hinduism

National Council of Hindu Temples
62 Oakdene Road
Watford
Hertfordshire
WD24 6RW
Telephone: 019 2335 0093
Email: info@nchtuk.org
Website: www.nchtuk.org

Humanism

British Humanist Association
1 Gower Street
London
WC1E 6HD
Telephone: 020 7079 3580
Email: education@humanism.org.uk
Website: www.humanism.org.uk

Islam

Muslim Council of Britain
PO Box 57330
London E1 2WJ
Telephone: 0 84 5 262 6786
Email: admin@mcb.org.uk
Website: www.mcb.org.uk/

Muslim Educational Trust
130 Stroud Green Road
London
N4 3RZ
Telephone:020 7272 8502
Email: info@muslim-ed-trust.org.uk
Website: www.muslim-ed-trust.org.uk/

Judaism

Board of Deputies of British Jews
6 Bloomsbury Square
London
WC1A 2LP
Telephone: 020 7543 5400
Email: info@bod.org.uk
Website: www.bod.org.uk

Jewish Education Bureau
8 Westcombe Avenue
Leeds
LS8 2BS
Telephone: 0870 800 8532
Email: jeb@jewisheducationbureau.co.uk
Website: www.jewisheducationbureau.co.uk

Sikhism

Sikh Education Council
27 Old Gloucester Street
London
WC1N 3XX
Telephone: 07870 138616
Email: info@thesikhway.com
Website: www.thesikhway.com

RE PROFESSIONAL AND RELATED ORGANISATIONS

Association for the Teaching of RE in Scotland
ARTRES is the professional organisation for those teaching, or in
training to teach, Religious and Moral Education in Scottish schools.
All contact through website
Website: http://www.atres.org.uk/

Interfaith Network for the UK
8A Lower Grosvenor Place
London
SW1W 0EN
Telephone: 020 7931 7766
Email: ifnet@interfaith.org.uk
Website: www.interfaith.co.uk
The Inter Faith Network fosters good relations between the communities of the
major faiths in Great Britain.

National Association of SACREs
Yvonne Cameron
Centre Administrator
South London Multifaith Resources Centre
Lewisham PDC
Kilmorie Road
London
SE23 2SP
Tel: 020 8314 7016 Telephone: 020 8314 7016
Email: secretary@nasacre.org.uk
Website: www.nasacre.org.uk/
Develops links between the activities of local SACREs.

Christian Education and RE Today
RE Today
1020 Bristol Road
Selly Oak
Birmingham
B29 6LB
Telephone: 0121 472 4242
Email: enquiries@christianeducation.org.uk, retoday@retoday.org
Website: http://www.christianeducation.org.uk/contact.htm, www.retoday.org.uk
Professional organisation that serves religious education by publishing resources and
offering training for teachers.

Religious Education Council of England and Wales
c/o CAN, 1 London Bridge
London
SE1 9BG
Telephone: n/a
Email: n/a
Website: www.religiouseducationcouncil.org
Provides a national forum for discussion of matters concerning RE. It promotes the
interests of RE at national level.

Scottish Joint Committee for Religious and Moral Education
The Educational Institute of Scotland
6 Clairmont Gardens
Glasgow
G3 7LW
Telephone: 0141 353 3595
Email: n/a
Website: n/a
Promotes RE, RS and Moral Education in schools and in further and higher educa-
tion. Advice is given in these subject areas, and conferences are organised at Scottish
and district levels.

Shap Working Party on World Religions in Education
PO Box 38580
London
SW1P3XE
Telephone: 020 7898 1494
Email: n/a
Website: www.shap.org
Established to encourage the study and teaching of world religions. Publications include a calendar of religious festivals and an annual journal *World Religions in Education.*

Welsh Association of SACREs
The Secretary
The Gables
Llanwern
Newport
South Wales
NP18 2DS
Telephone: 016 3341 1919
Email: n/a
Website: n/a
Develops links between the activities of local SACREs in Wales.

UNITARY AWARDING BODIES FOR RELIGIOUS EDUCATION AND RELIGIOUS STUDIES

AQA (Assessment and Qualifications Alliance)
Regional Offices in Guildford, Harrowgate and Manchester; see website for addresses and contact phone numbers
Email: list of contacts on website: http://www.aqa.org.uk/over/pdf/CONTACT-AQA.PDF
Website: www.aqa.org.uk

CCEA (Northern Ireland Council for the Curriculum Examinations and Assessment)
29 Clarendon Road
Clarendon Doc
Belfast BT1 3BG
Telephone: 028 9026 1200
Email: info@ccea.org.uk
Website: www.rewardinglearning.org.uk/

EDEXCEL
Edexcel Customer Service,
One 90 High Holborn,
London,
WC1V 7BH.
Telephone: 0844 576 0025
Email: enquiries@edexcel.org.uk
Website: www.edexcel.org.uk

OCR
OCR Head Office
1 Regent Street
Cambridge
CB2 1GG
Telephone: 01223 553 998
Email: general.qualifications@ocr.org.uk
Website: www.ocr.org.uk

SQA (Scottish Qualifications Authority)
The Optima Building
58 Robertson Street
Glasgow
G2 8DQ
Telephone: 084 5279 1000
Email: customer@sqa.org.uk
Website: www.sqa.org.uk/

WJEC (Welsh Joint Education Committee)
245 Western Avenue
Cardiff CF52YX
Telephone: 029 2026 5000
Email: info@wjec.co.uk
Website: www.wjec.co.uk

Glossary

Accreditation   The recognition of a programme of study by an institution, normally through certification on the successful completion of a course, thus providing it with value through formal public recognition.

Assembly   A meeting of the school community for purposes of administration and/or to celebrate an aspect of the life of the school, but not involving any dimension of collective worship.

Child-centred education   See *Progressive education*.

Cognitive learning   Learning rooted in reason and critical reflection rather than in the enhancement of experiential sensibility and/or practical behavioural skills.

Collective worship   A form of school-based worship stipulated by the 1944 and 1988 Education Acts, in which the collective religious beliefs of the school community are celebrated.

Concept cracking   A method of exploring religious concepts in the classroom associated with the work of Trevor Cooling.

Conditioning   A process or regime whereby a pupil is moulded, or conditioned, to adopt particular habits or beliefs without having much choice in the matter.

Confessional RE   A form of religious education which derives from a particular religious tradition's confession of faith. Its commitment to religious nurture and the transmission of faith is often taken by opponents to be anti-educational.

Critical realism   The philosophy that there is an objective reality external to our minds 'out there' waiting to be discovered, but that access to it is not immediately given; rather, it requires an ongoing exploration of the world by human wisdom and intelligence.

Curriculum   The subjects taught in schools. The 1988 Education Act distinguishes between: (1) the *whole curriculum*, all learning activities that take place in school, including cross-curricular themes; (2) the *basic curriculum*, RE plus the National Curriculum; and (3) the *National Curriculum*, those subjects prescribed for study at national level.

Developmental education   (1) All education that takes account of the variety of psychological models of child-development associated primarily with Piaget and his followers;

(2) education concerned with and for social, economic and cultural inequality and the Developing/Third World.

Differentiation   Pedagogy that seeks to take account of the variety of ability ranges represented in the classroom by presenting material and setting tasks differentiated to meet the specific needs and aptitudes of individual pupils.

Emotivism   The doctrine that our inner feelings and emotions reflect what is ultimately true or real, and consequently are the most appropriate guides of our actions.

Empiricism   The philosophy that human knowledge is grounded in our sense experience.

Enlightenment   Eighteenth-century philosophical movement, standing at the dawn of the modern era, in which the potency of reason was emphasised as the means of obtaining knowledge against obedience to religious authority.

Ethnography   A branch of anthropology which focuses on the study of human individuals in the own environment.

Experiential RE   RE which attempts to give pupils a foundational experience of what religion entails, by engaging them in activities which emphasise reflection, the use of the imagination and the development of an inner life.

Faith development   An approach to religious education grounded in James Fowler's belief that the universal phenomenon of human faith commitment and formation develops in sequential stages.

Formative assessment   The process through which the performance of pupils, schemes of work, schools and teachers are evaluated and reported in order to support and enhance further development.

Generic religion   The belief that religion as a phenomenon constitutes a distinct entity, and that specific religious traditions are alternative forms of a common generic human religiosity.

Hermeneutics   The science or art of human understanding.

Implicit RE   A form of RE, flourishing in the 1960s, grounded in the assumption that the capacity for religious experience and insight was implicit in all pupils and simply needed to be drawn out of them. It would often begin by unpacking general moral, cultural and aesthetic topics before attempting to relate them explicitly to religious themes.

Indoctrination   A process in which someone attempts to influence another to accept particular doctrines, or beliefs, without regard to whether they understand them and accept them voluntarily. The concept of indoctrination is often contrasted with the concept of education.

Interpretative RE   An approach to RE associated with Robert Jackson which focuses on the process of interpreting an individual or group's religious way of life. This approach draws particularly on ideas from anthropology and ethnography and arises partly through balanced criticism of phenomenology.

Liberal education   (1) Education rooted in the liberal values of freedom, tolerance and reason. (2) Following Paul Hirst, the term is also used in the more restrictive sense of education focusing exclusively on the acquisition of knowledge.

Logical positivism   A now largely defunct philosophical tradition that claimed that only statements capable of verification and testing through sense experience could be meaningful. Religious, moral and aesthetic language was held to be neither true nor false, but quite literally nonsense.

Multicultural education Education largely within the liberal tradition concerned to teach about cultural diversity as a means of enhancing mutual understanding and toleration.

Multi-faith RE (1) In its soft form, any approach to RE that takes account of the diversity of religious traditions; (2) in its harder form, the principle of the absolute equality of all religious traditions is brought into play.

Naturalism The philosophical belief that the natural world as described by natural science constitutes the sum of reality and that no transcendent religious realm lies beyond it.

Nurture A process whereby those who hold particular religious beliefs attempt to teach and transmit them to others, often children, in ways that encourage understanding and commitment.

Objectivism The philosophical doctrine that both reality and our understanding of reality must, if they are to be considered authentic, transcend our inner subjective feelings and desires.

Open RE An approach to RE that asserts the value of pupils' freedom to decide their response to religion. It is opposed to any form of indoctrination and deeply suspicious of closed forms of confessional religious teaching.

Phenomenological RE An approach to teaching religion associated particularly with Ninian Smart and closely allied with multi-faith RE. It seeks to balance an objective study of the world's religions with an empathetic understanding of the world-view of the religious believer.

Phenomenology A philosophical movement associated with Edmund Husserl that attempted to understand reality through the twin processes of description and empathetic understanding of the phenomenological world that presents itself to our senses.

Pluralism (1) In its soft form, the basic reality of cultural diversity. (2) In its hard form, the claim that truth is to be found in the plurality of cultural contexts.

Postmodernism A broad contemporary philosophical and cultural movement that, in opposition to the rationalism of modernity, stresses the value of *relativism*, *pluralism*, *emotivism* and cultural diversity.

Progression The structure built into a scheme of work that enables learning to progress through ordered, appropriate and coherent stages.

Progressive education A form of child-centred education that flourished in the 1960s and has its roots in the thoughts of the French philosopher J-J. Rousseau. It is concerned with allowing the pupil the freedom to develop naturally and tends to be opposed to the imposition of any traditional subject-based curriculum and suspicious of formal schooling.

Realism The philosophical and religious belief that objective reality exists independently of the observer. Whether God exists, or does not exist, is not affected in any way by our decision to believe or not to believe.

Relativism (1) In its hard form, the belief that truth is not universal but is relative to particular groups of people or individuals. 'This is our truth, now tell us yours.' (2) In its soft form, the recognition that all human claims to true knowledge are always partial, contingent and relative. 'We think this, you think that, but which of us is right?'

Religionism A term popularised by John Hull in reference to pathological forms of religious belief which treat their own claims as exclusively true and all other forms as false, and consequently tend towards sectarianism, bigotry, intolerance, oppression and even violence.

Religious education   (1) the teaching of the subject of religion in schools; (2) sometimes distinguished from religious instruction on the grounds that one is essentially 'open' and educational, whereas the other is 'closed' and confessional.

Religious pluralism   (1) In its soft form, it simply indicates the reality of religious diversity. (2) In its hard form, it refers to a particular interpretation of that reality, in which all religious traditions are held to contain some element of religious truth.

Religious Studies   The academic study of religion, normally from a neutral or scientific perspective, concerned primarily with the understanding of religious culture rather than the reality and truth of God.

Revelation   A category of theological epistemology in which knowledge of God rests not in human endeavour, experience and reason, but in the act of divine revelation.

Romanticism   A broad cultural movement that arose in reaction against the technical rationalism of the Enlightenment. It stressed the importance of feeling and intuition over and against reason, and was deeply influential in shaping liberal forms of religion, progressive child-centred education and experiential religious education.

Scientism   The philosophy that the only valid form of knowledge is that gained through the exercise of the scientific method.

Summative assessment   The process through which the performance of pupils, programmes of study, schools and teachers are evaluated and reported in order to indicate their actual standard of achievement.

Theology   The study of religion, normally from the perspective of faith commitment, concerned primarily with the understanding of the reality and truth of God, rather than religious culture understood as merely a human phenomenon.

Bibliography

Abbot, I. and Huddlestone, P. (2004) 'The Curriculum: 14–19', in V. Brooks, I. Abbot and
  L. Bills, *Preparing to Teach in Secondary School*, Maidenhead: Open University Press.
Abbott, C. (2000) *ICT: Changing Education*, London: RoutledgeFalmer.
Albans, P. (1998) 'Effective Questioning in Primary Religious Education and the Assessment
  of Pupils' Learning from Religion', *Resource*, 21(1): 3–6.
Arthur, J. and Wright, D. (2001) *Teaching Citizenship in the Secondary School*, London: David
  Fulton Publishers.
Astley, J. (1994) *The Philosophy of Christian Religious Education*, Birmingham, AL: Religious
  Education Press.
Barnes, L. P. (2001) 'What Is Wrong with the Phenomenological Approach to Religious
  Education?', *Religious Education*, 96(4): 445–61.
Barnes, L.P. (2002) 'Working Paper 36, Christian Confessionalism and Phenomenological
  Religious Education', *Journal of Education and Christian Belief*, 6(1): 3–23.
Barnes, L. P. (2007) 'Developing a New Post-Liberal Paradigm for British Religious Educa-
  tion', *Journal of Beliefs and Values*, *28*(1): 17–32.
Barnes, L.P. (2008) *Religious Education: Taking Respect for Difference Seriously*, Oxford: Philosophy
  of Education Society of Great Britain, Impact Series.
Barnes, L.P. and Kay, W.K. (2002) *Religious Education in England and Wales: Innovations and
  Reflections*, Leicester: Religious and Theological Studies Fellowship.
Baumann, A.S., Bloomfield, A. and Roughton, L. (1997) *Becoming a Secondary School Teacher*,
  London: Hodder & Stoughton.
Baumfield, V. (2002) *Thinking Through Religious Education*, Cambridge: Chris Kington
  Publishing.
Best, R. (ed.) (1996) *Education, Spirituality and the Whole Child*, London: Cassell.
Black, P., Harrison, C., Lee, C., Marshall, B. and Wiliam, D. (2003) *Assessment for Learning:
  Putting It into Practice*, Buckingham: Open University Press.
Broadbent, L. and Brown, A. (eds) (2002) *Issues in Religious Education*, London:
  RoutledgeFalmer.
Capel, S., Leask, M. and Turner, T. (2004) *Starting to Teach in the Secondary School*, London:
  RoutledgeFalmer.

Capel, S., Leask, M. and Turner, T. (2005) *Learning to Teach in the Secondary School*, 4th edn, London: Routledge.

City of Birmingham Education Committee (1975) *Living Together: A Teachers' Handbook of Suggestions for Religious Education*, Birmingham: City of Birmingham Education Committee.

Coles, R. (1990) *The Spiritual Life of Children*, Glasgow: HarperCollins.

Cooling, M. (1996) *Toolkit: Creative Ideas for Using the Bible in the Classroom*, vols 1, 2 3, Swindon: Bible Society.

Cooling, M. (1998) *Jesus through Art: A Resource for Teaching Religious Education and Art*, Norwich: Religious and Moral Education Press.

Cooling, T. (2000) 'The Stapleford Project: Theology as the Basis for Religious Education', in M. Grimmitt (ed.) *Pedagogies of Religious Education: Case Studies in the Research and Development of Good Pedagogic Practice in RE*, Great Wakering: McCrimmons.

Cooling, T. (2002) 'Commitment and Indoctrination: A Dilemma for Religious Education', in L. Broadbent and A. Brown (eds.), *Issues in Religious Education*, London: RoutledgeFalmer.

Cooling, T. (2003) *Try Something Different: Approaches to Teaching and Learning in RE*, Nottingham: The Stapleford Centre.

Cooling, T. and Cooling, M. (2004) *Concept Cracking: A Practical Way to Teach Big Ideas in RE*, Nottingham: The Stapleford Centre

Cooper, D. (1986) *Metaphor*, London: Blackwell.

Copley, T. (2008) *Teaching Religion: Religious Education in England and Wales 1944 to 2007*, Exeter: University of Exeter Press.

Copley, T. (2000) *Spiritual Development in the State School*, Exeter: Exeter University Press.

Copley, T. (2005) *Indoctrination, Education and God*, London: SPCK.

Crick, B. (1998) *Education for Citizenship and the Teaching of Democracy in Schools: Final Report of the Advisory Group on Citizenship*, London: QCA.

Dearing, R. (1996) *Review of Qualifications 16–19*, London: SCAA.

Department for Education (1994) *Circular 1/94. Religious Education and Collective Worship*, London: HMSO.

Department for Education and Employment (DfES) (2003) *14–19 Opportunity and Excellence*, London: HMSO.

Department for Education and Employment (DfEE) (1998) *Circular 4/98. Teaching: Higher Status, Higher Standards*, London: HMSO.

Department for Education and Science (DES) (1989) *Circular 3/89. The Education Reform Act 1988: Religious Education and Collective Worship*, London: HMSO.

Department for Education and Skills/Teacher Training Agency (2002) *Qualifying to Teach*, London: TTA.

DES/HMI (Her Majesty's Inspectorate) (1977a) *Curriculum 11–16*, London: HMSO.

DES/HMI (Her Majesty's Inspectorate) (1977b) *Supplement to Curriculum 11–16*, London: HMSO.

DES/TTA (2002) *Qualifying to Teach*, London: HMSO.

DfES (2005) *14–19 Education and Skills*, London: HMSO.

Erricker, C. (1998) 'Spiritual Confusion: A Critique of Current Educational Policy in England and Wales', *International Journal of Children's Spirituality*, 3(1): 51–64.

Erricker, C. and Erricker, J. (2000) *Reconstructing Religious, Spiritual and Moral Education*, London: RoutledgeFalmer.

Erricker, C., Erricker, J., Ota, C., Sullivan, D. and Fletcher, M. (1997) *The Education of the Whole Child*, London: Cassell.

Felderhof, M. (2005) 'RE: Religions, Equality and Curriculum Time,' *Journal of Beliefs and Values*, 26(2): 201–14.

Ferrigan, C. (2005) *Passing the ICT Skills Test (Achieving QTS)*, Exeter: Learning Matters Ltd.

Fisher, R. (1998) *Teaching Thinking: Philosophical Enquiry in the Classroom*, London: Cassell.

Fowler, J. (1981) *Stages of Faith: The Psychology of Human Development and the Quest for Meaning*, San Francisco: Harper & Row.

Francis, L.J. (2001). *The Values Debate: A Voice from the Pupils*, London: RoutledgeFalmer.

Gates, B.E. (1989) *The National Curriculum and Values in Education*, Frinton: Hockerill Educational Foundation.

Gearon, L. (2003) *Learning to Teach Citizenship in the Secondary School*, London: Routledge.

Gearon, L. (2004) *Citizenship through Secondary Religious Education*, London: Routledge.

Gearon, L. (ed.) (2007) *Teaching Citizenship in the Secondary School: A Practical Guide*, London: Routledge.

Geaves, R. (2006) *Key Words in Religious Studies*, London: Continuum.

Giles, A. (2002) *Religious Studies at Post-16*, in L. Broadbent and A. Brown (eds), *Issues in Religious Education*, London: RoutledgeFalmer.

Gilligan, C. (1982) *In a Different Voice*, Cambridge, MA: Harvard University Press.

Goldman, R. (1965) *Readiness for Religion: A Basis for Developmental Religious Education*, London: Routledge & Kegan Paul.

Grimmitt, M. (1973) *What Can I Do in RE?*, Great Wakering, Essex: Mayhew-McCrimmon.

Grimmitt, M. (1987) *Religious Education and Human Development: The Relationship between Studying Religions and Personal, Social and Moral Education*, Great Wakering, Essex: McCrimmon.

Grimmitt, M. (ed.) (2000) *Pedagogies of Religious Education: Case Studies in the Research and of Good Pedagogic Practice in RE*, Great Wakering, Essex: McCrimmons.

Hammond, J., Hay, D., Moxon, J., Netto, B., Raban, K., Straugheir, G. and Williams, C. (1990) *New Methods in RE Teaching: An Experiential Approach*, Harlow: Oliver & Boyd.

Hampshire County Council (2004) *Living Difference: The Agreed Syllabus for Religious Education in Hampshire, Portsmouth and Southampton*, Winchester: Hampshire County Council.

Hay, D. (1982) *Exploring Inner Space: Is God still Possible in the Twentieth Century?*, Harmondsworth: Penguin Books.

Hay, D. (1985) 'Suspicion of the Spiritual: Teaching Religion in a World of Secular Experience', *British Journal of Religious Education*, 7(1): 140–7.

Hay, D. (1990a) *Religious Experience Today*, London: Mowbray.

Hay, D. (1990b) 'The Bearing of Empirical Studies of Religious Experience on Education', *Research Papers in Education*, 15(1): 3–27.

Hay, D. and Nye, R. (1996) 'Investigating Children's Spirituality: The Need for a Fruitful Hypothesis', *International Journal of Children's Spirituality*, 1(1): 6–16.

Hay, D. with Nye, R. (1998) *The Spirit of the Child*, London: Fount.

Haydon, G. (1997) *Teaching About Values: A New Approach*, London: Cassell.

Hick, J. (1997) 'Is Christianity the Only True Religion?', *Resource*, 19(3): 3–7.

HMSO (1944) *Education Act*, London: HMSO.

HMSO (1981) *Education Act*, London: HMSO.

HMSO (1988) *Education Reform Act*, London: HMSO.

HMSO (1992) *Education (Schools) Act*, London: HMSO.

HMSO (1993) *Education Act*, London: HMSO.

HMSO (2000) *Citizenship Order*, London: HMSO.

Hookway, S. (2004) *Questions of Truth: Developing Critical Thinking Skills in Secondary Religious Education*, Norwich: RMEP.

Hull, J.M. (1991) *Mishmash RE in Multicultural Britain: A Study in Metaphor*, Derby: Birmingham University/CEM.

Hull, J.M. (1992) 'Editorial: The Transmission of Religious Prejudice', *British Journal of Religious Education*, 14(2): 69–72.

Hull, J.M. (1998) *Utopian Whispers*, Derby: CEM.

Ipgrave, J. (2003) *Building eBridges: Interfaith Dialogue by Email*, Birmingham: Christian Education Movement.

Jackson, R. (1997) *Religious Education: An Interpretive Approach*, London: Hodder & Stoughton.

Jackson, R. (ed.) (2003) *International Perspectives on Citizenship, Education and Religious Diversity*, London: RoutledgeFalmer.

Jackson, R. (2004) *Rethinking Religious Education and Plurality: Issues in Diversity and Pedagogy*, London: RoutledgeFalmer.

Kay, W. and Francis, L.J. (1996) *Drift from the Churches*, Cardiff: University of Wales Press.

Kelly, A.V. (1986) *Knowledge and Curriculum Planning*, London: Harper & Row.

Kennewell, S. (2006) *A Practical Guide to Teaching ICT in the Secondary School*, London: Routledge.

Kerry, T. (1980) 'The Demands Made by RE on Pupils' Thinking', *British Journal of Religious Education*, 3(2): 46–52.

Kincaid, M. (1991) *How to Improve Learning in RE*, London: Hodder & Stoughton.

Kohlberg, L. (1981) *The Philosophy of Moral Development*, San Francisco: Harper.

Kyriacun, C. (2007) *Essential Teaching Skills*, London: Stanley Thornes.

Leask, M. and Pachler, N. (2005) *Learning to Teach Using ICT in the Secondary School*, London: Routledge.

Loukes, H. (1961) *Teenage Religion: An Enquiry into Attitudes and Possibilities among British Boys and Girls in Secondary Modern Schools*, London: SCM.

MacGilchrist, B., Myers, K. and Reed, J. (2004) *The Intelligent School*, London: Paul Chapman.

Malone, P. (1998), 'Religious Education and Prejudice among Students Taking the Course "Studies of Religion" ', *British Journal of Religious Education*, 21(1): 7–19.

Marshall, P. (ed.) (2000) *Religious Freedom in the World*, Nashville, TN: Broadman and Holman.

Mercier, S.C. (1996) *Interpreting Religions: Muslims*, Oxford: Heinemann.

National Curriculum Council (1990) *The Whole Curriculum*, London: NCC.

Nodding, N. (2003) *Caring: A Feminine Approach to Ethics and Moral Education*, Berkeley, CA: University of California Press.

North Somerset SACRE (2004), *Agreed Syllabus: Awareness, Mystery and Value*, Taunton: NSSACRE.

Office for Standards in Education (Ofsted) (1994) *Framework for the Inspection of Schools*, London: HMSO.

Ofsted (1997) *The Impact of New Agreed Syllabuses on the Teaching and Learning of Religious Education*, London: Ofsted.

Ofsted (2003) *Promoting and Evaluating Pupils' Spiritual, Moral, Social and Cultural Development: Guidance for Schools*, London: Ofsted.

Ofsted (2004) *Promoting and Evaluating Pupils' Spiritual, Moral, Social and Cultural Development*, London: Ofsted.

Ofsted (2005) *Religious Education in Secondary Schools: Annual Report 2004/5*, London: HMSO.

Ofsted (2007) *Making Sense of Religion*, London: HMSO.

Ogden, V. (1997) *The Role of Religious Education at 16–19 in the Ascendancy of Work-related Learning and a New Framework for Post-compulsory Education*, Abingdon: Culham College Institute.

Parker-Jenkins, M., Hartas, D. and Irving, B. (2004) *In Good Faith: Schools, Religion and Public Funding*, Aldershot: Ashgate Publishing.

Parsons, G. (ed.) (1993) *The Growth of Religious Diversity: Britain from 1945. Vol. 1, Traditions*, London: Open University/Routledge.

Parsons, G. (ed.) (1994) *The Growth of Religious Diversity: Britain from 1945. Vol. 2, Issues*, London: Open University/Routledge.

Priestley, J. (1996) *Spirituality in the Curriculum*, Frinton: Hockerill Educational Foundation.

Priestley, J. (1997) 'Spirituality, Curriculum and Education', *International Journal of Children's Spirituality*, 2(1): 23–34.

Qualifications and Curriculum Authority (QCA) (1997) *Guidance for Schools: The Promotion of Pupils' Spiritual, Moral, Social and Cultural Development*, London: QCA.

QCA (1998) *Exemplification of Standards in Religious Education: Key Stages 1 to 4*, London: QCA.

QCA (2004) *The Non-Statutory Framework for Religious Education*, London: QCA.

Robson, G. (1995) *Interpreting Religions: Christians*, Oxford: Heinemann.

Robson, G, (1996) 'Religious Education, Government Policy and Professional Practice 1985–1995', *British Journal of Religious Education*, 19(1): 13–23.

Schools Curriculum and Assessment Authority (SCAA) (1994a) *Model Syllabuses. Model 1: Living Faiths Today*, London: School Curriculum and Assessment Authority.

SCAA (1994b) *Model Syllabuses. Model 2: Questions and Teachings*, London: School Curriculum and Assessment Authority.

SCAA (1994c) *Religious Education Glossary of Terms*, London: SCAA.

SCAA (1995a) *Spiritual and Moral Development, SCAA Discussion Papers 3*, London: SCAA.

SCAA (1995b) *Religious Education 16–19*, London: SCAA.

SCAA (1996a) *Education for Adult Life: The Spiritual and Moral Development of Young People*, SCAA Discussion Papers 6, London: SCAA.

SCAA (1996b) *Findings of the Consultation on Values in Education and the Community*, London: SCAA.

Schools Council (1971) *Working Paper 36: Religious Education in Secondary Schools*, London: Evans/Methuen.

Smart, N. (1973) 'What Is Religion?', in N. Smart and D. Horder (eds), *New Movements in Religious Education*, London: Temple Smith.

Smart, N. (1989) *The World's Religions*, Cambridge: Cambridge University Press.

Starkings, D. (1993) 'The Landscape of Spirituality', in D. Starkings (ed.) *Religion and the Arts in Education: Dimensions of Spirituality*, London: Hodder & Stoughton.

Thatcher, A. (1990) 'The Recovery of Christian Education', in L. Francis and A. Thatcher (eds) *Christian Perspectives for Education*, Leominster: Gracewing.

Thatcher, A. (1991) 'A Critique of Inwardness in Religious Education', *British Journal of Religious Education*, 14(1): 22–7.

Thiessen, E.J. (1993) *Teaching for Commitment: Liberal Education, Indoctrination and Christian Nurture*, Leominster: Gracewing.

Tomlinson, M. (2004) *14–19 Curriculum and Qualifications Reform*, London: HMSO.

Torrance, H. and Prior, J. (1998) *Investigating Formative Assessment*, Buckingham: Open University Press.

Training and Development Agency (2006) *Professional Standards for Qualified Teacher Status*, London: TDA.

Training and Development Agency for Schools (2007) *Professional Standards for Teachers*, London: TDA.

United Nations (1998) *Report of the UN High Commissioner for Human Rights*, Geneva: United Nations.

Watson, B., and Thompson, P. (2007) *The Effective Teaching of Religious Education*, London: Pearson Longman.

Watson, J. (2003) 'Preparing Spirituality for Citizenship', *International Journal of Children's Spirituality*, 8(1): 9–24.

Wayne, E. (1996) *Interpreting Religion: Hindus*, Oxford: Heinemann.

Webster, D. (1995) *Collective Worship in Schools: Contemporary Approaches*, Cleethorpes: Kenelm Press.

Wintersgill, B. (2000) 'Task Setting in Religious Education at Key Stage 3: A Comparison with History and English', *Resource*, 22(3): 10–14.

Wright, A. (1993) *Religious Education in the Secondary School: Prospects for Religious Literacy*, London: David Fulton.

Wright, A. (1997) 'Embodied Spirituality: The Place of Culture and Tradition in Contemporary Educational Discourse on Spirituality', *International Journal of Children's Spirituality*, 1(2): 8–20.

Wright, C. (1995) *Key Christian Beliefs*, Oxford: Lion.

Index

Note: References with *f* direct you to figures, *tb* to tables and *tsk* to tasks.